D1013328

STRICTLY
BUSINESS

◆

STRICTLY BUSINESS

Roger Craig

with Garry Niver

ST. MARTIN'S PRESS
NEW YORK

STRICTLY BUSINESS. Copyright © 1992 by Roger Craig and Garry Niver. All rights reserved. Printed in the United States of America. No part of this book may be used or reproduced in any manner whatsoever without written permission except in the case of brief quotations embodied in critical articles or reviews. For information, address St. Martin's Press, 175 Fifth Avenue, New York, N.Y. 10010.

Library of Congress Cataloging-in-Publication Data

Craig, Roger, 1960–
    Strictly business / Roger Craig with Garry Niver.
        p.   cm.
    ISBN 0-312-07854-4
    1. Craig, Roger, 1960– . 2. Football players—United States—Biography. 3. San Francisco 49ers (Football team) I. Niver, Garry. II. Title.
GV939.C73A3   1992
796.332′092—dc20
[B]   92-3630
                                                            CIP

First Edition: June 1992

10 9 8 7 6 5 4 3 2 1

This book is dedicated to the memory of my father, Elijah Craig, who gave me the spirit of life and instilled in me the rewards of hard work. Each new day begins with his love.

—Roger Craig

Contents

◆ Acknowledgments

We would like to thank our families for their patience and support in making this project a success.

My thanks to my mother, Ernestine, for getting me through the first part of my life; to Vernessia, my lover, confidante, best friend, and wife, without whom I couldn't have made it through these difficult times; to my children, daughters Damesha and Rometra and sons Rogdrick and Alexander Julian, for their kindness in understanding that Daddy can't be with them as much as he used to; and to my brother, Curtis, for being such a positive role model.

And a special thanks to my close buddies, Jerry Rice, Tom Rathman, Jamie Williams, Riki Ellison, and Ronnie Lott, for lending me their support and advice. Thanks to Eddie DeBartolo, Jr., Bill Walsh, and Al Davis for believing in me. A belated thank-you to Lou Williams, my junior high school coach, and Jim Fox, my high school coach. Finally, a special salute of gratitude to all of my teammates, both past and present, who have made the football part of my life so enjoyable. Guys, I couldn't have made it without you.

—Roger Craig

To my wife, Aileen, and children Garry Sean and Danielle, thanks for your encouragement and understanding.

My thanks go to the 49er beat writers, whose witty everyday insight helped form this book. They are, in no particular order, Ira Miller, Frank Cooney, Bill Soliday, Rich Weiner, Jim Jenkins, John Crumpacker, Jon Rochmis, Ann Killion, Eric Gilmore, Ron Thomas, Gary Swan, Mike Silver, Jarrett Bell, Nancy Gay, Andy Cox, and Kevin Lynch.

I would also like to thank Jerry Walker, Rodney Knox, Dave Rahn, Al Barba, Darla Maeda, and the rest of the 49er public relations staff for their cooperation. Special thanks to Christopher Stave, whose penchant for literacy cleaned up my act, so to speak. And to literary agent Laurie Harper, whose guidance was critical.

—Garry Niver

STRICTLY
BUSINESS

◆
1. Shedding Memories

Sunday, September 29, 1991, dawned very much like any typical Los Angeles morning. Kind of close, with a sulphuric aroma and a battleship gray sky outlined by a light, whiskey-colored haze.

Only it wasn't going to be a typical day for me. It was to be the day that I put all of the hurt and confusion behind me and got on with my life. It was the day I would play in a Los Angeles Raiders uniform against my former team, the San Francisco 49ers, in a regular-season game, the day I would start for the team that wanted me against the team that didn't want me. It was the first day of my new beginning.

It had been an emotional week, and both Ronnie Lott and I knew it was going to be chock-full of media hype, with the assembled reporters and TV types egging on the two ex-49ers to talk about the sweet taste of revenge. Like myself, Ronnie had been put on Plan B by the 49ers, offered a reduced salary, and decided to sign with the Raiders.

Truthfully, the game wasn't about revenge. It was about winning. Both teams were 2–2 coming in, and both were on the verge of losing sight of the divisional leaders. A Raider victory would put us back on track for the AFC West title; likewise, a San Francisco win would help them stay within reach of NFC West leader New Orleans.

When we came off the practice field Monday afternoon there was a horde of media from both Los Angeles and San Francisco waiting to ask us questions.

I was trying to approach this game as professionally as I could. I wanted to make sure I took care of my responsibilities and guarded against getting caught up in the hype. In a way, it was good for Ronnie and me to experience a situation like this; it forced us to focus even harder on our chores.

1

We decided that we would hold a joint press conference to answer everyone's questions, and then we would be unavailable for the remainder of the week. We wanted to get all of those media queries out of the way so we'd be able to concentrate on the game. That would be it. No more talking.

Most weeks I fly home to San Francisco following Monday's practice because the Raider players have Tuesday off. Riki Ellison, another ex-Niner, and I usually share a ride to the airport and take the same flight. We reverse the procedure Tuesday night after spending a very precious thirty-six-hour period with our families. Riki and I live about a half mile apart in Portola Valley, so we ride-share to the airport. United Airlines flight 1131 leaves San Francisco International Airport at nine P.M. every Tuesday night, and he and I are regulars on that flight. We're on a first-name basis with the flight attendants round trip.

It's really ironic that Riki and I have become united again through my new team. It seems like more than just coincidence. We both live in the same rural village, we both have four children, two girls and two boys, and we both make our living playing for the same team four hundred miles away in Southern California. I had called him for advice when I realized the Raiders were serious about signing me away from the 49ers.

Riki had been one of the first players San Francisco lost through Plan B, signing with the Raiders in May 1990. The Plan B concept was devised by the NFL owners in 1989 to keep the U.S. Congress from declaring the National Football League a monopoly. Basically, it limits teams to protecting thirty-seven players on their active rosters. The remainder of the players are declared unconditional free agents and free to negotiate with any teams interested in their services.

Theoretically, it provides a weak version of free agency. Truthfully, it gives teams an added opportunity to dump high-salaried veterans without the embarrassment of releasing them and allows the team to protect more younger and inexpensive players.

We were both drafted by the 49ers in 1983, myself in the second round and Riki in the fifth. We first met at the Dallas scouting combine when we were college seniors in 1983. I remember that Gil Brandt, who was the Cowboys' personnel director, told both of us that we weren't healthy enough to play in the NFL. Brandt told Riki he would never play because he had had three operations on his left knee and one on the right. He told me I wasn't durable enough to play pro ball because I got injured a lot my senior year at the University of Nebraska.

Because of that prejudgment by Brandt, Riki and I sort of bonded together, like a pair of misfit brothers. The 49ers played Dallas in the final game of our rookie season, and all week long before the game Riki and I kept reminding each other that we weren't good enough to play in the

NFL. By the time Sunday rolled around, Riki could have tackled a bus full of Cowboys, and I could have run through the walls of all those big oil buildings in Dallas. Come to think of it, we almost did. We used Brandt's snub as a motivational tool, and I scored two touchdowns and Riki slammed into everything that moved, including Cowboys running back Tony Dorsett. Thanks Gil, we owe you for that one.

Anyway, here we were eight years later, playing mind games off each other's emotions again.

But I had injured my shoulder against the Falcons the previous Sunday—actually I had separated it at the acromioclavicular joint (A-C joint), where the acromion process and the distal end of the clavicle meet—and I stayed behind Monday night so I could get treatment from Raider trainer George Anderson. With Marcus Allen still on injured reserve and rookie Nick Bell just coming off the injured list, I knew that my team would be depending on me, and I needed to be as physically fit as possible. As it was, I wouldn't be able to participate in any scrimmages during the week.

Ronnie also stayed that Tuesday, so we went to dinner Tuesday night. Believe it or not, we didn't reminisce about our 49er days, other than to remind each other that we had to go on living and that we were both happy where we were. We talked about where the Raiders were as a team and where we would like to be. We noted how much our new teammates respected and believed in us, and that now it was up to us to give something back to the organization—like a Super Bowl title.

Then we talked about our respective families—Ronnie had recently married and he and his wife Karen were expecting a child—and how much the responsibilities of parenthood would change Ronnie's life.

Wednesday when we came off the field for lunch, there were even more reporters waiting for Ronnie and me. But we told them they were too late, as we had said all we were going to say at our press conference Monday.

One of the reporters outside the locker room was Lowell Cohn, a columnist for the San Francisco *Chronicle.* Lowell had always treated me fairly; besides that, he is probably the best columnist in the Bay Area. I felt bad about stiffing him, so I snuck back out and gave him the phone number of the hotel I was living at during the season and told him to call me that night. I later explained to him over the phone that I was quite weary of talking to the media about the 49ers. I was a Los Angeles Raider now, and that was the career I wanted to focus on. I was tired of reliving the past and of having people keep bringing up the fumble that helped to derail the 49ers' drive for a third consecutive Super Bowl.

I told him that I was still grappling with the Raider system, but that

I was coming along and knew that my best games were in front of me. My positive demeanor prevents me from holding grudges or harboring regrets. If I had to play for a team on Mars, I would do it. Life is too short to dwell on all of the bad things that happen.

Lowell thanked me for my time and hung up. I tried to get some sleep, but I was already starting to become focused on the game, which was still four days away.

Thursday and Friday we put our game plan in, and I was real excited because I was a major part of the running game. Marcus Allen was still on the injured list, and I was the starting tailback. My shoulder was still sore, but I knew I would be able to carry my share of the load. Bell, the team's second-round draft pick, had just been activated, and I knew coach Art Shell was a little hesitant to throw him into the breach on the first series.

Saturday we had a short morning practice, and I ran my plays in a mock scrimmage with no contact. I knew it was a big game when I saw the Madden Cruiser pull up outside our training field. The Madden Cruiser is a specially outfitted Greyhound Bus for former Raider coach-turned-announcer John Madden, who has a phobia against flying. Madden and his crew watched practice and talked to our coaches. The ache in my shoulder was beginning to subside. It's amazing how therapeutic adrenaline can be.

The night before home games, the Raiders stay at the Hyatt Wilshire Hotel in Los Angeles, but before I reported that Saturday, I spent a couple hours with my favorite family, the Roger Craig family. Vernessia, Damesha, Rometra, and Rogdrick had all flown down for the game, and we went to the beach for a couple of hours.

Team members are required to check into the team hotel by five o'clock on the afternoon before the game. We attend a team dinner and then break up into position groups to go over the game plan one final time with the position coach, who in my case is Joe Scanella. Then we go to bed. It's a very standard schedule; most teams in the NFL adhere to it.

I went upstairs, turned on the television, but my mind was thousands of miles away from the TV set, in my hometown of Davenport, Iowa, sorting through the memories of my father, Elijah Craig. One of the things that has kept me strong through adversity are my recollections of him. As far back as I can remember, he always worked long hours so he could provide a better life for his family.

I always felt special when I was around him. My brother Curtis was heralded as the best athlete in the family, but my dad used to tell people to watch out for me because I was going to be better. He gave me lots of inspiration and encouragement and love.

It really hurt me when he died, but at the same time it gave me the incentive to succeed in whatever endeavors I might undertake. His memory has kept me strong and helped me grow up. During quiet times before big games like this, I often reflect back on his memory to help my focus.

I spent a restless night, dozing on and off, like I do the night before any big game. I'd wake up and my mind would skip back to my college days at Nebraska. Those were fun times, but they were also difficult. Our daughter Damesha was born during my freshman year and Rometra was born midway through my senior season with the Huskers. So most of my evenings were spent studying and changing diapers, instead of out drinking beer with the fraternity brothers.

But thinking back, the hardship of trying to make ends meet and balancing an athletic schedule with an academic schedule helped prepare me for the reality of life—certainly, for life after football. It wasn't like we were destitute; we lived in a comfortable little apartment about a mile from campus. Vernessia worked part time for State Farm Insurance, and we were quite disciplined about saving money.

I was confident that I would go pretty high in the NFL draft, and then our monetary problems would be over. The 49ers came to Lincoln and worked me out. The day before the draft, coach Bill Walsh called me and told me to stay by my phone. It was difficult to sleep that night, not knowing for certain where I would start my professional career.

San Francisco didn't have a first-round draft pick, having traded it to San Diego for a pair of second-round picks. The 49ers called me just before they selected and told me they were going to take me with the second of their second-round picks—ironically, the forty-ninth pick overall—and I was elated. I was going to sunny California.

I made it a point to sign my contract and report to training camp on time. I was really jacked up, and I didn't want to miss a day. I received a four-year, $860,000 contract, which included a $200,000 signing bonus. It was a pretty good deal for a mid-level second-round pick.

The first thing I did with my bonus money was buy my mother, Ernestine, a new home in Davenport, Iowa. I think it's every black athlete's dream to be able to buy his parents a home once he makes it in professional sports. My mother had spent most of her life as a machinist in the Caterpillar factory in Davenport; now she would be able to retire and not worry about making the monthly mortgage payments. It took a lot of pressure off her, and it made me feel good that I could in some small way pay her back for all of the years of nurturing and love she had given me. As I said, we were quite disciplined in handling our finances, and Vernessia and I invested the rest of the bonus money. And wisely, I might add.

Football is a funny game. I don't mean funny, ha-ha but funny as in strange. I remember my first day of training camp as a rookie in 1983.

As I walked out of the locker room and onto the cement tarmac at the 49ers' summer camp in Rocklin, a small town about 25 miles northeast of the state capital of Sacramento, where the 49ers have made their summer training camp since 1981, I was surrounded by the media. I figured they were going to ask me about that memorable day during my junior year against Florida State when I gained 234 yards on 20 carries, including a 93-yard touchdown.

But they wanted to talk about the two fumbles I had in my final game at Nebraska. I can never understand why the media enjoys dwelling on the negative. Certainly there are more upbeat things to talk about than fumbles.

It's ironic that I left San Francisco the same way I came in, trying to explain fumbles. Football has a strange symmetry to it. But I'm not complaining, because the game has been extremely good to me and my family, and I'm eternally grateful.

As I said, I didn't sleep too well Saturday night. I tossed and turned and had those flashbacks of my life. I also tried to visualize some of the runs I'd be making the next day.

I probably got a total of five hours sleep. But it's to my benefit not to sleep too soundly or get overly relaxed the night before a game. Sometimes you can get too much rest, and you go on the field thinking you have it made. I've always performed my best after a restless night.

By the time I got to the Los Angeles Coliseum, my focus was good. I was blocking out all of the exterior elements, and that meant the crowd, past loyalties and friendships, and anything else that would detract from my doing my job.

I was coming back down the tunnel after our early warm-ups when 49er quarterback Joe Montana grabbed me by the arm and asked, "What's wrong? Too good to say hello to old friends?" He said he had shouted my name three times and I had totally ignored him.

Joe had said some things in a recent newspaper article that had upset me. He told a reporter that the 49ers would have been in the Super Bowl a third straight time had it not been for my fumble. I mean, that was last season's news. Why did he have to bring it up again and reopen old wounds?

But that wasn't the reason I had ignored him. My focus was nearly complete when I walked by him, and I honestly didn't notice him until he grabbed me. I had already forgiven and forgotten that Joe had mentioned the fumble. He was probably just frustrated because of a chronic elbow injury that was keeping him on injured reserve. I will always consider Joe Montana my friend, and I believe that he will go down in history as the greatest quarterback ever to play the game.

I didn't go out of my way to say hello to any of the 49ers before the game. I didn't feel it would serve any purpose. It was time for business; there would be time for salutations and handshakes after the game.

There was a crowd of nearly 92,000, national TV, and all of the attendant hype. It was like a mini–playoff game.

Quarterback Jay Schroeder called my number our second offensive play of the game, and I gained four yards before 49er linebacker Bill Romanowski tackled me.

I really didn't know it was Romo until someone mentioned it to me after the game. I recalled how vicious the 49er defense could be, but when I stepped on the field, it didn't faze me. I really wasn't aware who I was playing against. They were just objects. I couldn't even tell whose faces were inside the helmets. The only thing I was aware of were colors, the black jerseys of the good guys and the white jerseys of the bad guys. It's real easy for me to focus because I don't get caught up in all of that macho rhetoric and inane banter that goes on. It never really concerns me whom I'm facing.

In the second quarter, I got around left end for a 10-yard gain. I high-stepped into the secondary, just like the Roger Craig of old, and I came inches away from breaking a really big one. Near the end of the third quarter, 49er linebacker Darin Jordan tackled me after a five-yard gain, and I reinjured my shoulder. There's another piece of football irony: Jordan played for the Raiders last season and was a Plan B signee by the 49ers.

Anyway, I was through for the remainder of the game. Even though my afternoon ended prematurely, I was the game's leading rusher with 44 yards on 13 carries. I also caught one pass for 15 yards and made three first downs in the first quarter. All in all, not a bad afternoon at the office.

There was an incident early in the third quarter that did disrupt my focus and brought me rushing back to real life for a few moments. Steve Young had passed high over the middle to Jerry Rice, and Jerry made a serious attempt at the uncatachable ball. At the same time, our cornerback Terry McDaniel came up and took Rice's legs out from under him with a perfectly legal hit. But Jerry landed upside down on his neck and just lay there. Ronnie was the first one there, and he tried to help Jerry up, but when he saw that Jerry appeared semiconscious, he motioned to the 49er bench for the team doctor. My heart stood still for a few anxious moments as I watched my best friend being attended to. I put my head down and prayed that he was all right.

Fortunately, Jerry only suffered a mild concussion, and he came back to make some key catches for his team. As soon as the game was over, I ran across the field to embrace him.

"J.R., don't you ever do that to me again," I scolded him. "You scared the hell out of me."

The nice thing was that the Raiders won 12–6, and we were back in the AFC West race again. I was also pleased that we didn't try to stick it in their face. The 49er defenders tried to take my head off, which was what they're supposed to do. I would have been disappointed if they hadn't tried their best.

Both Tom Rathman and Jerry visited me in the Raiders locker room after the game. They brought me up to date on what was going on with the 49ers and how disappointing the 1991 season had begun for them. Both were a little down at the mouth. Tom wasn't getting to carry the ball as much as he liked, and Jerry wasn't getting his usual steady diet of passes. I told Jerry that he couldn't take the weight of the whole team on his shoulders.

But Jerry is a competitor, like me, and every time the 49ers lose, he accepts the blame, because he feels responsible for making the big plays that lead them to victory. With Joe out for the season, he felt double the pressure to pick up the slack. They both seemed happy that I was doing well again.

I guess my glee over beating the 49ers was hard to disguise, and that didn't help matters any. We wished each other good luck and cautioned each other to stay healthy. I watched them disappear through the door into the sunlight, their heads a little bowed.

I retired to the training room to get some treatment on my shoulder. Little pangs of exhaustion were starting to make their way into my body. It had been an extremely emotional week, and now it was all over. My emotional system had been taxed and purged, and I was completely drained.

When I made my way back to my locker, the locker room was almost completely empty except for a few attendants and an equipment man. I dressed hurriedly and rushed outside to where the 49ers park their buses. I had forgotten to say so long to the rest of the guys. But I was too late. Their buses had already left for the airport.

I felt a slight twinge of sadness because I didn't want to let my old teammates go away without saying good-bye. We had shared too many good memories together, good times, bad times, and funny times. We had been a close-knit family at one time, with one heartbeat. We had vigorously chased a dream that only two other teams in the history of pro football had been in position to pursue—three straight Super Bowl championships.

And damn, we had come close, closer than any of them. We had two hands and one foot on the summit.

I slowly made my way to my car, where Vernessia and Rogdrick were waiting. We joined up with my two daughters, who had opted for Disneyland Sunday instead of the game, and we all went out and had a nice quiet dinner.

By now I was really tired, but it was a good tired, the kind you get when you know you have accomplished something. In my case, the benefits were twofold. I had helped my new teammates to a victory, and I had helped heal some old wounds that had been festering.

I quickly shed consciousness and slipped off into dreamland, feeling contented for the first time in a long while. I knew that the loneliness over being away from my family and living out of a suitcase would quickly return once the weekly routine started again. But for now, all of the inconveniences were retreating. I buried my emotions under a blanket of contentment and dreamed of the future. I already had a lot of great memories and now I knew there were a lot more in front of me. It's been a helluva ride so far, and the meter is still running.

◆
2. Disappointment
7, 49ers 0

People are always coming up and asking me to explain when the 49ers really started their quest for the "Three-peat." What type of motivation was involved in getting a team to rally together for one common goal? How is a diverse group of grown men with different thoughts and different goals able to assemble the character to overcome all of the adversity? I tell them that it's difficult to explain. It's too simplistic to say that we just got better or that we peaked at the right time.

Then again, I don't think that we did much differently in 1988 than we had the previous season. Or the year before that. Certainly, luck is a factor. Talent is a factor. The injuries, or lack of them, are a big factor. But I think the major factors are the intangibles—the bitter and lasting memory of losing, of knowing another team is going on to the playoffs, of saying good-bye, or just the memory of a tear in the eye of a teammate. There was an unseen inner strength that bonded us together and made us scratch and claw for a common goal. How did we acquire it? I really don't know, except that determination and a work ethic passed on from one team generation to the next certainly contributed. I think that it has to do with the unselfish team concept in its purest form. How else can you explain it?

I honestly believe you have to go back to our 36–24 loss to the Minnesota Vikings in the 1987 NFL playoff game on January 9, 1988, at Candlestick Park. That is the genesis of our Three-peat quest. Looking back, it might have been the biggest disappointment in the franchise's history. By all accounts, we were supposed to win that game. We had come into the playoffs with a 13–2 record, the best in the NFL, and were a solid favorite to beat the Vikings, who barely made the playoffs as a wild-card team. I mean, everything pointed to us winning that game, big-time. A blowout. No contest.

We were on a tremendous roll and had beaten our final three regular-season opponents, Chicago, Atlanta, and the Rams, by a cumulative score of 124–7. That was impressive, even awesome. Plus, as the NFC West champions, we had that extra week off, which allowed our players to heal. Players like guard Bruce Collie, who was nursing a shoulder injury, started feeling better.

Before the game our injured tackle, Keith Fahnhorst, a holdover from the 1981 and '84 Super Bowl teams, addressed us in the locker room and told us how much it meant to win a Super Bowl, and how there was no other feeling in the world like it. He told us that we should want to give it our all because you never know when it could be your last playoff game, or your last football game for that matter. There is no reason to hold anything back, because the playoffs are a brand new series of one-game seasons. The teams that are able to turn it up a notch are the ones that go on to be successful. The others go home.

That should have been motivation enough, because we all sensed that Keith had played his last game, at least as a 49er. He had played nearly a full fourteen seasons without an injury of consequence, and then a neck injury in the second game of the regular season, against Cincinnati, had sapped all the strength from his left arm. He was placed on injured reserve when we returned from the 1987 players' strike; rookie Harris Barton replaced Keith and had been doing a great job ever since. Even if Keith had come back from his injury, it is doubtful that he would have reclaimed his old job. And there isn't much room in the NFL for thirty-six-year-old backup tackles who are making $342,000 a year. But Keith had attained a rare dream; he played on a Super Bowl team (1984) with his younger brother Jim, who was a linebacker for San Francisco through the 1990 season.

In addition to Keith, wide receiver Dwight Clark had announced earlier that this was going to be his final season. Dwight had a bad knee, and he had been relegated to a backup role behind Mike Wilson. I give Dwight credit for being very honest. He said he didn't want to sit on the bench and collect his salary under false pretenses. He was making about $550,000, and he said that was too much money for a backup. However, he added it would sure make it sweet if he could go out on top with a third Super Bowl ring. It was Dwight's catch during the 1981 NFC Championship Game against Dallas that propelled the surprising 49ers into their first Super Bowl. I think that he is San Francisco's favorite son when it comes to professional football. I would have loved to have won that one for Dwight.

Then there were our fans. We have some of the greatest fans in the world at Candlestick Park, and when they get to roaring during the pregame introductions, it sends chills up your spine.

Personally, I felt good. Some of my bruises had gone away, and I felt strong for the game. This had been the strike-shortened season. I had missed two of the three strike games and another one was canceled, so my body wasn't as abused and bruised as it would be after a normal, 16-game season. I felt that I was ready to make a major contribution. In previous seasons we had been beat up and had had to take our show on the road, which is a distinct disadvantage. But here we were at home, sleeping in our own beds, eating home cooking, and experiencing very little disruption to our normal life-style.

Even the Bay Area media was on our side for this game, which was a pleasant switch. Sometimes I believe they go out of their way to create an issue, or at least they belabor an actual issue until you're sick of reading or talking about it.

But now everything you read in the press heralded a 49ers' victory. We were the team of the eighties, the team of destiny, we were this and we were that. All of the front-runners were hopping aboard our cable car, clanging our bell, and riding along with us halfway to the stars.

Before the game, Vikings defensive coordinator Floyd Peters was quoted by the Bay Area media as saying that he liked his team's chances. He insisted the Vikings were peaking at exactly the right moment, and that a narrow 27–24 overtime loss to the Washington Redskins in the final game of the regular season two weeks earlier, plus the surprising 44–10 demolition of the New Orleans Saints in the NFC wild-card game the past week, underscored his premise. He said he couldn't believe that the 49ers were an eight-point favorite. Well, I guess we should have listened to Peters—or at the very least heeded his warning.

It's not that we were cocky or anything. It's just that we were brimming with confidence and believed that it was our year. There was a lot of talk in the media speculating on who our Super Bowl opponent would be, and I guess maybe some of us got caught up in that.

During the final week before the game, Coach Bill Walsh kept us loose with his usual pranks. The one that really cracked me up occurred a couple of afternoons before the game at our practice quarters in Redwood City. We had just finished eating lunch and were preparing to go out on the field for the afternoon practice when Bill strutted through the locker room dressed in black spandex cycling tights and a sweatshirt, with Jerry Rice's Flash '80 towel (Rice's good luck towel with his jersey number on it) tucked into his waistband. He really cracked me up—I told him that he would make a nice ice skater.

One thing that did detract from our preparations was the news that our owner was being fined $50,000 because he had announced he was doubling our playoff money for the game from $10,000 to $20,000. When the team had returned to play following the players' strike, team owner Eddie DeBartolo, Jr., told us that he would double the playoff money for each player that season. That meant that we were playing for twice as much as the Vikings were, and I suppose that upset the Viking players, whose management had a reputation for being tight-fisted. Eddie did that as a goodwill gesture, because the league had canceled one game, and some of us had missed up to three games' salary during the strike. One thing our owner wasn't, and that was cheap. He was a very generous owner all through the eighties.

Which is exactly what got him in trouble. Some of his fellow owners felt that this was carrying goodwill a little too far. They fumed that the 49ers were receiving an unfair incentive to make it to the Super Bowl. Perhaps we were, but they had the same prerogative to pay their players a bonus, as Eddie was doing. Instead they went to NFL commissioner Pete Rozelle, stamped their expensive brogans, and demanded that he do something about it. I guess in the end, it's the owners who have the ultimate say in the NFL. So Rozelle notified the 49ers that he was fining Eddie $50,000 for, as he put it, "violations of league rules regarding the form and timing of the bonuses and for failing to follow proper procedures in the filing of player contracts which contained the bonuses." But Rozelle said he would not rescind the bonuses, as some owners were demanding.

We still hadn't seen any money, so we didn't know what was going on. But Thursday after practice, Bill informed the media that the team was accepting the NFL's ruling and that the 49ers would pay the fine. He told the media, "We're going ahead with the incentive clause we've committed to with our team, and we're accepting the NFL decision related to a substantial fine for the act itself. I'm glad the decision was made." Bill then took a swipe at some of the other owners, saying they "took real issue with what we've accomplished."

So now we had an even bigger incentive to win the game, because we had a much larger stake in the pot. And that pot at the end of the rainbow, assuming we followed the path of the experts right into the winner's circle at the Super Bowl, was now $74,000 per player, instead of the traditional $64,000. At the same time, I'm sure we had every other owner in the NFL rooting against us. They will put aside any petty jealousies among themselves when it comes to hard cash. I could just picture Eagles owner Norman Braman dancing with Saints owner Tom Benson when we were losing. And I bet you that Benson was leading.

Anyway, we didn't think it was right that our owner had to pay a fine just because the other owners were shortsighted and vindictive. So at our team meeting Friday night before the game, Ronnie Lott, Dwight Clark, and Joe Montana stood up and suggested that each player chip in $1,000 to help pay the fine that was levied against our owner. We all agreed. I don't think there was a dissenter in the group. Later, Eddie said he was genuinely touched by the gesture. And I think he was. I truly believe that we were more to him that season than just a cog in the wheel of a machine that could bring personal satisfaction to a very wealthy person.

I can remember game day. We had the usual pregame jitters, but nothing out of the ordinary, nothing I can put my finger on. I know we had trained hard that last week, but I thrive on hard training. So we trotted out on the field and looked the Vikings over, and trotted back to the sidelines, almost like we had already played the game and beaten them. Most of us probably were thinking about who we were going to meet next, instead of who we were getting ready to meet that day.

That was the biggest mistake we made. Minnesota scored first, on a 21-yard field goal. We came right back and scored on Ray Wersching's 43-yard field goal, and we went into the second quarter all tied up. But we were beginning to realize we were in a battle. Whenever I went out for a pass, there would be someone in a purple jersey waiting right where Joe wanted to throw the ball. I'd circle right, and he'd circle right; I'd pop out into the flat, and he'd already be in the flat. It was uncanny, like they had a copy of our game plan or something.

They scored again on their next drive to go up 10–3. Then Joe Montana tried to squeeze a sideline pass in to Dwight Clark, but he didn't see Viking defensive back Reggie Rutland hanging back until after he had already released the ball. Rutland stepped in front of the ball, grabbed it, and ran 45 yards for a touchdown.

Going into the game, our coaches felt we could pass on Minnesota because their secondary supposedly was weak. So our game plan primarily was a passing plan, which was to be supplemented with a running attack after we had built up a substantial lead. But we went into the locker room at the half trailing 20–3, and now we had no choice but to pass. There was some confusion, and we were really shocked at the way the game was going.

It seemed like we were getting all of the bad calls and that the ball kept bouncing their way. On a third-and-ten pass from their own 26, our cornerback Don Griffin made a terrific play on the ball and tipped it away—only it fell right into the hands of Anthony Carter for a 63-yard gain. Things like that were killing us. Bill said that we would stick with the game plan, which was to get the ball to Rice, our big-play guy. That meant I wouldn't be given much opportunity to run the ball. Rice was getting a lot of double coverage, but we still tried to get him the ball. While everything had gone right for us in the previous three games, nothing was going right for us that afternoon.

Still, there was no panic at halftime. Bill didn't rant and rave, nor did he swear at us like he sometimes did. He calmly told us to just regroup. That was one major character asset of those 49ers; we weren't the type of football team that ever gave up just because someone tossed a little adversity in front of us. We'd fight down to the last second, and I think that's what distinguished the 49ers from other teams.

Minnesota took a 30–17 lead into the fourth quarter, and we just couldn't catch up. The final score was 36–24, and the team that everyone had predicted would be in the Super Bowl was packing its bags and going home. It was an extremely bitter defeat.

Afterward, Peters said that the Vikings' game plan was to deny the ball to our two big-play guys, Jerry and myself. He admitted that he took a risk by playing strictly for the pass and by keeping a linebacker or safety on me every time I'd pass the line of scrimmage. I guess they had a better grasp of our game plan than we did. There are some things that I will never understand about that game, like trying to force the ball in to Jerry when he was double-covered.

Still, I don't like to second-guess a coach. That's not my job. I never did it in college and I'm not about to start now. I just accept whatever a coach tells me, because he's the one being paid for coaching.

So if the blame is to be passed around for the debacle against the Vikings, I'll accept my share along with the others. Looking back, I do believe that we got a little complacent with ourselves. Perhaps we believed all of those newspaper stories about how the road to the Super Bowl led right through San Francisco, how we were the team to beat.

I don't think we were mentally prepared to play Minnesota. They were not one of our big rivals, and they got to the playoffs with an 8–7 record. So maybe we didn't harbor as much respect for them as we should have. Also, I believe that we overtrained for the game that last week. I think that we played the game against each other during the extra week we had. We were so excited; we finished the season with the best record in the league, and we were overanxious to get the postseason under way. So we went at each other with such ferocity that we burned ourselves out.

Plus, our fields at Redwood City were flooded, so we spent most of the time practicing down at Stanford University's football field. I'll never forget the muddy field we practiced on that week, and I think it took something out of us. It was like running in sand. I know that Jerry complained to me during the week that his legs were tired. Thinking back, my legs were a little dead too. Minnesota flew to Arizona to practice on dry fields in the sunshine. I remember thinking to myself during the game that they seemed to be just one step ahead of us.

Then again, perhaps the Vikings wanted it more than we did. They had an extremely tough defensive line, and they had nothing to lose. They were pumped up and ready to play. It was like they turned it up another notch after they beat New Orleans in the wild-card game. We had played well in the previous three or four weeks, but now we didn't have enough steam to carry us through the first game of the postseason. It was one of the worst days of my life.

The truth was that they played better than we did, and I guess a blow to your pride is the hardest blow to accept.

Minnesota was the better team that afternoon, and we were, at best, mediocre. But more than anything, that loss shocked us back to reality. It made us realize that the only way you get to the Super Bowl is through hard work and teamwork. Those are the two indispensables. It gave us a stronger resolve not to let it happen again. Press clippings and television interviews don't win games.

After the game I was so depressed, so mentally drained that I just wanted to go home and go to bed. We were supposed to go to dinner with friends, but I told Vernessia that I just couldn't do it. I was emotionally empty, and I knew that I didn't want to have to keep explaining over and over and over again to people why we lost. Don't get me wrong; I love my friends and the fans, but I just couldn't accommodate them after this game. It was better for everyone concerned that I went home and went to bed.

Bill met with us the next morning in Redwood City and told us that we had nothing to be ashamed of. He basically said that when you go into the competitive arena you always expose yourself to disappointment. Only one team can win, and it just happened to be Minnesota's day. He also told us that we'd be back, that this loss was just a temporary setback.

But I could tell that the loss bothered him more than he let on. He looked older, and his eyes were tired and his voice didn't have that positive lilt that it usually does when he's around football. I know that our local media requested to meet with him later in the day, but he sent word to them through public relations director Jerry Walker that he would be unavailable. Walker also informed the press that Bill was going out of town for a week and would not be available for comment until he returned. I guess that's more or less how all of us felt, like we'd like to get out of town and not have to stand around and offer explanations.

Anyway, after he met with the team he called me aside and asked me to come up to his office for a few minutes. I didn't have any idea what he wanted, and given the mood of the meeting, I wasn't about to speculate.

That's when he told me that I was going to be the halfback the next season. I had split that role with Joe Cribbs and shared fullback duties with Tom Rathman. Because I had to know both positions, I think I might have played overly cautiously at times so I wouldn't .confuse the two. Bill's decision was one of the few bits of sunlight that I experienced during the next few days. I was really happy with the change, because it would enable me to concentrate on one position.

I told him, "Coach, I'm ready for the challenge. I'll really prepare myself for it." I weighed about 226 then, and I told him that I would get my weight down and get my mind and body in tune, that both would be ready for the pounding I would take next year.

I remember my disappointment at Nebraska when coach Tom Osborne called me in just before spring practice before my senior year and informed me that he was switching me from tailback to fullback, and that Junior Mike Rozier would be the tailback. We had shared that position the previous season. "I think by alternating you and Mike, we're hurting the team," he told me.

I said, "Look coach, you have nearly a two-thousand-yard-rushing tandem. How could it be hurting our offense?" But he didn't answer me.

I was coming off a fantastic year, something like 1,200 yards rushing and 12 touchdowns, including a 234-yard game against Florida State and I figured that they would pump me up for the Heisman Trophy.

At the time, it bothered me because I had been a tailback my entire career. I didn't cry about it, because I'm a team man, but that doesn't mean that I agreed with it.

All my life I had been running away from linebackers, and now I had to run at them and block for Mike. So I trained hard during spring ball, and I beat out the two guys who were in front of me. Rozier got the headlines, and I got the blocks. But I dealt with it. As long as we won, that was the most important thing.

I never had a falling-out with Osborne. After all, he offered me a scholarship when my home-state school, Iowa State, ignored me. Still, I just never understood why he did what he did, and I thought that I was entitled to an explanation. In the long run, though, I guess it helped me out, because it made me work all that much harder to achieve my goals.

I received some vindication when the 49ers drafted me and Bill Walsh showed me the scouting reports: they said that Nebraska hadn't utilized me to my full potential. Bill said that the 49ers were disappointed in the way I was used there. That gave me motivation and made me feel good.

So here I was with Bill, in the reverse role, getting a chance to return to the position I grew up at. Personally, I think halfback is the natural position for me. I was getting used to playing halfback most of the time, and I felt that if I could lose ten to fifteen pounds, I would be that much quicker. For one thing, I was never the big, powerful blocking fullback Tom was. I kept that extra weight on just so I could block for Joe Montana and whoever was playing halfback.

I think my key attributes are my ability to run with the ball and catch it and to block if I really have to. I thought that I would be more effective as a halfback. I told Bill that he wouldn't be sorry about making that decision.

My legs almost had a happy spring to them as I came down the hall from his office and started downstairs to the team locker room. But the reality of the situation came rushing back to me as soon as I opened the door. I very quietly went to my locker, keeping the good news to myself, and started cleaning out my shoes and whatever else I had accumulated during the course of the season.

The saddest part of a football season, I believe, is when you clean out your locker after the final game. You've lived side by side with your teammates for what seems like an eternity, all working for a common goal. The heat of summer camp, the long two-a-days, the separations from your family, the fun times, the parties, the team meetings, the night before a game in the team hotel, your roommate on the road—it all makes you realize that you're part of a very special family. And then one day *poof*! it's over.

I looked slowly around the room at the guys cleaning out their lockers. What made this especially nostalgic was the fact that this would be our last time in this locker room. The locker room in Redwood City was old and crowded and smelly, and we were always bumping into each other. But like the San Francisco fog and Candlestick itself, it had a certain charm or mystique to it. After all, this was the birthplace of the 49ers' era of respectability, and there was a well-worn mental comfortableness about it. We would be moving into the new $10-million Marie P. DeBartolo Sports Centre in Santa Clara when we broke summer camp the next season. But none of us knew who would be there and who wouldn't. For some, like Keith Fahnhorst and Dwight Clark, this was it. This was the last time they would clean out a locker as 49ers. And as it turned out, there were quite a few others who would not be back.

Center Fred Quillan, who had missed the last part of the season after suffering a severe concussion in the Rams game, would be traded to San Diego during the off-season. He and I used to stay after practice and lift weights, and we'd built a special relationship. Ray Wersching, Joe Cribbs, Derrick Crawford, Ken Margerum, George Cooper, Clyde Glover, Dana McLemore, and Calvin Nicholas wouldn't make it through our next training camp. Linebacker Milt McColl, who had recently obtained his medical degree, would be traded to the Los Angeles Raiders, and linebacker Todd Shell's career would end on the practice field at our summer camp in Rocklin the next July following a violent collision with tight end Ron Heller. Finally, punter Max Runager would be waived following our first game of the 1988 season, and both defensive end Dwaine Board and linebacker Darren Comeaux would be lost when the 49ers tried to sneak them through waivers during the 1988 season.

I know that's all part of the game, and we're all professionals. Still, you never get used to it. You share lunch and dreams, you talk and joke with a guy for days, months, even years, and then you come to work one day and there's nothing but an empty locker. Your heart drops, and next you think, Hey, that could have been me. And then you wonder if that's the way you'll leave this game, too embarrassed to say good-bye to your teammates.

The only evidence of their years of contribution and hard work and sweat is that empty locker, and the next day there's some stranger with a new jersey occupying it and telling jokes. I'm a people person and I enjoy the camaraderie, so the transitional aspect of football is something that I'll never get used to. Never. But if you're looking for security, you're certainly in the wrong business if you choose football. I eventually learned that the hard way; little did I realize that day that the Fahnhorsts, Clarks, and Boards were giving me a peek into my future.

I cleaned out my locker and went home to contemplate my future. We were living in San Carlos, a small San Francisco suburb about twenty miles south of the airport, and the comfort of Vernessia, daughters Damesha and Rometra, and my little live-wire son Rogdrick was very important to me at this time. The innocence and trust of children have a unique quality that cleanses all of the mental hurt and makes distant the bad memories. Every day more sunshine and laughter filled our home.

The Minnesota who?

Still, I must admit that it was difficult sitting around the house waiting for the Super Bowl between the Redskins and Denver to finally be over. I had been selected to the Pro Bowl again, and I was really looking forward to those two weeks in Hawaii. I knew that it wouldn't take me long to get out of the funk I was in and enjoy football once more.

But first, I owed my family something. Football can be a lonely occupation, and it takes an understanding wife and understanding children to make it a success. When I was in camp for five weeks and on the road some ten weekends and at the team hotel the night before every home game of the season, Vernessia took care of all of the family matters. When the children cried, it was she, not me, who was there to tend to their scrapes and bruises, wipe away their tears, and tuck them into bed at night.

So we packed our bags and flew down to Disneyland for a few days. The kids really loved it, and we just relaxed. I found that I actually could have a good time. The best thing was that no one recognized me. I was finally away from people who kept asking me, "What happened?" "Why did you lose?" "Where was your offense?" "How come you didn't score more touchdowns?" I had to get away from that because it was really frustrating.

I also was able to find some quiet time for myself, and that's when I started gathering my thoughts for my off-season training regimen. In the past, I had usually taken a month off after the season was over and gone back to Davenport, Iowa, to visit family and friends. That gave me time to relax and let my body heal. But now I felt that I'd made a commitment to Bill to be his halfback, and the sooner I got back in training the better.

So I set some goals for myself. After the Vikings had beaten us to start 1988, I vowed to gain some retribution and erase the bad start on the new year by going to Hawaii and having a good game in the Pro Bowl. Even though we lost to the AFC, 15–6, I thought I had a decent game. I was scheduled to compete in the Super Teams the week following the Super Bowl. The Super Teams competition was one of those zany television shows featuring well-known professional athletes, created to fill the TV programming void between the football and baseball seasons. The friendly competition between teams featured such events as a bicycle race, swimming, and running an obstacle course. And the following week, I was scheduled to go to Miami for the Super Stars competition. It was basically the same format, only it was individual competition instead of team. I told myself I wanted to finish in the top three, and I finished second to Herschel Walker. So I had accomplished two of my goals right off.

My third goal was to lose the weight I had promised Bill I would lose and come into camp in great condition. Oh Lord, there went my ice cream, milk, and cookies. One of the simple pleasures of life, and one that had become quite a habit with me, was eating a bowl of vanilla ice cream with some oatmeal raisin cookies and drinking a couple of glasses of milk just before bedtime. Man, I can taste it now, the coolness of the milk and the richness of the ice cream and the crunchiness of the cookies. I don't do drugs, I do cookies. With ice cream and milk.

And I think about them a lot. There's no simple way to give up a vice like that. I knew there was no way I could do it on my own.

So Vernessia had to help me. First she hid the cookies on me. But I'm a great sleuth, and I would find them. So she stopped buying them, and when I would go to the supermarket with her and slip them into the shopping cart when her back was turned, she would take them out at the checkout counter. So my new bedtime snack became popcorn and ice water.

I also wanted to cut down on red meats, so I had my wife prepare chicken and fish, with lots of fruits and vegetables. I guess I wavered a few times, but I tried to keep my goal of being the best player possible always in focus. If I lost the weight and came into camp in great condition, everything else would take care of itself. Because I felt sure that if I were physically and mentally prepared, I would have a great year.

At the same time I called Dr. Arthur Ting, an orthopedist who was part of the medical team that took care of the 49ers. Dr. Ting is a former marathon runner, and he knows a lot about conditioning. He knew of a park right near where I lived, which had horse trails that wound up a mountain. He explained that running hills would be a lot less stressful on my legs than other types of running.

When I got back from the Super Stars competition, I was actually still in pretty good shape. I had been involved in strenuous competition since the season ended, and I don't think that I really ever got out of shape. I only took a week off and started my conditioning program right around the first of March.

Running the hills was tough at first. I even stopped a few times in the middle of one of those steep trails, only to hear Ting behind me screaming, "Keep pushing, keep pushing!" So I kept pushing, and in a week or so I was running all the way to the top. After a while I mastered it, and it seemed like a piece of cake—make that ice cream and cookies. I started laughing all of the way up, shouting to the mountain, "Ha ha, I beat you." The mountain became my opponent, and all of the anguish I had built up after that Minnesota game, all of the nightmares were lost in the sweat dripping over those hilly paths.

It got so that I actually looked forward to getting up at six o'clock every morning and driving over to the hill. I'd look up at the forest paths, shake my fist, and say, "I'm going to beat you today."

I think it's important to pass down the work ethic, just as Walter Payton and Jack Reynolds, our crusty old former linebacker, passed it on to me. I invited some of my teammates to run the hills with me, but until the second year it was usually only a one-shot appearance. Tom Rathman—we're both from Nebraska and real good friends–came out one morning, but he said that six-thirty was too early. Other players have run with me; Barry Sanders came out and ran with me.

But, of all the people who I've invited to run with me, only one really got into the routine, until last year, when Jerry Rice also joined us, and that's Eric Wright, although Tom slowly has returned to run on occasion. When we first started doing it, Eric would tell me that he would be there and then he wouldn't show up. So I'd go over to his house and get him out of bed. After I rousted him out of the sack a few times, he finally got with the program.

I guess that my dedication to fitness borders on religion. But that's how I felt about things going into the 1988 season. I had been delegated an extremely important role in our offense, and I didn't want to let either Bill or my teammates down.

According to Dr. Ting, who has worked out a program for the sports rehab clinic he worked for, Sports, Orthopedic and Rehabilitation Medicine Associates (SOAR), an athlete must simulate the activity he or she participates in to maximize performance. So I visualize myself running through safeties and past linebackers when I run the hills.

He also has studies that show running hills decreases the stresses on the lower extremities and at the same time greatly increases one's endurance. He has all of these technical terms, but basically he's explained to me that running uphill decreases the effect of gravity and the pounding on the lower back. He's also showed me studies that explain how running hills eliminates excessive tearing and stress on muscles and supporting soft tissues.

In the succeeding years I have added sprints, and I work out with weights, pulling them in a harness, like a plow horse. Jerry Rice and I probably do sprints three times a week, finishing up with ten or more hundred-yard dashes.

But Dr. Ting doesn't have to convince me. I've always tried to be in tune with my body, and I know when it's telling me that it feels good. The hill-running program, as prescribed by Ting, made me feel good. It got to a point where I actually couldn't wait until football season started. I wanted to give my body the ultimate test and show that I could be an even better football player.

The best was yet to come, and I knew it—I could feel it. It was almost as if I had an extra vision, as if I was tuned in to the future. I could also feel that no amount of adversity was going to shake my prediction of a great season for the 49ers in 1988. We had the talent, the maturity, and we certainly had learned how to be humble.

3. The Commitment

Every preseason begins with the same hopes and dreams and optimism as the previous one did. I think that even the less talented teams feel at the start of summer camp that this could be their year, that a miracle will come along and sweep them right into the Super Bowl for the ultimate sixty minutes of the sport. Certainly, the 49er team of the eighties always believed it was the best, because we had been to the playoffs every year since 1983, my rookie season. In my second year we went all of the way, posting an 18–1 record, the most wins ever in a single season in the NFL, en route to beating Miami 38–16 in Super Bowl XIX at Stanford.

But the preceding three seasons we had been eliminated in the first round of the playoffs, and people were beginning to suspect our legitimacy and question our motivation. Football fans are very fickle. Once you win it all, they will accept nothing less from that day forward, and if you fall short of their expectations, you are open to criticism.

Twice we were eliminated by the New York Giants in the first round of the playoffs, and now we were coming off a humiliating first-round loss to the Vikings. So the big question around the Bay Area was, whatever happened to the real 49ers, the Super Bowl champions?

And the team was beginning to wonder too. Not that we were doubting our talent or our coaches; the team's draft picks were among the best in the NFL, and our game plans were beautifully crafted. But it was like we were snakebit. Somewhere, somebody had this little 49er doll and was sticking pins in it.

But 1988 felt different. I think we were all brimming with confidence about the upcoming season. We knew that most of what went wrong against the Vikings was correctable, and that we were just a few centimeters away from taking it all the way. But we were hesitant to go public with our feelings, because we knew from past experiences that those kind of predictions could backfire.

I was really pumped up about my off-season running program and truly looking forward to summer camp and the 100-plus-degree days in Rocklin. Honestly, it was hard for me to contain my enthusiasm. In addition to building up my stamina and helping me lose the weight I needed to get rid of in order to play halfback, the hill-running also helped me construct an inner strength that would become a valuable tool for me during the coming season. It was a strength that I'd possessed all along, but one I hadn't exploited or tested the limits of. I'd just taken it up to another level.

Right before our May minicamp a bunch of us decided to enter the centipede division of the Bay to Breakers footrace. The Bay to Breakers is a race in San Francisco that started out as a sporting event and has evolved into a happening. It's really hard to describe, because of the aura it creates; its mood actually transcends competition, which has become a peripheral component of the race. Every kind of person participates in it, from men on roller skates dressed like nuns to people with no clothes on at all to human floats of the Golden Gate Bridge to world-class athletes. And at the end of the 7.45-mile race, out at the Pacific Ocean near the edge of San Francisco's Golden Gate Park, there is this giant picnic, or festival. It seems like the entire Bay Area unwinds and laughs and is happy on this one magical Sunday.

A bunch of us, including wide receiver Mike Wilson, fullback Tom Rathman, linebacker Michael Walter, our conditioning coach Jerry Attaway, and two very popular ex-players, Bill Ring and Ron Ferrari, decided that we would enter the centipede race, a separate division of the Bay to Breakers, in which teams of runners race linked to one another by ropes. Some of those guys practiced together, but I had my own running group and didn't see them until the day of the race. We were being sponsored by Milky Way, which meant that we would be outfitted in Milky Way T-shirts and hats while we ran through the streets and up and down the hills of San Francisco.

I was in the middle of the centipede, in front of Rathman and behind Wilson. It was like a big tug-or-war, with Wilson pulling me one way and Rathman pulling me the other. I think I ended up pulling Rathman nearly the entire way. I kept hollering, "Tom, pick up your feet!" But it was fun, and it made you feel good inside to see so many people, such a varied cross-section of humanity, enjoying themselves. It is an event, like a big Hollywood party. And we did pretty well. I don't know where we finished, but I think it was in the top ten. And they have some world-class centipedes in the race.

A couple of weeks afterward the 49ers went to Santa Clara, where we had our final minicamp, at our new practice facility. The building wasn't completed, so we couldn't use the locker rooms, but the fields were ready, so we had a sneak preview of our new state-of-the-art facility. It was second to none in the NFL.

This was going to be an exciting summer for us. We were scheduled to play the Miami Dolphins in the American Bowl on July 31 at Wembley Stadium in London, England. Joe Montana and I had gone over to London for a week in early June to promote the game, and I could see it would be a little more special than your ordinary exhibition game.

For some of our players, free agents and time-worn veterans, this might be their only trip to England. A lot of them were going to be cut as soon as we returned from the trip, and they knew it. Plus, the NFL selected different teams every year to play in the game, so the 49ers would have to take its place in line to get back. Many of the fringe players were really looking forward to this free trip. The team was chartering a 747, and we could bring along our wives and girlfriends on the trip. Usually we're lucky if we see our wives and families one weekend during the entire summer camp.

We reported to our summer headquarters at Sierra College, a community college in little Rocklin, California, on July 17, two weeks before the game. Rocklin is the exact opposite of San Francisco. While San Francisco is sophisticated and cosmopolitan, Rocklin is down-home and country. Life in Rocklin is the way I imagine it used to be back in the forties and fifties. The people are very friendly and will go out of their way to help you. And they know only two speeds—slow and slower. I think they are forced to be slow because it gets so hot during the daytime that you have to limit your physical activity.

The 49er coaches like the location because it gives them better control over our environment. I know some of my former teammates are going to think I'm crazy, but I liked Rocklin too. I think it is an ideal location for a summer camp. First, there are few distractions because it's in such a remote area, way out in the Sierra foothills, and it's difficult for the players to find any trouble. We took over the campus, and everything was centralized for us. And the heat is great for conditioning.

Maybe I'm from the old school, but I truly believe that you have to make sacrifices if you want to be the best and be known as the best. I think it's good to get away from the comfortable home surroundings and totally concentrate on football. The fewer distractions, the better. That goes for temptations, too. When football season starts, all of that nightlife and extra stuff is over. For me, anyway.

We stayed in air-conditioned dorms right on campus, and usually there was an 11:30 bed check. Once in a while they'd let us stay till one A.M., but with meetings scheduled just about every night until 9:30, we didn't have much of an opportunity to get out to visit beautiful downtown Rocklin, population 7500.

But even when we did, there wasn't much to see: a couple of country bars with Merle Haggard and Tammy Wynette on the jukebox, a bowling alley, and a few fast-food places. Most of the players, when they did get a night off, liked to drive down to Roseville, which is about ten miles west of Rocklin. Danny Bunz, formerly a linebacker with the 49ers, has a large bar and restaurant, a good place to get a cold beer or a plate of barbecued spareribs. Once a week I liked to go out and pig out at a Mexican or Italian restaurant. I might even have a Corona.

As I said, though, usually it was lights out following our night meeting. I would sit around and watch some films of our first opponent, or even films of our practice. When I got a free moment, I sometimes drove down to my masseur, Dr. Don Sanchez, and he worked on my body. His offices are right near Sierra College, so that made it convenient.

The 6:30 wakeup horn came awfully early—before the end of round one of my dreams, most mornings. The two-a-days, coupled with the intense heat, really took it out of you. Some nights it was all I could do to crawl into bed and turn out the lights.

But this summer was different. We were only in Rocklin for a week before we packed our bags and headed off to London. And after seven days of temperatures over 105 degrees, we were really looking forward to that jolly old London Fog. That first week of practice seemed to fly by, and before we knew it we were boarding our charter at San Francisco International Airport.

On the plane on the way over we were too excited to sleep. Vernessia kept telling me about all of the shopping she was going to do, which had me thinking that I would have to get another job on the side when we got back to pay the extra bills.

Once we got there, we mixed business with pleasure. We'd scrimmage against the Dolphins, usually in the morning, and be free to spend the afternoons with our wives and girlfriends. London is an exciting city, and there are so many things to see and do. And Eddie De-Bartolo had gone to great expense to set up special tours and activities to keep everyone entertained. So I tried to have fun, right along with tending to business.

People had cautioned me before I left that I might not like the food, but I found I didn't have any trouble. I love Italian food, and I discovered plenty of great Italian restaurants in London. The water might have been a little strange, but the food was great.

Vernessia and I enjoyed the time we spent together. Sure, we missed the children, but both Damesha and Rometra were born while I was still in college, and this was our first vacation away from the kids. Vernessia really loved checking out the fashions. I was all for it too, as long as it was just window-shopping. After visiting all of the chic fashion houses we would go out for dinner or to one of those cozy pubs that are so prevalent in London. We also took in a couple of plays, including *Phantom of the Opera.*

It was a great experience for me and for the team to go to a foreign country like that. Sort of a cultural exchange, if you can equate sports with culture. But I also had to make sure that I kept my mind on my job. I had worked hard during the off-season to attain a high level of conditioning, and I didn't want to blow it with too many linguini and clam sauce dinners. Tortellini in cream sauce maybe, but not linguini.

Football is growing rapidly in Europe, and the NFL smells some big bucks over there, so I guess games in foreign countries will become a regular part of our preseason itinerary in the near future. Europeans collect all of the NFL team memorabilia, and that market is economically healthy for pro football.

It was quite an experience playing in front of a foreign audience. I really didn't know what to expect, because I knew that most of the people in the stands didn't understand our rules or the subtle nuances of the game the way the fans back in the United States do. But they were very enthusiastic, if a little more eager to learn about the athletes than the game itself.

When we stepped onto the field that Sunday, the people went crazy. Wembley is a huge soccer stadium, and it was nearly packed. The atmosphere was charged with excitement from the fans; it was like a mini–Super Bowl. Whether a player caught a pass or fumbled, the same fans would stand and cheer. That part of it struck me as being really weird. But who knows? I might cheer at a similar transgression during a cricket match.

We won the toss and elected to receive. But it was Jerry Rice, not I, who carried the ball first in this American Bowl. He gained 21 yards on a sweep, and on the next play Joe passed 13 yards to Wes Chandler. We were on a roll, and then I got my chance. Two carries, seven yards, and an incomplete pass, and we had to punt. So much for the Roger Craig roll.

Miami went on to win, 28–21. I carried the ball only four times for 23 yards and caught one pass for 22 yards. Not scintillating numbers, but I felt that I was on schedule. I felt good about our team and our upcoming season. I can't explain why, I just did.

We left for home on the charter right after the game, and we had a good time on the flight. The biggest prankster on the plane was Joe Montana, who got a few laughs at the expense of Vernessia and myself.

While we were in London, one of those notorious English tabloids ran a front-page story, complete with fabricated quotes from my wife, that suggested we had done more than sleep on the flight over. The article was entitled, "Roger's 49 Ways to Please His Missus." When I saw it on the newsstands with my picture next to the headline, I couldn't believe it. Somebody is real sick over there. There is an abundance of that type of newspaper in Britain, and I soon forgot about it.

But Montana had bought a copy and saved it, and on the flight home he got up and showed it to anyone who hadn't seen it yet. A real pal. He got a few laughs, and I just slouched down in my seat. Vernessia took it a lot better. She laughed along with the rest of the group.

On our way home I confided to my wife that I thought that our team was going to have a super season. I felt much better about going into the 1988 season than I had at the start of any of my previous six. I'd had a great off-season, my weight was down, and I was in top physical condition. Plus I knew where I was going; for the first time I had my mind exclusively focused on playing halfback. I looked forward to practice every day, instead of counting the days down the way you usually do before a season starts.

The bottom line in football is to have fun. If you get involved in contract hassles, if you don't know your role on a team or you have problems with your teammates, you're not going to perform at your best. Life is too short to go around with a chip on your shoulder. I think you should enjoy your job on a football team, no matter what your role is. Sure, I got paid more money than most of the players, and I had a so-called glamor position, but the 49ers were a first-class organization, and we all had a lot to be thankful for.

So here I was in the best frame of mind I could be in and raring to get the season under way. I couldn't see any obstacles that could prevent the 1988 San Francisco 49ers from going all the way from the American Bowl to the Super Bowl.

But I guess life is just not like that. Immediately following the game in London, Bill Walsh was asked by a network television reporter in the locker room about the quarterback position and he offhandedly remarked that it was an "open competition" between Joe Montana and Steve Young. None of us on the team was aware of what he had said at the time, but we sure were by the time we got back to Rocklin the next day.

Most of the media that follow the team had picked up on the televised interview, and some took it to mean that Joe no longer had job security. They wrote that he and Steve would compete for the starting job, and some of them were even predicting that Young would beat Joe out.

The first crisis of the new season, and we weren't even over jet lag yet.

Naturally, Joe wasn't too happy about what was said. And he was even less happy about all of the attention the media was focusing on the incident. Bill didn't do too much to clear up matters. On one hand he said, "Joe had the greatest season of his career, is at the top of his game, and has a history of excellence and consistency." Then in his next breath, he would tell the media, "We'll go back to the same response: it's open competition. Roger Craig can be replaced, Harris Barton can be replaced, and Jerry Rice, theoretically, can be replaced. I would be awfully dogmatic and bullheaded if I were to say that only Joe will be considered the starting quarterback this year."

Roger Craig can be replaced? Hey, I was just getting started in my new role with the team. I wasn't ready to abdicate my position just yet.

Joe confided to some of us that he was a little perplexed by Bill's failure to give him a vote of confidence. Even before the season started there had been a rumor circulating that the 49ers were offering Joe to the San Diego Chargers. Nothing ever came of it, but Joe was aware of the rumor, and it no doubt lent credence in his mind to Bill's statement that he considered Joe replaceable.

Joe said it appeared as if his entire football career was judged by one performance—the loss to the Vikings. It was eating at Joe, and we could tell. Let me tell you one thing about him: he's not a complainer. He told the media that he didn't want to talk about it because he didn't want to "be labeled a complainer or a whiner. I'm going to do what I have to do. If he [Walsh] makes up his mind that way [that Young would start], then it's going to happen whether I want it to or not."

We had done some pretty good things the previous season, even if it did end on a sour note, and Joe was a big part of that success. I was ready to roll, and the last thing I wanted to see was a full-blown controversy. But the way the media was acting, it appeared that it would end up that way.

Joe is really a classy individual. Around us players, he tried to downplay the controversy. Once he steps between those white lines there is nothing but football and the will to win on his mind. He blocks out all exterior pressures and focuses on the game. That's what makes him such a great quarterback.

In any case, the debate that raged in the newspapers and on television and on the radio talk shows didn't appear to have any effect on the stability of the team. I don't know if it affected Joe mentally, because he was the one who had to constantly deal with the media, but Joe is strong enough to handle something like that.

The only thing that might have disrupted us somewhat was having two different voice commands on the field. When a football team is operating at its optimum performance level, when all components are functioning as one team, it reacts more than it thinks. And this team was used to reacting to Joe's voice, and now we had to learn to react to Steve's voice.

Don't get me wrong. Steve is a great quarterback in his own way, and the 49ers quarterback of the future. It's just that when you get used to one quarterback and his cadence and then you get another guy in there with a different cadence, it can mess up your timing.

But I thought we adjusted well. The potential was there for it to be a disruptive force, but it never was. Both men are great at what they do. It's just that Joe has a little edge over Steve because of his experience and the big games he has participated in throughout his career. Steve does certain things better than Joe, like running the ball, and he puts added pressure on a defense because of that ability.

But with Joe you have a quarterback who can dissect a defense with the precision of a surgeon. He can cut through a zone with a perfectly thrown ball, and he can dismantle a man-to-man defense with a perfect timing-pattern to his receiver. He has an uncanny knack for reading defenses, and perhaps his greatest asset is his ability to improvise when his primary receiver is covered. Many times I'd be the third or even the fourth option (receiver) in the pattern, and I'd look up to see the ball coming my way. It's a special gift that not many quarterbacks possess.

But who knows? Maybe in time, Steve will be able to do the same thing with the football. That's a mindblower. If Steve had Joe's innovative skills to go with his running skills, the Niners would be practically invincible.

Getting back to the controversy, though, I thought it was blown out of proportion. I think that Bill wanted to ensure that Joe would last the entire season, so he created a way to rest him. And Steve is a real competitive guy and it just kills him to sit on the bench; I know I have a hard time watching him agonize on the sidelines because I know that deep inside he would give anything to be out on that playing field.

So by creating an open-ended issue, Bill was keeping Steve's hopes alive. I think that might have been more important than declaring Joe the starter. Steve had a lot of youthful enthusiasm, and he might have lost some of it if he thought he wasn't ever going to get a fair shot at the starting quarterback job.

I have to give Walsh credit for keeping the potentially disruptive situation from hurting the team. He told us at a team meeting that we had to keep all the negative forces, such as the quarterback controversy, away from our family. He said that if they got inside our sidelines or in our locker room, they could devastate a team. He kept reminding us at every opportunity to keep all of the negative forces outside and to keep the family strong.

So it never reached a serious level with us. If anything, it lent a little more interest to summer camp. We still had four exhibition games left and that usually means alternating quarterbacks, so the media would have enough ammunition to carry them halfway through the regular season. One paper even ran one of those public opinion polls asking who should be the 49ers quarterback.

That's all we need in this game—a popularity contest to determine who the starters will be. If it were decided that way, our third-string quarterback John Paye most likely would have seen the starter, because he's a local product and had a large local following to stuff the ballot box.

But I shouldn't complain. Everything was going great for me, and Rathman was blocking better than he ever had. Putting me at halfback and moving Tom up to starting fullback looked like a great move. It was the Husker Connection, two Nebraska boys running the football for the 49ers.

Our preseason, though, was nothing to brag about. Our first game after we got home from London was a Saturday night game against the Los Angeles Raiders. They used to be the Oakland Raiders, and when we played them at Candlestick it seemed like half the stadium was rooting for the Raiders. I mean, really. We beat them 24–10 to even our preseason record at 1–1. I carried the ball 12 times for only 31 yards. But Terrence Flagler, my backup, had 37 yards on just seven carries. In his postgame press conference, Bill praised Terrence, saying that he was a "much-improved player this year."

Myself? I told the media that I was still adjusting to the halfback position and that I wasn't concerned about personal statistics. I told them that I would rather return to the Super Bowl than worry about how many yards I did or didn't make. There were those two words again, *Super Bowl.*

The next week we went to Denver and lost 34–24 at Mile High Stadium. I only carried five times for 18 yards. Locker room rumor had it they were getting ready to make a decision on Joe Cribbs, and they wanted to see if he had anything left. But he only carried twice for seven yards, so I guess they had already made up their minds. We closed out our 1988 preseason with a pair of victories, beating the Seahawks 27–21 at home and the Chargers 34–27 in San Diego.

Right before we flew to San Diego to play the Chargers, we broke camp. Just as Rocklin is a good place to train in the summer, it's an even better place to leave when the time comes. Your mind has been totally focused on football, and now it's time to apply your newfound skills. Your body tells you that you've logged your boot-camp hours, and now it's time to go to war. The mind is clear and fresh, the physical and mental components are in harmony, and the concentration honed to perfection by all of those repetitions that they put you through in camp.

You definitely know it's time to go home when you start to get tired of seeing your teammates' faces all the time. I got weary of living with all of those males in the dorms and I started craving female attention. It's such a relief to see my family. My wife tends to all of my needs—at least for the first few days—and the kids are really glad to see their daddy.

We didn't play as well as we wanted to as a team in the preseason, but personally I had one of my better campaigns. Even though I didn't play as much as in previous preseasons, I ran effectively, and I could feel that my off-season regimen was on the verge of yielding huge dividends.

I felt good at halfback, just like I had during my sophomore and junior years in college. And that feeling that this was going to be a special year was still with me, beating stronger than ever.

The coaches were still playing the younger guys during the exhibition season, which I used as a motivating tool. Flagler and Doug DuBose were taking my reps, but I was razor sharp when I was out there. I would start the game really hard and finish it off with the same determination and speed. I heard people saying that the competition was affecting me negatively, but that just wasn't true. It was making me hungrier to prove to myself and my teammates that I could be the best.

So I tried to encourage Terrence and Doug to run hard, and to push me to my limit. I wish I could have persuaded Doug about the importance of taking care of your body. I did my best to convince him that you're only as good as you train yourself to be, but I guess he was beyond helping by the time he got to the 49ers.

While we had both played at Nebraska, he had hung out with a far different crowd than I did. By the time Doug got to the pros, according to reports I have since read, he was already a heavy cocaine user. He was caught once during the 1987 season through testing, and he eventually tested positive more times than announced, because the 49ers released him following the 1988 season. No other team picked him up.

His plight is a sad testimony to what the drug can do. Doug was one of us; he was family. At one time he had a bright future. He was a very gregarious guy with an ingratiating smile. Tom and I made him a part of our Husker Connection when he arrived in 1987.

He was a very quick running back, and he would have done well in this league. I read a news story in 1990 that said he was sitting in this darkened bedroom in his mother's home back in Connecticut, afraid to answer the door. I feel sorry for him, and I wish I could have taught him the importance of taking care of yourself. Maybe I could have done more, I don't know. I do know that it's a waste of talent. Not many collegians get such an opportunity. The 49ers did bring him back for a tryout in 1990, but he was cut after the first minicamp. I guess he's forever branded.

In 1988, I could actually feel that I was faster in training camp than I was in any of my five previous camps. Everything was intact, and I was starting to set goals. I was hitting the holes a little quicker, and I had that crucial extra step on the linebackers. I could feel the extraordinary season coming—I honestly could.

◆
4. Bitter Memories Revisited

I was starting a new season at a new position, and the job was mine to lose. There was some concern that I might not be as effective, because our line was in a state of transition. Randy Cross had replaced the departed Fred Quillan at center, Jesse Sapolu had moved into Randy's vacated right guard position, Harris Barton had replaced Keith Fahnhorst at right tackle, and Steve Wallace had replaced Bubba Paris at left tackle. Left guard Guy McIntyre was the only incumbent.

I really felt sorry for Bubba, and that had nothing to do with my feelings toward Steve. Bubba had played some outstanding football for San Francisco, but he just couldn't say no to food. To paraphrase Will Rogers, Bubba never met a fried chicken leg or a donut he didn't like. The previous year the 49ers sent him to the Pritikin Clinic, a sophisticated fat farm for the wealthy, and this year he had come in somewhat lighter. But he was still well over 300 pounds. He's a very talented player, yet it seemed like he was always in the coaches' doghouse. I often wondered what would happen if he reported to camp at 275 pounds. He probably wouldn't have played worth beans.

The Bubba saga has a rather sad ending because the 49ers eventually released him on the final mandatory cutdown day of the 1991 season when he couldn't make their prescribed weight. He signed with the Indianapolis Colts, but they to gave up on him after week twelve of the season following a horrendous game against Cleveland in which he was called three times for holding and gave up two sacks. He finished the 1991 season with the Detroit Lions.

We were back home and preparing for our regular-season opener against the Saints in New Orleans. It was a particularly important game

34

for us because the Saints, for some inexplicable reason, are in the NFC West with us and they had come on strong the previous season under new coach Jim Mora.

Their biggest asset at home is the crowd noise in the Superdome. When you get down inside the 20 yard line, near the end zones, you can't hear your quarterback's signals. If he changes the play you're in big trouble. It's like trying to call an audible at a Rolling Stones concert. And the Saints fans know they are disruptive, so they holler just that much louder. Some teams unravel under the acoustical onslaught, because they haven't prepared for it. But not the 49ers.

Bill Walsh was one of the most thorough coaches I've ever been associated with, and he left very little to chance; he used to go over every detail, no matter how small or insignificant it seemed. Which is why we practiced all week in front of loudspeakers blaring rock music. Huey Lewis and The News were the 49ers' group of choice. They sang the national anthem at many of our home games and joined us on the sidelines during the game. Occasionally, they even flew with us on our charter to road games.

And now during practice they were in our huddle with us—at least, their music was, drowning out our signals. Every time we would run a successful play, our equipment assistant Ted Walsh (no relation to Bill) would crank up the decibels. Joe Montana practiced his hand signals, so the backs and receivers would know when he changed a play at the line of scrimmage. That way we didn't have to waste a time-out getting a new play to the receivers and running backs.

Bill kept reminding us that this game was going to be a dogfight, that it was us against the world. We already knew that the Saints seemed to play harder for Mora and that he was a great motivator.

But if Mora is viewed as a great motivator, then Bill is an even greater one. He and I had a relationship that no one knew about. He would call me into his office before a big game and say, "Okay Roger, I need a hundred twenty-five yards today. And we're going to give you the ball twenty to twenty-five times." Now how could you not come through for a man like that? I would walk out brimming with pride because he had so much confidence in me. There was no way I would let him down; I knew it and he knew it. It was our little secret.

We left for New Orleans late Friday afternoon, and I had a new roommate. Tom Rathman and I decided to unite the Husker Connection and be roomies. The previous season wide receiver Mike Wilson and I roomed together, and Mike is pretty quiet and easy to get along with, but through the years I really haven't had much luck with roommates. One year safety Carlton Williamson and I teamed up. But Carlton snores like a grizzly bear chewing on an alligator. He'd be coming down that mountain after me all night long.

Another year I roomed with running back Carl Monroe, bless his soul. Carl was a quiet little guy, but he could make big noises when his head teamed up with a pillow. Between the 1987 and 1988 seasons, Carl choked to death in his sleep. It was a very strange and tragic ending for an upbeat guy. Carl forever will be known for scoring the first touchdown in Super Bowl XIX against Miami. He will always have a special place in my heart.

I've also had center Jesse Sapolu as a roommate. Now, Jesse can block for me any time he wants, but those offensive linemen snort and grunt in the pits all game long, and I think that Jesse must have dreamed about 90-yard drives every night of his life.

Our families are close. Vernessia was in the delivery room with Tom when his wife Hollie had little Nicole. We played one year together at Nebraska, so we have that line connecting us also.

I really love the guy and would like to see him get a thousand yards some season as a reward for all of the hard work he's done for me. If Tom hadn't helped out blocking during the 1987 season, I wouldn't have had such a good year. He could be one of the best fullbacks in the league.

But you can carry love and friendship just so far. Asleep, he sounds like a pack of wounded hyenas. I mean his head wouldn't even hit the pillow and the room would be full of all these wild-animal sounds. It was like trying to go to sleep in the zoo. And you know what? Tom had the nerve to complain to me that I kept him awake with my snoring.

So it was by mutual agreement that we decided to go our separate ways. No hard feelings. We just felt that in the best interests of our deep friendship and for the preservation of our fond memories, it was best for both parties if we got separate rooms.

After we split up we could both concentrate, and there were fewer distractions. When my phone rang at night, I knew it was for me, and when Tom's phone rang, he knew it was for him. I could visualize and concentrate on what I had to do the next day during the game; there was just me and four corners, and I enjoyed the serenity and privacy.

So the combination of noisy practices and quiet rooms enabled us to sneak away from the Superdome with a 34–33 victory, as tight end John Frank caught two touchdown passes and Mike Wilson another.

In week two we hit the road again, moving on to the Meadowlands to play the New York Giants. I'm not a particular fan of the Meadowlands, because back in 1986 in the first round of the NFC playoffs, I had my worst game ever as a professional there. I went into the game with a hyperextended right knee and a bruised left knee, and I had also injured my hip earlier that season against Miami. I was just not prepared for the pounding I took that season.

I thought I could play against the Giants, but I couldn't perform at my peak level. It was cold and miserable, and I was dropping all kinds of passes. There was just no way I could perform physically, and our team was battered and bruised, both offensively and defensively. Before the afternoon was over Montana was sent to the hospital with a severe concussion. So perhaps it was just as well we lost 49–3. Even if we had won, I doubt we would have been able to find twenty-two healthy guys the following Sunday for our next opponent.

So that was my most recent memory of the Meadowlands as I took the field for the pregame warm-ups. Steve Young started because Joe had dinged his elbow the previous Sunday in the victory over New Orleans, but Bill sensed that Steve was struggling, and Montana came in for the second half. With time running out and the 49ers trailing 17–13, Joe found Jerry Rice behind the Giants secondary on a third-down play. Just as New York's safety Kenny Hill and cornerback Mark Collins collided, Jerry grabbed the ball and raced 78 yards for the go-ahead touchdown with just forty-two seconds left in the game. The Meadowlands crowd stood in shocked silence. I went up to Jerry afterward and said, "These are the kind of finishes that produce Super Bowl champions."

Flushed with a 2–0 record on the road against playoff-caliber opponents, we came home the following week to meet the Atlanta Falcons. Ordinarily, there are three things you can count on in life: taxes, death, and beating the Falcons, who usually finished last in our division. With that type of attitude going in, you can guess the rest. Atlanta spoiled our home debut before the Candlestick Park crowd with a resounding 34–17 victory. It was a real eye-opener for us, and the following week's practice was intense.

We traveled to Seattle for week four, and I could sense that everyone was ready to take out their frustration on whoever stood in front of them. Ever since 1979, when the Seahawks poured it on during a 55–10 preseason game, Bill had enjoyed beating them. We won big-time, 38–7, as I gained 107 yards on 21 carries.

Tight end John Frank, who caught those two touchdowns against New Orleans, caught another against Seattle and was off to the best start of his five-year career. John was a second-round pick out of Ohio State who had played in the rather large shadow of Russ Francis his first three years. But now he was coming into his own and appeared to be on his way to having a lengthy and productive NFL career.

After that game we all knew what we were capable of doing. We knew that if we played 49er football, no team in the league could beat us. But there was something lacking, though I couldn't put a finger on it.

We came back home against Detroit, and struggled against an inferior team. We won 20–13, but there wasn't much celebrating in the locker room afterward. Offensively, Joe was playing well despite a sore elbow and sore ribs, and our running game had never been better. I had 90 yards against the Lions, and Rathman added 74.

But something happened in that game that would have a profound effect on John Frank's professional career. Early in the second quarter, John fractured a bone in his left hand while blocking. He went on injured reserve on October 9. During that time I guess he started thinking about the perils of the game, and he must have had a long talk with himself. John wanted to be a surgeon and had already completed nearly two years of med school at Ohio State during the off-season.

He was activated November 9 and went on to have a successful season for us. He even recovered one of my rare fumbles later in the season against Atlanta, thus saving me an embarrassing moment. John kept his thoughts pretty much to himself, but about two months after the season was over he called Bill and told him that he was quitting to concentrate on becoming a doctor. He said the Detroit game made him realize that he could permanently damage his hands and that he then would never realize his goal to become a surgeon.

He wanted the 49ers to know his plans before they went into the draft so they could make plans to pick a tight end. He said it was one of the most difficult decisions he ever made. Personally, I could never understand why he would walk away from the game just as his career was starting to blossom. But John is a very sensitive and articulate person, and I will always respect his decision.

We got a better idea of our shortcomings the following week when we hosted the Denver Broncos. Bill had never beaten Denver in his ten years as head coach of the Niners. He knew that he wouldn't get many more opportunities, so our practices were pretty spirited during the week, and we could tell that our coach had turned it up a notch.

Little did any of us know at the time, probably not even Bill himself, that this would be his final opportunity to get a win against Denver. The game started out just as we expected, a hard-fought defensive battle. We took a 10–3 lead into the locker room at halftime, feeling pretty confident.

But as we took the field for the second half, we noticed that the flags on the north side of the stadium were standing straight up, like Don King's hairdo. Those sinister and turbulent Candlestick winds had snuck out of the shadows during the intermission and were raising havoc. There was dust flying in every direction, and hotdog wrappers were taking off and landing on a regular schedule.

Joe's arm is perhaps the most accurate in pro football, but it's not overpowering, and he had some real problems throwing both against the wind and with it in the second half. John Elway wasn't having much more success. Denver tied the game up with a little more than six minutes left when Elway hit Butch Johnson with an eight-yard touchdown pass. The game went into overtime and Denver eventually won it, 16–13, on Rich Karlis's 22-yard field goal with 6:49 remaining in the sudden-death stanza.

We were still 4–2 and not yet in any danger of losing sight of our goal to get to the Super Bowl. Still, you could sense an uneasiness. Bill seemed more abrupt than usual, and practices weren't as spirited as they had been.

Football is a very strange game. If you're doing well and winning, then practices can be fun. You almost look forward to going out there and going through the preparations for the next game. But when you're losing, it seems more like drudgery than anything else. You hate putting on your uniform and going out on the field, and the practices seem twice as long as usual. Losing is the greatest argument for winning that I know.

The following week we traveled to Anaheim to play the Rams. If we lost this one, we would fall two full games behind NFC West leader New Orleans and probably have to play catch-up for the rest of the season. The Rams also were playing well and their swarming "eagle" defense, with five linebackers and only two down linemen, was creating havoc on passing teams. But I felt really good in the pregame warm-ups, and once I touched the ball I knew I was going to have a banner day. Everything just seemed to fall into place. I was running well, and I could see my blocks before they happened. It was uncanny.

Early in the first quarter I took a handoff from Joe and stepped through a hole off tackle. I can remember Jerry Rice and John Taylor blocking for me, and all of these arms in blue and gold jerseys grabbing at me. But I just kept my legs churning, and when I looked down I was stepping on guys. I did that all of the way to the end zone to complete a 46-yard touchdown run. Afterward, Rams coach John Robinson said it was the greatest run he had ever seen. It made all of the highlight films that season.

We took a 17–7 lead to the dressing room at intermission, but that is nowhere near a big enough lead when the Rams and 49ers get together. Los Angeles scored twice in the third quarter to take a 21–17 lead. The shadows were growing long late in the third period when we got the ball on our own seven yard line. And with Montana at quarterback, we knew that this was the time to seize the opportunity.

Jerry Rice made eight yards on a simple out pattern, and then I picked up a first down with a three-yard run on the 15 as the third quarter ended. But then we started to lose our rhythm. Joe threw an incomplete to me on the first play of the final quarter, and on second down he threw an out pattern to Mike Wilson, but the officials ruled that when Mike made the catch for an apparent first down, he had one foot out of bounds. On third and ten, Rathman caught a little swing pass and turned it into a 17-yard gain to our 35 yard line. But guard Jesse Sapolu was flagged for holding, and we were now faced with third and 19 from our own nine yard line.

In the huddle, Joe called an "all-go," the same four–wide receiver set he had called to beat the Giants in the second game of the season. Terry Greer had worked his way free down the middle and Joe waited until the very last second to release the ball. Terry caught it on our 40 and was immediately leveled by Rams safety Johnny Johnson. The hit echoed throughout the stadium. But by some miracle, Terry held on to the ball. It was Terry's first NFL catch, even though he had been kicking around the NFL for three years, following an all-star career up in Canada.

So it was first down 49ers. Six plays later I capped off the drive with a 16-yard touchdown run up the middle. There were still some twelve minutes remaining in the game, but our defense came on to shut them down, and we flew home that night a winner. I didn't need a plane; I was still flying on my adrenaline when we landed in San Francisco. I'd had my greatest afternoon as a professional, rushing for 190 yards and three touchdowns.

Monday night games are the absolute worst for a football player. You wait around all day—and half the night if you are in the Midwest or the East—for the game to start. Your anticipation is stretched out. I have to keep telling myself, "Slow down, slow down. You've still got a long wait." I must put on my game face and take it off four or five times waiting for the game to get under way. I really don't like them, but we have to play them, and the better you finish one season, the more Monday night games you have on your schedule the next. Still, you are showcased before the entire nation and you get a chance to display your talents and wave to your mother before a national TV audience. So I guess in the final analysis, the good outweighs the evil.

In week eight we were scheduled to meet the Bears at Soldier Field in Chicago in the ABC Monday Night game. I had only played in Chicago once before, in my rookie year in 1983, and we had lost 13–3 in a chilling rain. It was miserable, and this experience proved to be no different.

I never got untracked, ending up with only 31 yards on ten carries. Bill Walsh had told the media going into the game that he didn't think we would be able to run effectively on the Bears, and as usual, he was right. Joe's 23-yard touchdown pass to Jerry Rice in the first quarter and a third-period sack of Chicago quarterback Jim McMahon for a safety were our only points.

Steve Young had always done well against the Bears, so Bill substituted Steve for Joe in the late going. I could tell that Joe was miffed, but the coaches get paid to make the decisions. Steve couldn't do much better, though, and we lost 10–9. After the game Bill said that Joe was still weak from the flu he had suffered two weeks before and it was affecting his throwing.

We appeared to be at the crossroads. The season was half over and we had a 5–3 record and had fallen a full two games behind the 7–1 New Orleans Saints. We were scheduled to play the Minnesota Vikings Sunday at Candlestick Park, and Bill still was sitting on the fence as to which quarterback would start. He told the media that he would "explore my options. I'll have to see how Joe moves and feels."

I could've told him how Joe felt. He'd have to have been stabbed two hundred times and have forty bullet holes in him and an arrow through his heart before he would concede that he wasn't well enough to start a football game—and then only if the coach agreed to let him start the second half. He is one of the most competitive people I've ever met. I've seen him get clobbered by a pass rusher and stagger back to the huddle with glassy eyes and call another pass play. He's incredible, and he has a lot of pride. There's no doubt in my mind that he's the best quarterback ever to play pro football.

Bill is the coach, and Steve took most of the snaps in practice that week, which usually meant that he would be the starting quarterback. But on Wednesday Bill told the media that "you can expect Joe to start, but we hold the privilege of starting Steve if we think it's appropriate." On Saturday Bill surprised even the players as he announced that Steve would start, so some of the suspense was over.

Steve guided us to a come-from-behind 24–21 victory over a team that many were predicting would be in the Super Bowl. Late in the fourth quarter, with less than two minutes remaining, Steve was flushed out of the pocket, ran into one of his own offensive linemen, spun through three or four Vikings, and escaped from the clutches of what seemed like twenty or thirty more Minnesota players to score, a 49-yard touchdown run. He fell exhausted into the end zone, and we mobbed him, just jumped all over him. It was a wonder we didn't hurt him.

Almost lost in the excitement of the dramatic victory was the fact that we'd gotten retribution from the Vikings for their knocking us out of the playoffs in the first round the previous season. We couldn't have been happier after that game—everyone, I guess, except Joe. He knew now that it would be tough to convince Bill he was well enough to start the following week against Phoenix.

We were 6–3 and talking about the playoffs again. But just as every cloud has a silver lining, so does every brightness have a dark side. I mean, losing to Phoenix was an incomprehensible thought. The Cardinals then were the type of team that you looked at on the schedule before the season and said, "Well, this is one victory we can count on."

But you can't do that in pro football the way you can in college. Nebraska may be a dozen touchdowns better than Kansas, but in the NFL, teams are so close in ability and talent that even the worst team is capable of beating the best team on any given Sunday.

Hello, any given Sunday. As expected, Steve started for us again, and everything was clicking, both offensively and defensively. We were up 23–0 late in the third quarter, and it seemed just a matter of running out the clock, jumping on the plane, and going home with the victory. Our defense had been the cornerstone of our team. George Seifert, who was then the defense coordinator, managed to come up with game plans that confused rival offenses.

But for some inexplicable reason, our secondary couldn't stop the Cardinals in the fourth quarter. Stop them? Hell, they couldn't even slow them down. Cornerback Don Griffin, perhaps our best cover man, suffered a dislocated left shoulder in the second quarter and was replaced by rookie Darryl Pollard. But that's not an excuse. Nor was the defense entirely to blame; we had problems on offense too. It seemed that we went into a conservative mode when we got that big lead, and then we couldn't crank it up again. On third down during one drive, Steve ran for what looked like an easy first down, but the officials said that he was an inch short. An *inch*. I couldn't believe it. Not helping the situation was the fact that we were assessed a club-record-tying fourteen penalties for 111 yards. It seemed like every time we got something going in the second half, a little yellow flag would come fluttering from somebody's back pocket.

Still, we didn't lose the game until the very last play. There were six seconds left and Phoenix was on our nine yard line. The crowd noise was deafening as Roy Green, a ten-year veteran, lined up across from Pollard. He ran down to the goal line and then cut his pattern across the back as Neil Lomax, the Cardinal quarterback, threw low and hard. Pollard was all over him with good coverage, but there was no way you could defense that play. It was just the perfect throw and the perfect catch.

Afterward, Bill was livid, and I can't say that I blame him. There was just no way we should have blown a 23–0 lead and lost 24–23. I finished with 162 yards on 26 carries for my second-most-productive day of the season, but I felt like I'd lost yardage.

Bill screamed at us about the penalties and he screamed at the assistant coaches too. As soon as he finished addressing the press, which took all of about thirty seconds, he stormed into the coaches locker room and slammed the door right in the face of running backs coach

Sherm Lewis, who had just come from taking a shower and was bare-assed naked. I was especially upset because I wanted to win this game for our owner, Eddie D. It was his forty-second birthday, and the team had been planning on presenting him a victory as his birthday present. So much for plans. We couldn't wait to get on that plane and get out of there. If I never see Sun Devils Stadium again, it will be too soon for me.

Were we some bumbling, stumbling team prone to committing penalties at the most inopportune times, or was there a sinister, unwritten code among officials to make the 49ers examples to the rest of the league? We currently were third in the league in penalties, trailing only the Houston Oilers and Minnesota Vikings.

Now the little things, a missed block here and there, were starting to become important. Our team pysche had been severely bruised. No matter how much you brace yourself for the letdown, you are never prepared for it. And just when you think matters can't get any worse, they do.

The following Sunday we were home against the Raiders, a struggling team with quarterback problems. They were no longer a factor in the AFC West, and on paper they appeared very vulnerable. We had handled them relatively easily in the preseason, 24–10, and there was no reason to believe that we shouldn't do the same. There certainly wouldn't be any lack of intensity in practice during the week after our debacle against Phoenix.

The defense held up its end of the bargain on this Sunday, but I'm afraid that the offense didn't. Our defense held the Heisman Trophy tandem of Marcus Allen and Bo Jackson to 143 yards rushing and allowed Raider quarterback Steve Beuerlein only eight completions in 12 attempts for 112 yards. Los Angeles scored only nine points, but our offense could only generate three points—a 44-yard field goal by Mike Cofer in the second quarter. We had a good chance at winning the game in the last two minutes. We had third down and one at the Raiders 20 and Bill sent in a play that was designed to catch the Raiders in a goal line defense. It went just as planned: they dug in in the pits, Joe play-faked to me, and I was mobbed at the line of scrimmage. In the meantime, Jerry Rice angled toward the middle, but a split second after Joe had released the ball, Raider defensive back Mike Haynes shoved Jerry to the ground and the ball sailed harmlessly over his prone form into the end zone. Jerry screamed, Joe screamed, and Bill screamed, but we didn't get a flag. On the next play, Bill called a reverse to Jerry, which the Raiders were waiting for. And that was it.

We only got 83 yards rushing, with myself accounting for just 58. It was a subpar day for the entire offense. I think that we might have been telegraphing our plays. They strung out their defense on our sweeps, and someone mentioned to me that every time Tom Rathman cheated up a little to pull out, they knew it was going to be a sweep. They would just load up everybody on the right side to take away the cutbacks and outside sweeps. Matt Millen, their middle linebacker, played like he was computerized. He knew exactly what was going to happen, and he would shoot the gap on trap plays. Maybe that's why Matt ended up with San Francisco after the Raiders released him.

We had fallen three games behind the New Orleans Saints in the race for the NFC West title, and our playoff hopes now appeared to depend on a wild-card berth. Even Bill's voice sounded a little weary as he implored the team not to lose sight of our goal, pointing out that the Vikings had made the playoffs the previous season with an 8–7 record.

The main thing was not to start pointing fingers and blaming each other. Once a team gets in that mode, you can forget it. It just tears a team apart emotionally, and it can take years to overcome the damage. But we were a pretty close-knit bunch, and none of us was so immature as to push the blame off on any one individual. We all understood the team concept of football.

My brother-in-law Michael Nunn, then the middleweight champion, was due in later in the week for a visit, but I wasn't in the mood to be entertaining relatives. Still, Michael and I were childhood friends growing up in Davenport. Plus I married his sister, Vernessia—he's family. So he was welcome, but he knew that I probably would be moody.

When the Niners arrived in Santa Clara the following day, we decided it was time to call a team meeting. We were 6–5, at the crossroads of our season. One more loss and we knew that we would be watching the playoffs from a soft seat in the family room in front of the television set, something we weren't accustomed to doing.

So Randy Cross and I went to Bill and told him that we wanted to have a team meeting, strictly for the offense and with no coaches present. Ronnie Lott asked Bill for the same thing with the defense.

Randy and myself did most of the talking at the meeting. As a team leader, it's something that's expected of you. I told the guys that I didn't want to get any deeper into this rut. I had been on teams that had lost two games in a row before, but I was never on one that lost three in a row, and I wasn't too keen on finding out what it was like. I told the younger players that we had to look within ourselves and redefine the direction we wanted to go in. We had to get everything back into focus and start pulling together, get our bodies and minds in sync. Forget about partying, forget about making money, and forget about what car you're driving, just get involved and play basic 49ers football. I told the younger players to go back to when they first started playing football and to remember how much fun it was. I suggested that they recapture that attitude, get back those lost thrills.

I especially directed my speech toward the younger guys. We were going into week twelve, and that was like the final game of the season for them. They had never played beyond that in college. So I explained to them that there was a lot of mental stress involved, but that they had to be able to fight off the distractions and concentrate on the things that would make them better players.

I impressed upon them that we had a championship-caliber team, and it was up to the other teams out there to rise up and beat us. I told them that they had to be totally devoted to this team and its fortunes, that we weren't in the habit of giving anything away to other teams.

You never know how one of these speeches is going to be taken. Some of the older guys might scoff at your effort, but then again I think that most of our veterans agreed with what Randy and I had to say. Mainly, it's for the benefit of the younger guys on the team. I know that when I was a rookie I'd listen to every word that a veteran would tell me and take it as gospel. You hope that what you say makes sense. Maybe it works on you more than the people you're talking to. I know that I honestly felt more pumped up and more focused when I left that meeting room. I was ready, determined to put forth my best effort.

We were taking on the Washington Redskins in a Monday night game at Candlestick Park, and many of the media doomsayers were predicting our demise. But in the back of my mind I knew that we were going to win that game. As I said, I've never been on a team that lost three games in a row.

I couldn't wait to run out on the field for the pregame warm-ups. After our meeting, I could sense all that week in practice that everyone was a little more intense. Blocks were finished off, and running backs and receivers were running out their plays. Even Bill seemed a little less tense than usual. It definitely was a good sign for the team.

We suffered a loss that Thursday before the game which shook everyone up. Dwaine Board, a popular defensive end whom we called "Pee Wee," and who is now on the 49ers coaching staff, had been on injured reserve and Bill and general manager John McVay decided to try and sneak him through waivers and then activate him in time for the Redskin game.

Each team gets five free moves per season in which to bring a player off injured reserve and back onto the active roster without exposing him to waivers. San Francisco had already used three of its free moves on other players, and had two left for the final six games of the season. It was a calculated chess move and team officials were trying to get Board back on the roster without having to spend one of the two remaining free moves.

That process involved waiving Dwaine off the injured reserve list, thus making him available to every other team in the league, for a twenty-four-hour period. If no team files a claim for him during that time, he is free to re-sign with the team that waived him. Dwaine was a nine-year veteran who was in the twilight of his career. He carried a pretty hefty salary, so it was felt that no other team would want to foot the bill for a player who probably only had a few games left.

But the 49er braintrust proved wrong in this instance. The New Orleans Saints reached in and claimed Dwaine off the waiver wire, officially making him a Saint. We had already started our afternoon practice when McVay walked out to the field and called Dwaine aside. He and McVay left the field together, and that was the last time I ever saw Dwaine in a 49ers uniform. By the time practice was over, Dwaine's locker had already been cleared out, and he was on his way to New Orleans.

I never figured out why the Saints would claim him. Some of the writers said it was a payback for a 49ers claim in 1985, when they stole linebacker Jim Kovach from the Saints in a similar situation. Maybe New Orleans was just waiting for the chance to get even. As I said earlier, this can be a cold profession at times. The nice thing about the 49ers was that they never forgot those who were loyal to them. When we had our rings award ceremony later the next year in Eddie's hometown of Youngstown, Ohio, Dwaine was there to accept his Super Bowl ring, even though he finished the season with another team.

Losing Dwaine meant we would face the Redskins with a somewhat weaker pass rush. We went out to Candlestick Sunday night and practiced under the lights. It was chilly, but there really wasn't that much wind.

Monday night the crowd was alive as we took the field. It was a pretty close game until about three minutes into the second quarter, when John Taylor fielded a punt on our 5 yard line and ran it back 95 yards for a touchdown. He took a risk on that play because coaches always teach you never to field a punt inside your own 10 yard line. Taylor defied that rule, and he ended up being the game's hero. Had he fumbled or failed to score, no doubt he would have felt the coaches' scorn.

We took a 23–7 lead into the locker room at halftime and went on to win, 37–21, thus preserving my record of never having been on a team that lost three games in a row. I rushed for 75 yards and led all receivers with five catches. I even lined up at wide receiver on one play, which I think confused the Redskin defense. They weren't sure who they were supposed to cover. We received a scare in the second quarter when Joe tripped over Steve Wallace while dropping back to pass and sprained his left knee. Steve Young replaced him for two series, but Joe came back to finish the game.

That old excitement was back in the locker room after the game. I know it wasn't the Super Bowl or even a playoff game, but it certainly felt like it had extra meaning. Personally, I think it was a great lesson for all of us. It showed us that we couldn't afford to look past anyone, that we had to take on one opponent at a time. If we did that, cut down on the errors, and played our style of football, we'd be tough to beat. It also showed that our offense was capable of putting some big numbers on the board. The victory pulled us into a second-place tie with the Rams in the NFC West at 7–5 and moved us to within two games of the division-leading Saints, whose record was 9–3. Life had taken on a whole new meaning with that one win.

Many of our fans and most of the media were talking about a wild-card berth, but I honestly believed that we could still win the division title, even though we were two games back. To me, we were sitting in the driver's seat, in control of our own destiny. We still had games left with the Rams and the Saints, and we had beaten them both already. There were some teams, most notably the Saints, that were starting to slip backward. It was gut-check time, time to see who wanted the division title the most. If we were to beat both the Rams and the Saints again and win our other two games, we were the champs. It was as simple as that.

The following Sunday we played the Chargers in San Diego, and we weren't about to overlook another AFC West foe. We exploded against them. I gained 87 yards in 17 carries, and I only played about three quarters of the game. DuBose, my backup, enjoyed the biggest day he'd ever had as a pro, gaining 60 yards on seven carries. Joe connected on 14 of 22 passes for 271 yards and three touchdowns. Everything was clicking now as we went back on the road the following week to play the Falcons at Atlanta's Fulton County Stadium.

I knew now that we weren't saving anything. The little meetings Randy Cross and I and Ronnie had held a couple of weeks back must have had their effect, because everybody was putting forth every ounce of effort. Even the younger players seemed to find renewed energy. I asked them, "Do you want to go home for Christmas or do you want to keep playing?" This was my sixth year in professional ball, and I had been in the playoffs every year. I didn't intend to spend this Christmas singing carols and watching football on television. The only chorus I wanted to sing was "Moon Over Miami," which was where the Super Bowl would be played.

Going into week thirteen I was once again leading the NFC in rushing with 1,204 yards and needed only 30 yards to break Wendell Tyler's single-season team record of 1,233 yards. But my goal wasn't to become the 49ers single-season rushing leader; my goal was to make sure we won this game and then moved on to the next one.

Atlanta was and still is always tough to play because their linebackers are so active. Their soft zone gives you the first five yards and then they converge on you and knock the piss out of you. The key against the Falcons is not to try to get all of the yardage at once. I felt that we could take advantage of them with short passes. Once you catch the ball, you just head straight upfield and get as much as you can get. It's foolish to try to fake their linebackers out and search for angles to run at. The Falcons had won four of their last five games, so we knew it was going to be a dogfight.

We had a good practice the week before the Falcons game, and we were real loose when we boarded the plane Friday afternoon for our flight to Atlanta. In addition to having a good game plan against the Falcons, we also were looking for retribution. After all, it was the Falcons who ruined our homecoming party back in week three at Candlestick, with a 34–17 whipping.

This time the offense held up its end of the bargain as we tallied a 13–3 victory over the Falcons. Joe found Jerry Rice with a 20-yard scoring toss just before the end of the first half, and Mike Cofer added a pair of field goals in the fourth quarter to secure the victory. It was the first passing touchdown against the Falcons defense in eighteen quarters. I think it was a matter of our offense wearing their defense out near the end. We controlled the ball for 36:49, compared to Atlanta's 23:11. We also eliminated Atlanta from the battle for a wild-card playoff berth.

I guess I was more fired up than usual, because I got flagged for something I had never been called on before: a unsportsmanlike conduct penalty for punching Atlanta defensive back Scott Case in the face, or actually in his face mask. I kind of lost it a little bit. But you have to expect that sometimes. No doubt, though, that it hurt our offense. We were moving the ball, and then we got the penalty.

However, I still felt justified. The officials didn't see Falcon strong safety Robert Moore ramming my head into the ground several times after I had made the first down. Then, while I was walking back to the huddle, someone grabbed me from behind and said something to me. It was Case, and that's when I went after him. I just let my emotions get away from me, but I think that it served a purpose, because the incident seemed to fire up our offense. Up to that point, it had pretty much been in the doldrums. I also got a lecture from center Randy Cross, who told me in rather colorful language to knock it off. Randy was very good about explaining the alternatives to playing in the NFL. That cooled me down, and I went back to the business of beating the Falcons.

So all in all, it was a very fruitful if not exciting Sunday. I had one of my better afternoons, gaining 103 yards on just 23 carries and catching seven passes for an additional 73 yards. Heck, I had ten more receiving yards than Jerry. Plus I became the team's all-time single-season rushing leader with 1,336 yards. My big day also enabled me to take over the NFL's all-purpose yardage lead from Herschel Walker with 1,831 yards. How sweet it was.

5. Sweet Revenge

Before we boarded the plane for the flight home to San Francisco, we received word that the Saints had lost to the Minnesota Vikings, big-time. They were blown out, 45–3.

That meant that we were both tied for the NFC West lead with 9–5 records. And to think that three weeks earlier we were three full games behind them and the media was writing our obituary. Guess who we were playing the following Sunday at Candlestick Park? That's right: the Saints.

But now wasn't the time to get cocky or overconfident. This was a new lease on life for us, and it would mean playing a new level of football. Now it was time for us to rise to the occasion and make certain that we didn't lose sight of our goal of getting to the Super Bowl.

I was the focal point of the media attention during the week because of my productive Sunday against the Falcons. I told the press, and I was sincere, that all of those personal accomplishments didn't mean a thing unless we were winning. Now we had a three-game winning streak, our longest of the season, and a chance to take command of the NFC West.

When I rush for more than a hundred yards it's probably more of a tribute to my offensive line than to me. The 49ers line was really a solid group. What made me mad is when I read that we were a finesse offense. *Finesse* may have a positive ring to it around the Paris fashion shows or lingerie parties, but in the pits it's downright insulting. We were an aggressive team, not a finesse team. Believe me, those guys up front use their strength to move people around. They're not in the least bit intimidated.

I woke up early Sunday morning and started thinking about the game. I could feel the excitement starting to take hold of me. All we had to do was to beat New Orleans and then sit back and see if anybody could catch us.

I hardly noticed the ride to Candlestick Park from the team hotel in Burlingame, where we always stayed the night before a home game. I guess I was too preoccupied with going over my plays and lining up what I wanted to do. When I went out on the field for the pregame warm-ups, it was almost like a balmy summer day, although it was December 11. The flags were hanging limp.

I scored our first touchdown on a one-yard run to put us up 7–3 early in the second quarter. New Orleans came back to take a 10–7 lead, and you could sense their confidence rising. But five minutes after they scored, Joe took it in from two yards out on a quarterback keeper. Then, with a little more than three minutes left in the first half, Joe caught the Saints in a three-deep zone, with the safety cheating toward the middle. Once the cornerback passed Taylor off, he was all alone, and Joe knew that the safety couldn't get over. It was as easy a 68-yard touchdown as you will ever see, allowing us to take a 21–10 lead off the field at halftime.

We went on to win 30–17 to take sole possession of the NFC West lead. I had another hundred-yard day, gaining 115 yards on 22 carries. The amazing thing about this game is that we were only called for one penalty, a holding call on Paris. And that ended up not costing us a yard, as Saints linebacker Pat Swilling also grabbed my face mask on the same play. We had been averaging 66.1 yards per game in penalties.

During halftime they retired Dwight Clark's number, 87. Dwight had retired the year before, and this was a big moment for him. He and Eddie D. were real close, and I guess this was Eddie's way of thanking him. Dwight, a tenth-round draft choice in 1979, had decided to hang it up after the 1987 season. His knees had betrayed him, and he just wasn't effective anymore. But he had been a great player for the club. Although I wasn't there, people tell me that his dramatic catch to win the 1981 NFC Championship Game against Dallas was the biggest single moment in the franchise's history.

We were in the locker room and I didn't witness the ceremony, but friends told me his voice cracked and his eyes glistened when he thanked the San Francisco fans. I wondered how I would go out? I wouldn't have minded doing it just like Dwight, except I wouldn't have wanted injuries to dictate to me when I had to quit. But I would never get that opportunity, and not because of injuries.

Clark is part-owner of Clark's by the Bay, a popular restaurant on the Peninsula. He was always a very charismatic person and popular with the fans. Being a good friend of Eddie's, he also traveled with us on the charter to a lot of our road games. It was like he was still one of us, without the uniform and the bumps and bruises. Early in 1990, Eddie gave him a job as head of marketing for the club. He has since moved up the ranks, learning scouting and personnel. It wouldn't surprise me if one of these days he becomes the general manager of the 49ers. So I guess there is life after football.

We were really becoming a close team. The love was back, and it reminded me of the 1984 team, which went 18–1 and won Super Bowl XIX. Before the past few games, we'd all held hands in the locker room and said a prayer. We loved each other, but we were still mad at the world. I think that's the type of attitude you have to have. I call it the Ronnie Lott attitude. Don't ever try to discuss something with Ronnie before a game—you might lose your head, or at the very least your ears. That's the only way players can keep our edge; if we love our teammates but stay mad at the world.

We were scheduled to close out our season against the Rams with a five o'clock Sunday night game at Candlestick Park. New Orleans was playing Atlanta earlier that day, and if the Saints beat the Falcons then it would be over, we would be the 1988 NFC West champs. But if Atlanta knocked the Saints out, then the Rams could claim the title by beating us. If that happened, we would both finish the regular season at 10–6, but they would have the better intradivision record. And if we beat the Rams, then the New York Giants would be one of the two NFC wild-card teams. If the Rams beat us, they would get the wild-card berth, and the Giants would be staying home in front of the fireplace for the holidays. It was probably the first time in history that the Giants ever rooted for the 49ers and we rooted for the New Orleans Saints.

Well, the Saints held up their end of the bargain by beating the Falcons. That meant that we were the NFC West champs and assured of playing the first game of the playoffs at home. By winning the game, New Orleans was actually ahead of the Rams, who were 9–6, when we took the field for the kickoff. Philadelphia won the NFC East with a 10–6 record, the same mark as the Giants. It was a real wild finish to a crazy year. I mean, how many people gave the 49ers a chance to win the division when we were 6–5 and on the verge of losing three straight? Not many, I can tell you that. I remember after the loss to the Raiders that Los Angeles linebacker Milt McColl, who spent seven of his eight years in the league as a 49er, said that we weren't the same team we had been, that we had slipped a notch and lacked the intensity of previous years.

Now we were the champs, and it didn't matter what we did against the Rams. On the other end, Los Angeles was in a sudden-death situation. If they lost, their season was over. If they won, there was a chance that they would get another shot at us somewhere down the line.

It's a good thing that we had it sewed up, because we played like it was an exhibition game. The last time the 49ers and the Rams met, I gained 191 yards; this time I was lucky to get 51. We got on the board first with Mike Cofer's 23-yard field goal, but it was all downhill after that, as the Rams scored three touchdowns in the second quarter to take a 21–13 lead at the half. Our fans, who were in the holiday spirit, kept waiting for us to make one of those patented comebacks, but it wasn't to be. Bill took Joe and myself out, and he also rested a lot of other players. He didn't want to risk any injuries with the playoffs only two weeks away.

The Rams really kicked our butts in the second half to become the NFC's final wild-card team—Minnesota was the other one—with a very convincing 38–16 win. It was San Francisco's largest margin of defeat in eight years, the worst since a 35–10 loss to Atlanta in the dog days of 1980. It was also the first 49er defeat in the final game of the season since 1982, and gave us a 10–6 record.

I have to admit that I agreed with Bill, who told the media that the atmosphere in the locker room before the game lacked the intensity it had had before our other games. He said he could feel it change when Saints placekicker Morten Andersen kicked the field goal against Atlanta that clinched the title for San Francisco. We just weren't pysched up. I didn't even play the last quarter, and that might have cost me the NFL's total yards from scrimmage title as Herschel Walker barely beat me out. But honestly, that didn't concern me at all. It would have been selfish thinking on my part if I had insisted on going out there in the fourth quarter and then gotten hurt and been forced to miss the playoffs. I would have let my teammates down.

Bill also said that our composure got rattled midway through the contest. Now, I'm not so sure I agree with him on that issue. One thing was certain, and that was that we were always very composed. Pandemonium could be swirling all around us, but we were always very professional in our approach, sort of like we were in the eye of the hurricane. I think we just let down our intensity level a little when we knew we had won the conference title and would be playing at least the first playoff game at home. Our 10–6 record precluded us from playing any of the others at home, even if we beat the Rams.

Many of us were afraid that we might have lost the momentum that saw us win four straight games, and our critics pointed out that championship-caliber teams don't suffer lapses like that.

But if you thought Bill and our critics were upset, you should have heard the New York Giants. Since we didn't beat the Rams, the Giants were out of the playoffs. It must have been very painful for them to watch us disintegrate right before their eyes in their own living rooms. Giants quarterback Phil Simms even accused us of "laying down like dogs" before the Rams. But if we had to eliminate one team, I'm glad it was the Giants. I still remember that playoff game on Jan. 4, 1987, when they embarrassed us 49–3. Once you have a team beat, I don't think you should rub their noses in it. Over the long haul, it will come back to haunt you. Which is what happened to the Giants in this case. I don't know why we played so poorly. What I do know is that we were in the playoffs and Simms was home scratching his dog's fleas.

Now we had two weeks to prepare for either the Minnesota Vikings or the Philadelphia Eagles. The Vikings, despite having a better record than us (11–5), finished second to the Bears (12–4) in the NFC Central and would meet the Rams in the wild-card game. If the Rams won that game, they would play Chicago—because two teams from the same conference can't meet in a divisional playoff game—and we would play Philadelphia, which won the NFC East with a record (10–6) identical to ours. But if the Vikings won, then they would travel to San Francisco and Chicago would host Philadelphia in the two divisional playoff games. When the media asked which team I preferred to play, I replied that I was fresh out of predictions, and I didn't expect to make any until after the Super Bowl. I wasn't even going to talk about our prospective opponents, nor was I going to watch the wild-card game. I wanted to stay away from it and all other distractions. That way I wouldn't be burnt out by game day.

The coach gave us the following weekend off, including Monday, when the Vikings and Rams played. I decided to relax, maybe take the family shopping. Deep down, though, I was glad that Minnesota beat the Rams, 28–17. First, there was this little matter of revenge. Even though we had beaten the Vikings in the regular season, we weren't about to forget that they'd knocked us out of the playoffs the previous season. And the Rams had just beaten the pants off us, and they might have held a slight pyschological edge. So Minnesota at Candlestick Park was just fine with me.

Right away the oddsmakers installed us as three-point favorites—the same margin by which we beat the Vikings in the regular season. Our game was scheduled to follow the AFC playoff game between Houston and Buffalo.

That week I received a prestigious honor when the Associated Press selected me its Offensive Player of the Year. I looked on it as more of an honor for my offensive linemen than for myself. They are the guys who really deserved the kudos. All I did was run through the holes they created. But it is nice to be recognized as being someone special in the NFL, which has so many superstars.

I knew that the key to my success against the Vikings would be how well my line could get me to the outside. Once I got out there, I would make big yardage. The Vikings play a gambling defense with lots of stunts and loops, but it is effective because their main objective is to tear the quarterback's head off. And with Keith Millard leading the charge, they sometimes did that. They led the league in sacks that season, and the pressure was on our offensive line to keep them off Joe.

In 1988 I think that we were fresher both mentally and physically than we'd been the previous year. For one thing, we didn't hold a lot of long, tiring practices. Most of our afternoon sessions were short and sweet and to the point.

On a usual workday, we talked with the press when we broke at noon for our lunch—at least, some of us did. The players lounge, the training room, and the weight room are off limits to the media, and many of the players made it a habit to stay in there the entire half hour or so we got before the afternoon practice, thereby avoiding questions. But I don't mind talking to the press. As long as they understand that I have a job to do, I'll understand that they do too. I don't think that I ever ducked questions or my responsibility to the media. They are an important connection to our fans, and I think that most players don't understand this.

But that week at lunchtime I decided to keep a low profile. I knew that the reporters would be seeking me out because I had been so vocal and visibly upset after we had been eliminated by Minnesota the previous year. It's not like I didn't enjoy talking to them, it's just that I wanted to make sure that there were no distractions this time, that if we lost to Minnesota again, there would be nothing we could point to as an excuse.

Meanwhile, I kept telling the players, especially the younger ones, that we had to turn it up a notch. I reminded them that this was an entirely new season—a one-game season—and that the level of play in the playoffs is considerably higher than it is during the regular season. I told them that whoever is around the ball is going to have the chance to make something happen, so everybody has the opportunity to be a hero. There was no need to hold anything back.

As far as revenge, I tried to keep that way in the back of my mind because I was concerned that it could detract from the businesslike atmosphere that we were trying to maintain for this game. But I suppose that there was a certain motivation factor in it, as long as we kept it under control and didn't let it consume us. I told the rookies that if they won this game, they would feel very good about themselves.

Personally I felt that we were a cinch, but I kept that premonition to myself. The previous year we had been riding high going into the first playoff game, and I don't think we had the experience to adjust once things started going bad. Whereas in 1988, we'd been hit with numerous frustrations: players suspended for drugs, a quarterback controversy, rumors that Bill's job was in jeopardy if he turned in a losing season. There was nothing that could happen out there on the field that could be worse than what had happened to us already.

You could sense that mentally and physically we were ready. We checked into our team hotel New Year's Eve and tried to get a good night's sleep, though there were a lot of revelers about. We were hoping we'd get our chance to celebrate the next night.

It was cool and crisp out when I drove to Candlestick Park the next morning. Perfect football weather. When I arrived in the locker room, Randy Cross was already there, giving small pep talks to the younger players, as I had been doing. He was telling them that this was their opportunity to show that they could perform. He said that you might be physically tough, but you aren't mentally tough until you do it. He told the team that if you're going to pick somebody to crawl into a foxhole with, you want somebody who's done it before, not somebody who has read all the books or watched all the films. I wish I had thought of saying it like that.

Before we took the field, cornerback Eric Wright stood up and made a speech. Eric is a very dedicated and intense guy, but he'd had this nagging groin problem for two seasons and he sensed that his time for leaving the game was getting near. He still had some brilliant football left in him, but when he played he did so in constant pain, and he was then on the inactive list.

Usually Eric doesn't say much, but he got up, and with his eyes glistening and his voice choked with emotion, he told the squad that even though he wouldn't be playing, this game was very important to him personally. He pointed out that you never know when you will get the opportunity to return to that level, and that you have to make the best of it while you've got the chance. Even I had a couple of tears in my eyes. I think the speech really impressed the younger players, because we all charged out of there ready to breathe fire.

When they make a how-to film about blocking, they ought to use the films of this game. Our offensive line was about as perfect as you can get. They completely neutralized the defensive line's rush; neither Keith Millard or Chris Doleman laid a hand on Joe. Myself? I had a superb afternoon: 135 yards rushing and two touchdowns on 21 carries. My big play was an 80-yard touchdown run with 9:04 left in the game. We had practiced the play all week in short-yardage situations because Bill had detected something watching the Minnesota game films.

So it was a matter of calling the right play against the right defense, and then executing it. Guard Jesse Sapolu pushed Millard to the inside, and immediately there was this tremendous hole. As soon as I high-stepped through it, I looked up and saw that I only had the safety Joey Browner to beat. Minnesota had everyone on the line in a short-yardage defense. It was a piece of cake.

On the other side of the ball, our defense did its part, surprising the Vikings with a five-man line and constantly harassing their quarterback, Wade Wilson. It was a total team effort.

My 80-yard touchdown was an NFL playoff record and also a 49er playoff record. The 34–9 victory over the Vikings also was very sweet indeed. That night I allowed myself a little champagne and gave Vernessia a huge New Year's kiss. I felt on top of the world; I didn't even want to think about the Chicago Bears, who defeated the Philadelphia Eagles 20–12 in the other NFC playoff game. We would be traveling to Chicago the next Friday to play the Bears in their own lair, Soldier Field, on Sunday for the NFC championship and a berth in the Super Bowl. But this night rightfully belonged to my wife and family. God knows, they put up with enough from me.

Whenever you go into an important football game, you try to gain the edge. Because players are so equal in ability and there haven't been any real innovations in football since the forward pass, you try to get that slight advantage that can make the difference between victory and defeat. With me, of course, it's my off-season training regimen. I train hard to be able to withstand any type of physical or mental pressure. You never reach the point where you become so good that there aren't little things you can work on to better yourself. That fine-tuning is how you get the extra edge.

I remember back in 1983 when I was a rookie. Hacksaw Reynolds was a linebacker for us, and I used to marvel at his dedication and preparation for a football game. He was near the end of his career, but he could still play football, and most of the time he outthought the opponent. He used to watch films all day and halfway into the night, filling notebooks with diagrams. He had a very frugal side to him, and he used to go around collecting half-used pencils. Then he would diagram opposing teams' offenses in these notebooks. They tell me that he had a garage that filled with so many notebooks that you couldn't put a car in there.

Lots of people probably thought Hacksaw was crazy for doing what he did, but not me. He was able to visualize things before they happened because he had gone over every possible sequence of events. Somewhere in one of his playbooks was the answer to every play. That was Hacksaw's edge, and at times it could be considerable enough to win games for you.

Though I might not be quite as eccentric as Hacksaw, that's the type of player that I want to be. I want to be able to predict what is going to happen on any given play. Then I will have the edge.

I believe in natural ability, but nowadays that isn't enough. Players are bigger, faster, quicker, and tougher than ever before. Your body must be fine-tuned to play this game. You also need a maintenance program, just like an automobile does, to stay at your peak. So many players are worn down when the playoffs arrive because of the rigors of the long season, but I think I thrive on postseason play because my body is finely tuned. That's probably why I was able to run 80 yards in the fourth quarter against the Vikings. They were getting tired, and here was this player seemingly getting stronger. That can really deflate a defense, or an offense if it's a defensive player getting stronger. You can look across the line and see the weariness in the opposition's eyes. It also makes you play that much harder. I'm a workaholic, and I accept that.

Preparing for Chicago was going to be fun. Immediately after we beat Minnesota, the oddsmakers made the Bears 7-point favorites. That automatically took the pressure off us; if we won it was going to be an upset and if we lost, hey, we were supposed to lose. We had good practices all week long. The team appeared loose, which was a good sign. Bill Walsh appeared loose, which was an even better sign. We laughed and joked during practice, but we took care of business too. Our practices were short, probably only about an hour and a half, and only one was with pads. Bill's theory was that we weren't going to get any better or learn any more with pads on at that juncture of the season, and you cut down on the risk of injury when you practice without them. I agree with him. At this time of year, you want to keep your body as fresh and as healthy as possible.

The talk that week centered around the weather. The national media, which was now hot on our trail, took it for granted that being from California, we would have a severe allergic reaction or something to playing in cold weather. They would ask us questions about snow and ice, and then they'd write about how the game was going to be played in Chicago Bears weather. I kept waiting for one of them to ask me how well I played wearing snowshoes.

The lower the temperature dropped in Chicago, the higher the odds rose against us. All California teams are considered fair-weather teams because the state gets so much sunshine. We're all suppose to be surf bums who fold in the face of cold weather.

But I for one don't agree with that theory. In the first place, teams are made up of players from every area of the country. Both Tom Rathman and I had played in the snow at Nebraska, and Steve Young was a quarterback at Brigham Young, where I understand it snows 365 days a year. And our track record in cold weather wasn't that poor. In 1986 we beat New England in the snow at Foxboro, and the following year we defeated the Packers on a frigid December day in Green Bay.

But the media insisted on making it an issue, though I didn't believe that it was worth talking about. We even had a little laugh on Tuesday when we came back to practice. A chilly norther had blown down from

Alaska, and the hills behind our practice facility in Santa Clara were covered with a thin layer of snow. In Chicago it was cold, but there wasn't any snow. So here were these "Surf City" guys from California working out against a snowy backdrop, while the Bears were working out under blue skies. Some fair-weather team, huh?

Anyway, there are different kinds of cold. Cold is what the 1981 AFC Championship Game between the Chargers and Bengals in Cincinnati was. There was a wind-chill factor of something like 56 degrees below, and two people actually froze to death in the stands.

Bronco Hinek, our equipment manager, was at that game. He was with the Chargers then, and he tells a couple of chilling anecdotes about the cold that day. Hinek said that Ed Luther, the backup quarterback who held the snaps for field goals and extra points, forgot to wear his gloves and came running back into the locker room before the game to get them. There he confronted James Harris, another backup quarterback, and told him how cold it was out on the field. Harris started screaming, "You have to call off the game, you have to call off the game."

According to Hinek, Harris finally started removing his uniform. When an assistant coach asked him what the heck he was doing, Harris replied, "I'm getting ready to retire and I don't want to freeze to death in my last game." Hinek said that Harris had a point, because Charger quarterback Dan Fouts, who didn't wear gloves, had to be treated for minor frostbite of the fingers.

The main thing is not to get your clothes wet. That's what makes you cold. We wear special garments under our uniform that help keep us dry, so that wouldn't be a problem, and they told us that there would be heaters underneath the players' benches, blowing hot air up through the small holes in the bench. Heck, we didn't want to get too comfortable. We might think we're in Hawaii and fall asleep.

We went through a light workout Thursday afternoon and a short walk-through Friday morning, and then we went home to get ready to leave that afternoon on the charter to Chicago. Bill Walsh preceded us to Chicago, leaving on a commercial flight earlier in the day. The NFL had set up a press conference with Bill and Bears coach Mike Ditka, and it was mandatory that he be there.

We were also without receivers coach Denny Green. Very popular with the team, Denny recently had been named head coach at Stanford University and he had to perform a couple of recruiting missions. But if we won, he would be with us at the Super Bowl in Miami. I didn't want to even think about the Super Bowl until we beat the Bears. I wanted my concentration totally on this game.

After an uneventful flight we landed in Chicago, just another road town with hotel food as far as we were concerned. We were supposed to work out Saturday, but the weather was so dismal that we had a short meeting and took the rest of the day off. Several of the players headed for those deep-dish pizza houses that Chicago is famous for. I decided to take it easy and relax in my room. It was a rare opportunity to just do nothing.

For some reason, I woke up in the middle of the night and looked out the window. I did a double take. The ground was completely covered with snow. Sometime during the night it had started snowing, and the whole city was cloaked in a white mantel. I bet those oddsmakers were working late cranking out new odds. I soon drifted back to sleep.

We were the second half of the NFL doubleheader, with Buffalo and Cincinnati meeting earlier that day in the AFC Championship Game. That meant that we wouldn't get under way until four o'clock, which also meant that the field was going to be without what little warmth daylight might provide.

No matter. We were ready. No one had to tell us how important this game was. Even the rookies could see by looking at Ronnie Lott or Joe Montana or myself how much was riding on this game. We had come too far, gone through too much to turn back now. This was it. Beat the Bears and the 49ers are back in the Super Bowl. Lose, and it would be a long, quiet plane flight home and another entire off-season to painfully ponder what might have been.

Like the Vikings, the Bears liked to disrupt your passing game, mainly with their inside tackles, Dan Hampton and Steve McMichael. So we knew the key was not to let the Bears pass rush take us out of our game plan. Defensively, we felt pretty good.

Ditka kept the media—and us—guessing for most of the week as to who would be the starting quarterback for the Bears. Jim McMahon, who had had pretty good success against us, was still hobbled by a sprained knee, and Mike Tomczak had been very effective in his absence. They both had pretty good records going into the game. Tomczak was 16–3 as a starter, while McMahon was 34–4. But in games against the 49ers, McMahon was 3–0, while the Bears were 0–2 against us in games he did not start. In the previous season's 41–0 loss to us, Tomczak started and threw four interceptions.

So it came as no surprise on Friday before the game when Ditka announced that McMahon would start. Ditka was banking that the emotional lift McMahon would provide the Bears would offset his potential rustiness. And I think I would have gone the same way. I've always believed that you stick with a proven winner in this game if he's physically able to play. Also, while Tomczak probably was their most effective quarterback at the time, he had spent most of the season in and out of Ditka's doghouse.

Not that I really cared. I wasn't going to play against him. I was only concerned about the Bears defense and how our younger guys would stand up to the cold. I wasn't worried about our veterans, especially the line and Joe, Tom, Jerry, and myself. We knew what cold weather was all about, and it had never been a distraction to us.

Good thing, too, because at game time the temperature reading was 17 degrees Fahrenheit. That coupled with a chilling norther that was blowing off Lake Michigan put the wind-chill factor at 26 below. I checked out the parking lot at Soldier Field, and there weren't too many tailgate parties.

The field, surprisingly, was in good shape. It was a little hard, but not as hard as I expected. The crowd booed us lustily when we came out for our pregame warm-ups, which I think was a good thing for that 49er team. It just seemed to bring us closer together and help us work for a common goal. We went about our business, and I could sense that we were ready—more ready than the Bears or their fans.

And none of the 49ers seemed aware of the cold. Randy, I think, said it best. He said that he was only going to be out there for three and a half hours, and that you can hang by some very important body parts for three and a half hours, if need be, and endure the pain.

It didn't take Joe and Jerry long to take advantage of the Bears' undermanned secondary. On our third series of the first quarter, Montana fired a 20-yard sideline pass that Jerry turned into a 61-yard 49er touchdown. Then in the second quarter, after our defense held the Bears and a frustrated McMahon, Joe caught the Bears in a blitz and quickly threw a pass over the middle. Jerry picked it off his shoe tops, split two defenders, and ran it in to complete a 27-yard touchdown play. Now it was 14–0, and the Chicago fans couldn't believe what they were seeing.

Kevin Butler put the Bears on the scoreboard later in the second quarter with a 25-yard field goal, but by then our confidence was soaring. We marched into the locker room with a 14–3 lead, mad at ourselves for missing a couple of royal opportunities. We figured it could just as easily have been 21–3.

On our first drive of the second quarter, Joe took us on a thirteen-play, 78-yard drive. John Frank, bless him, caught a five-yard touchdown pass on third down to extend our lead to 21–3. Now we knew we had the Bears pretty much where we wanted them. It was night, and the lighting at Soldier Field isn't the best in the NFL, and they would be forced to throw the ball if they wanted to get back in the game.

But our defense was just too much for them. It was probably Jeff Fuller's best game ever. He had ten tackles and an interception and was all over the field. I hope that he looks back on that game with deep satisfaction during the ensuing years, because he was an important part of our success story that season. Linebacker Michael Walter also had a great game, setting a team postseason record with 11 tackles.

And I don't want to leave out my former college teammate and ex-roommate Tom Rathman. When he tumbled into the end zone head first following a four-yard touchdown run midway through the fourth quarter, he put the final nails in the Bears' coffin. Tomczak replaced McMahon, but he wasn't any better. The game ended as a resounding 28–3 49ers victory.

Hey, we were going to the Super Bowl. What had been denied us the previous year was now a reality. We were going from the frigid climes of Chicago to tropical Miami.

Ironically, the team we would meet in Super Bowl XXIII was the Cincinnati Bengals. The modern-day history of the 49ers is forever linked with the Bengals. Bill Walsh was spurned as head coach of the Bengals back in the mid seventies when he was an assistant for owner Paul Brown, which galls him to this day. When the 49ers won their first Super Bowl in 1981 it was against the Bengals. And one of the most popular assistants ever for the 49ers was Sam Wyche. He was Bill's protégé. When Bill coached quarterbacks at Cincinnati, Sam played for him, and when Bill was named head coach of the 49ers back in 1978, Sam was one of the first people he offered a coaching job to.

I don't know Sam all that well, because he left in 1983 to become the head coach at Indiana University, the year that I came to the 49ers. But I've heard plenty of stories about him from the players, about how he used to sit in the back of the plane on road trips and regale the team with his bag of magic tricks. I know that he and Joe Montana are real tight, Sam having been Joe's quarterback coach during Joe's formative years. So you can see how this shaped up to be a very interesting Super Bowl.

And Sam had something to prove to the football world. We played the second game of our 1987 season against the Bengals in Cincinnati. They were coming off a winning season and many of the Midwest gridiron experts were mentioning the Bengals in the same breath as the Super Bowl.

We had lost our first game to Pittsburgh, 30–17, and were in dire need of a victory to give us a shot of instant confidence. Bengal placekicker Jim Breech had kicked a 46-yard field goal with 1:56 left to give the Bengals a 26–20 lead, and the Bengals were all looking very smug on the sidelines. We again gave up the ball, and the Bengals took over near their goal line with the clock running out. On fourth down and inches, however, with about six seconds left, Wyche had several solid options with which to run out the clock—none of which included going for a first down. They could have taken the safety while running out the clock or they could have punted the ball, taking the slim chance we'd run it all the way back for a touchdown.

I never did understand his decision. Perhaps he panicked. Or maybe he was just so arrogant that he thought he could stuff it down our throats. But Kevin Fagan stopped James Brooks cold at the line for no gain, and we took over with about four seconds left. On the first play—the only play—Joe lofted a pass to the right corner of the end zone, and Jerry beat his man for the catch. Ray Wersching kicked the extra point and we went home 27–26 winners. The newspapers ripped Wyche for his call, and there was some speculation that he might lose his job over it. But he survived it, and here it was a year later and he had his Bengals in the Super Bowl.

We had two weeks to get ready for the Bengals, and Bill made sure that we didn't peak too early. He gave us the next two day off following Monday's short team meeting. That was real nice, because it gave us a chance to catch up on our family life. What wasn't nice, though, was all the people—old friends, long-lost relatives, and whatnot—calling for Super Bowl tickets. I finally told Vernessia to let the answering machine take care of the calls. If I'd gotten tickets for everyone who requested them from me, I'd have filled up half of Joe Robbie Stadium.

When we reported back to camp, the controversy had already begun. The Bengals were famous for this no-huddle offense, and some of the other NFL teams had complained bitterly about it. Marv Levy, whose Buffalo Bills lost to the Bengals in the AFC Championship Game, was extremely vocal in opposition to the ploy, and the result was that Commissioner Pete Rozelle had cautioned Wyche not to use it.

Wyche, meanwhile, defended his no-huddle offense and said that it was within the NFL rules. Bill Walsh, curiously, kept pretty quiet about the entire matter, preferring to let Wyche argue it out with the league. Bill even halfway defended it, saying that maybe every team should use it. What the no-huddle does is keep a particular defensive alignment off the field, like our nickel, which we used in certain passing situations. We used a lot of situation defense, and it definitely would have been detrimental to us if the Bengals were allowed to use the no-huddle.

However, since that time the no-huddle has become a popular innovation in the NFL. Houston and Detroit use it almost exclusively and, ironically, it has become an important tool in the Buffalo arsenal.

But we decided when we reported back to camp Wednesday that we weren't going to concern ourselves with it and let it become a distraction. If they used it, fine; we could handle it. And if they didn't, fine. We weren't about to lose any sleep over it. We practiced Wednesday,

Thursday, and Friday, and Bill gave us Saturday off. We really didn't put in many new plays. Mostly we just brushed up on some which we hadn't used for a couple of months.

What amazed me was how mature our team seemed. Our practices were conducted in a very businesslike manner. Everyone seemed focused. Many times teams let down when they get that far. It's like, "Whew, we finally made it here; now let's take a breather." They act like they're happy just to be there.

But not us. Our goal was those Super Bowl rings that go along with the winner's trophy at the end of the day. We had worked too hard and come too far to be satisfied just being there. We had overcome all types of adversity, and to stop now and marvel at our progress, to risk making all of our achievements worthless, would be cheating ourselves. We'd had enough veterans who'd been on the team in 1984 to know what it takes to win a Super Bowl.

The flight to Miami was uneventful, and when we stepped off the plane we were greeted by 80-degree weather and high humidity. I was glad I hadn't packed my snowshoes for this game. The week started out with a bang when center Randy Cross announced that the Super Bowl was going to be the final game of his illustrious thirteen-year pro career. It was typical Randy. He waited until he had all of the national press assembled, and then he made the big announcement. It took most of us by surprise. Personally, I thought that Randy was at the top of his game and had at least five more years left.

But I guess that's why football players, like spurned mates, are the last ones to know. We think we can play forever, and then one day the coach sends out a couple of big rookies and they drag you off the field kicking and screaming. That's the way most of us exit this game because we don't recognize that enough is enough. But not Randy. He stepped away with dignity.

Randy has class and style. He was our foremost spokesman. After a game, the media would flock to his locker for some wisdom and one-liners. I didn't know who was going to miss him the most, the team or the media. I admire him for how he went out. I think that's the way that I would like to do it; make an announcement before the Super Bowl and have that be my last hurrah. When you think about it, it's the perfect exit, like it was scripted in Hollywood.

Usually our team had to battle distractions, but this time it was the other team. The night before the Super Bowl, Bengals running back Stanley Wilson was discovered in a drugged stupor in his room. He was sent back home, and I guess that his predicament had an adverse effect on the morale of the Bengals. It certainly couldn't have helped any.

Stanley and I were old rivals. He was at Oklahoma when I was at Nebraska. He was drafted by the Bengals in the ninth round the same year that the 49ers took me in the second round. But he had already missed the 1987 season after testing positive for drugs. Now his career was probably over. It was very sad, just as Doug Dubose's plight was to be a sad note for our team the following off-season.

But the game goes on, and we had a date in Joe Robbie Stadium to play the Bengals for the championship of the world. We were ready, and I was still carrying that good feeling that I'd had when I reported to summer camp at the beginning of the year. Boy, that seemed like a long time ago.

All week long a crew had been assembling this giant circus tent next to our hotel. Let me tell you about the hotel. It was on an island outside of Miami. There was only one road in and one road out, and security was very tight. A guard would stop you on your way in and ask you to state your business. With the exception of a few of our beat writers, the hotel was nearly all 49er people. The second and third floors, where we stayed, were completely secured. The only way you could get to those floors was with a special pass signed by Bill Walsh or the pope.

I really don't understand all of the NFL's paranoia about security, but I guess they have their reasons. In a way it's good for the players, because we don't have a lot of people bothering us. I don't mind signing autographs, and I'm real appreciative of the fans; I understand that if it wasn't for them there wouldn't be any football. Still, you have to respect the players' free time, too. It's one thing to have someone come up to you on the street and ask for an autograph and another for people to practically knock each other down in the gift shop when you're just trying to make a quick stop to buy some toothpaste.

People, without being conscious of it, can be rude. I guess the hardest thing to understand is when you're out to dinner with your family and someone comes up and thrusts a piece of paper under your nose. I find that repulsive. If someone sits back and waits until you're finished and then comes up and asks politely, that's fine, I'm more than happy to sign. But don't be rude and demanding.

Vernessia came in with the family charter on Thursday, and Eddie D. gave a big welcome party at this other hotel across from the island, where the families were staying. There were two bands, ice sculptures, and all kinds of food, including prime rib, lobster, and shrimp. You can save the shrimp with me because I'm deathly allergic to it. I once had shrimp at a barbecue and Keena Turner nearly had to call 911. My breathing passages closed up and I thought I was going to choke to death. Since then I've kept my distance from shrimp.

Anyway, there was this huge tent erected next to the hotel. Eddie D. had put it up in anticipation of our winning. It was to be for our victory party. Now tell me, how are you going to even think about losing when your owner does this? I mean, I didn't want to be the one who spoiled Eddie's party.

I slept pretty well that Saturday night before the game. After the team dinner we had a short meeting, went over a few plays, and then spent the rest of the time in our rooms watching television.

Our buses left early for Joe Robbie Stadium the next day, which was a good thing. A lot of people who left about two hours before the game didn't get there until the middle of the first quarter. Bill had learned his lesson in Super Bowl XVI when the second team bus got stuck in traffic and almost didn't make it.

The field was in great shape, and it is a beautiful stadium. After we got taped, I went out on the field and ran a couple of sprints. The turf was real bouncy, and I still had the feeling: we were going to win the Super Bowl.

The game started out on a bad note. First, Steve Wallace got blocked from the side and suffered a broken left fibula on a running play on which I picked up ten yards. Steve was our left tackle and Joe Montana's main line of defense, and the game was barely two minutes old when he went down. Next, Bengal nose tackle Tim Krumrie got tangled up on an inside blocking scheme and fractured his left tibia.

Our first possession ended in a punt, but when the Bengals offense got their turn, our defense stopped them. It was going to be one of those days. We thought we had a touchdown when Joe passed 24 yards into the end zone to a diving Mike Wilson. However, the instant replay camera showed that Wills (his nickname) never had complete possession of the ball before it popped out. It was the correct call. That's one of the few times I can recall when I wish the NFL didn't have instant replay. Mike Cofer kicked a 41-yard field goal right after that so at least we salvaged three points out of the drive.

I guess the play I remember most, and the play I'll never forget for the rest of my life, was the one by Ronnie Lott midway through the first quarter. Bengals star running back Ickey Woods took a handoff, stepped through the line at right tackle, and was hit head-on by Lott. Normally, I don't pay that much attention when our defense is on the field because I'm usually on the phone talking to our coaches up in the press box. But this is one you couldn't miss seeing—or hearing, for that matter. The sound of that hit bounced into every nook and corner in Joe Robbie Stadium. It could be heard in the rest rooms.

I remember looking out on the field and thinking to myself that neither player was going to get up. Woods was on his back, and the ball just sort of dribbled out of his hands. Ronnie rolled over and pulled himself to his feet, shook his head a couple of times, and jogged back to the defensive huddle. Woods got up and wobbled back to his huddle, but he was never the same. He ran tentatively after that, like he was looking for Ronnie to bust him again. I think I would have done the same thing. I know I never want to get hit like that. Even my hair would be sore.

Fortunately, our defense was playing superbly. Every time we would mess up, our defense would hold the Bengals.

We had second and 24 on our own 42 when it happened: my worst nightmare became a reality. I took the ball from Joe and sprinted around left end. The lane was wide open, and I was thinking to myself, Hey, I'm going to get a first down and maybe even more. I remember trying to tuck the ball away when Bengals strong safety David Fulcher hit me from the side, and all of a sudden the ball left my grasp. People were grabbing at everything, including me. I couldn't get back to the ball, and Cincinnati defensive end Jim Skow fell on it at their 41. I felt sick. I knew I had let my teammates down. I don't think there is any worse feeling in football.

One minute you're on top of the world and the next minute you feel like you've betrayed the human race. When I first came to the 49ers, the media jumped on me about a game at Nebraska in which I fumbled two times, and I was forced to defend myself. But I've never had a problem holding on to the ball. I said going into the game that the team that made the fewest mistakes was going to win. And here I was, contributing to what could have been our demise. But I knew I had to stay positive. I had to play strongly and wait for the opportunity to make up for my transgression. It wasn't the first time that season that we'd had our backs to the wall.

But I wasn't the only culprit. It seemed like every time we would start to get something going, an offensive lineman would be called for holding or someone would get whistled for illegal motion.

By excitement standards, the first half was a real yawner. It ended 3–3, and I could visualize the people around the country getting bored with a game being decided by placekickers. But a defensive purist had to love it, because both teams' defenses were playing with reckless abandon. Both quarterbacks were having to run for their lives when they dropped back to pass, and the inside hitting was ferocious.

The offensive tempo picked up in the second half after Breech's 43-yard field goal had given Cincinnati a 6–3 lead. With fifty seconds left in the quarter, Cofer drilled a 32-yarder to knot the score at 6 all. But on the ensuing kickoff we had a breakdown on special teams, and Bengal returner Stanford Jennings ran it back 93 yards for a touchdown. Terry Greer made a diving attempt to get Jennings, but he just missed him. I looked over at Bill and saw him glaring at special teams coach Lynn Stiles.

To make matters worse, John Taylor fielded the kickoff at the 2 and only got it back to the 15 yard line with twenty-four seconds left in the third period. But Joe was the master when our backs were to the wall. On first down, he passed 31 yards to Jerry to give us a first down on our own 46. On the next play, I went in motion to the right and then turned upfield, took a throw from Joe and raced 40 yards down the right sideline to the Bengals' 14 before left corner Lewis Billups knocked me out of bounds. Another first down.

Billups broke up a pass intended for J.T., but on second down Joe hit Jerry on a fade in the right corner of the end zone for the touchdown. We had gone 85 yards in four plays and we felt a welcome surge of confidence.

But the Bengals defense toughened up again, and the two teams battled through the final period. Finally, Breech again broke the ice with a 40-yard field goal for a 16–13 Bengal lead following nearly a six-minute possession. There was only 3:20 left, and time was on their side.

To make matters worse, we were penalized for holding on the ensuing kickoff and now we had first and ten at our own 8 yard line. Hardly the place to mount a game-winning drive.

But I was confident. We all were, because we had Joe Montana. The huddle was completely quiet, and we all looked at Joe. His blue eyes turned steely, and he spoke very deliberately. It was like we had all the time in the world.

On third and two from our own 31, Joe handed me the ball, and I picked up four yards for the first down. Now we had four more downs to play with. After two more completions, Montana tried frantically to use our second time-out because he had been hit after the throw and had lost his breath. He was hyperventilating, but neither the officials nor his teammates realized it, and the time-out was never called. Joe threw out of bounds on the next play to buy himself a little time.

On second and ten from the Bengals 35, he passed over the middle to me on a delay, and I picked up ten yards and the first down on the 25. But Randy Cross had ventured too far downfield, and the flag came out. My heart dropped, and so did Randy. He was crouching there on his haunches, holding his head. This definitely is not the way he wanted his career to end. With first and ten on the Bengal 18 and thirty-nine seconds left in the game, Joe called our final time-out.

Bill sent a play in from the sidelines with me as the primary receiver. I was supposed to line up on the left side, but in the excitement of the moment I lined up on the right side and didn't notice Joe frantically trying to wave me back to the other side. I ran my route, but I wasn't open. However, J.T. was running a post, and when he made his cut toward the crossbars, he broke clear. That was all the opening Joe needed—*zing!* an 18-yard touchdown and a 20–16 lead with just 34 seconds left. Talk about high drama.

It still wasn't over, though. We kicked off, and the Bengals had a first down on their own 26. But on second down, with seventeen seconds left, Charles Haley broke through and sacked Bengal quarterback Boomer Esiason. And that was it, the end of one of the greatest comebacks in Super Bowl history. A 92-yard winning drive in 2:36.

Boy, I bet that Eddie D. was sweating it for a while. I mean, he had all of that food and drink under that big tent. It could have turned out to have been a real downer. But it didn't, and the celebrants partied long into the night. Me, I was tired and dehydrated. I made an appearance with my family and then retired to the sanctity of my room.

I had a pretty good afternoon, rushing for 71 yards and catching eight passes for an additional 101 yards, and there were a few moments that I wanted to relive. I went upstairs to my room, took a deep breath and savored the victory. To think of all the adversity that we endured to get there. It made it just that much sweeter.

6. He was a Helluva Coach

The team flew home the next day to a victory parade, all except Jerry, Ronnie, Charles Haley, John Taylor, and myself, who flew straight to Hawaii. We were going to the Pro Bowl, with a disgruntled Rice.

Now, don't get me wrong. Jerry is a great guy, but he was upset because although he was the Super Bowl MVP, Joe got to do the Disneyworld commercial where the announcer says, "Joe Montana, you've just won the Super Bowl. Where are you going?" and Joe answers, "I'm going to Disneyworld." I think it pays something like $75,000.

It came out wrong. Jerry was quoted as saying that there was racism behind the selection of Joe to do the commercial. He said that the MVP should have been selected. Jerry had not been told that the commercial was shot several days before the Super Bowl, and that both quarterbacks were filmed saying it. If the Bengals had won and Ickey Woods had gained a thousand yards and scored ten touchdowns, it still would have been Boomer Esiason telling the world that he was going to Disneyworld. I'm not saying that it's right, but that's the way it's done. I just don't think Jerry should have hinted at racism. We were a family, and there's no place for racism in it.

By the time we got to Hawaii, Jerry had calmed down. He's certainly come a long ways from Crawford, Mississippi. When he first came to the 49ers as a rookie, he had a hard time expressing himself. But not anymore.

I was especially proud of the young guys. There were plenty of times when they could have packed it in and said we'll try again next year. But they didn't. They hung in there. You have to understand that the rookies were used to playing ten or eleven games in college. Here we had played five preseason games, sixteen regular-season games, and three postseason games; that's more than two college seasons rolled into one. You have to be able to fight off the distractions and concentrate on the things that will make you a better player.

I also was proud of Bubba. People got on him pretty good about his weight, and I knew that deep down inside it hurt him. Then he got benched in favor of Steve Wallace, and that bothered him. Bubba is a very proud person and he has aspirations of someday playing in the Pro Bowl. But his career had seemed to be taking a downward trend the past two years.

But he was ready when Steve went down injured on our first series in the Super Bowl. Even though he was listed as a backup, Bubba was physically and mentally prepared. He stepped in and did a great job. His teammates were depending on him and he came through.

Personally, I never had any doubts that we would win the Super Bowl. I never got caught up in what team would beat us or looked ahead to which teams I thought we could beat. I just thought about giving it my best every time I stepped out on the field. The bottom line is your work ethic, and thinking positive. I honestly believe that you can do anything you set your mind to.

Being happy is also important. You can't really work effectively if you're not happy. You can't just be a football player making a lot of dollars. It's a total commitment, and that's what I tell all the younger players. It's a full-time job, and that means working out in the off-season.

There are a lot of former pro players out there right now who have to duck every time they go by a mirror. They can't honestly gaze at themselves and say, "I gave it my all." My theory is that you have to work hard when you have the chance. Tomorrow that opportunity might be in somebody else's pocket.

I try to play every play like it's going to be my last, like it's going to be absolutely the last time I see the football. That way, when it's all over you have no regrets.

You can't sit back and think about how well you are doing. If you know for certain that you gave it your all every time you were on that field, then someday you can walk away with a smile on your face knowing that you made the most of every opportunity. You utilized every last inch of your natural ability and you have no regrets.

In my rookie year, Hacksaw, who was at the absolute tail end of his illustrious career, probably played two or three years after his physical abilities had left him. The younger players used to make fun of him for spending so much time on preparation. They said he was crazy.

Hacksaw used to wear this T-shirt which proclaimed TOO SHORT, TOO SLOW, AND CAN'T COVER. Which in a way was true. But he made up for his physical deficiencies by being able to predict which way a play was going to go. He would see a play start to unfold and he knew exactly where the ball was going. He would be there waiting for the ball carrier.

He was a throwback to another era, and I listened to him. That's the type of player I want to be. I want to be Hacksaw Craig. I want to be able to predict what is going to happen and where it's going to happen on any given play. That's the edge I want.

You can't go out and predict that you're going to gain a hundred yards every game or that you're going to score x number of touchdowns. I have no control over that. But I do have control over my mental and physical condition.

Even when I have a good game, I don't think about that part of it. I go to bed and think about the negatives. I think about what went wrong and how I can better myself. I might have made an 80-yard run, but if I miss a block, then I can't let that happen again. Maybe I could have faked a little better on this play or that play and Joe would have had more time to throw. I never like to think that I'm on top of the world. If I make a mistake, I thrive on coming back and doing something positive.

I remember the game against the Rams when I gained 190 yards. It was hot down there on the floor of Anaheim Stadium, probably close to 100 degrees, and I was exhausted. But I didn't let the Rams know I was tired, and I think that they eventually got discouraged. I played my heart out and probably lost ten pounds during that game. But I never gave up.

I think my dedication stems from my childhood, watching my father Elijah and brother Curtis. My father worked hard all his life. When he lived in Mississippi, he worked in a lumberyard during the day and played guitar at night. He had many diverse talents and worked hard every day of his life so his family could have a better quality of life.

My father died of cancer in the spring of my senior year of high school, right before I graduated. Two days before he died, he said to my mother, "I don't think I'll be around to see Roger play football at Nebraska, but I know he will do well." That comment has stuck in my mind throughout my career and has been a source of strength whenever I start feeling a little down.

Curtis was an outstanding high school athlete at Davenport's Central High before me, and I remember how hard he worked to get where he wanted to be. He was a star in wrestling, football, and track. He made All–Big Eight at Nebraska for two years and also made the All-Academic team. He had a tryout with the Buffalo Bills, but by that time his bum knee was giving him too much trouble for him to be able to make it in the NFL.

Curtis was a great role model for me and helped keep me out of trouble. I watched him come in first all the time, and he was always the leader of the pack. Curtis's type of dedication affected my development. I always wanted to be a team leader, just like Curtis.

My mother Ernestine was a good athlete in her own right. She played basketball at Drustan High School in Mississippi. That's probably where I get my natural athletic ability.

Then there is Jim Fox, my old high school coach. He encouraged me to train when I was younger, and that made my life easier. Jim impressed on us youngsters at all times that we should be team players. He said you work for team glory, not individual glory; if you work hard, it will pay off for you. Jim is a legend in the state of Iowa. Currently he is the athletic director at Ambrose College.

Luck also has to play a role in success. Even though I worked hard, who could have predicted that I would go to the Super Bowl three times? When I think of the way I ended up in San Francisco, I really have to believe in luck.

When the 49ers traded for defensive end Fred Dean in 1981, they promised San Diego the option to swap the Chargers' second-round pick for the 49ers' first-round in the 1983 draft. The Chargers exercised that option in 1983 and chose linebacker Billy Ray Smith with San Francisco's first-round pick. San Francisco then traded their own second- and fourth-round selections to the Los Angeles Rams for running back Wendell Tyler, defensive end Cody Jones, and the Rams' third-round pick.

With their number-two pick from the Chargers, the 49ers chose me. Eight of Bill Walsh's picks made the team that year, and, strangely enough, only one, center Jesse Sapolu, remains. Safety Tom Holmoe recently retired and linebacker Riki Ellison preceded me to the Raiders in 1989.

I often wonder what would have happened if I had been drafted by another team, say Tampa Bay or New England. It just wouldn't have been the same, and I doubt that I would have had the impact on the game that I've had. For one thing, Bill Walsh knew how to utilize me. When he drafted me out of Nebraska, he sensed that I could be a pass receiver even though I had caught only five passes during my college career. When I was a rookie he saw me as a blocking back, and I played fullback. Then he saw that I had an even better flair for halfback, so he made me a halfback. The year that I created the thousand-thousand club, that was Bill's invention. He designed an offense that took advantage of both my running and catching abilities. I know deep down in my heart that it wouldn't have happened in any other program.

Therefore I was both surprised and shocked when Bill said that he was quitting. I had just gotten back from Hawaii when Eddie DeBartolo and Bill made the announcement down in Monterey, where Eddie was getting ready to play in a golf tournament. I should have guessed it, though, because Bill broke down in the locker room after our Super Bowl win when CBS's Brent Musburger asked him if it was his final game as a head coach. Bill hugged his son Craig and cried on his shoulder.

There are always all kinds of rumors when a season is over, and after a period of time passes and nothing happens, you just forget about them. But this rumor proved true.

Bill and I had a special relationship, and not just because he recognized my talents. He would confide in me, he trusted me, and he gave me responsibility. He knew I could do the job, and that meant a lot to me. He knew the type of athlete I am and he knew that he could count on me, that I would get the best out of myself.

Bill could be stern, and I guess he might have treated some players harshly. But really, we're adults and we have to expect to be treated as such. We're getting big money to play this game, and if we mess up we should be confronted with the fact. You shouldn't expect a pat on the back every time you do something good. I mean, I don't see any of our players offering to give money back when they have a bad game.

So Bill had a right to scream. If you're not doing the job or not doing it right, not concentrating, then you have to be reminded. If you make the same mistake over and over, any coach is going to get tired of seeing it. Bill never did scream at me, though, because I made sure that I was doing the right thing at all times. And if I did make a mistake, I'd do all I could to make certain it never happened again.

Bill is a very business-oriented person, and he is extremely well organized, and I think those are positive attributes for a football coach. He wasn't lost in some foggy world of *X*s and *O*s. He had a master plan that included all facets of the game, and he wasn't afraid to implement it. I heard that he and Eddie had a couple of fallings out, but that's to be expected when you are in charge of as many areas of the operation as Bill was.

Some players complained that he was too aloof, but I don't see anything wrong with that. He was there to lead us, not be our best friend or drinking buddy. In a way, he almost had to establish some distance; he didn't want to get too close to any of the players because then it would appear that he was playing favorites, and that could have had a disastrous effect on morale. I think he handled his role superbly, treating everybody equally.

Me, I had no complaints. I just did whatever he asked me to do, and I think he respected me for my attitude. That's all you can ask of a coach. I was brought up to respect my boss and trust that he would lead me in the right direction. And that's what Bill did. If you want to argue with me, I'll show you three Super Bowl rings to prove that you're wrong.

So yes, I was surprised when he stepped down. We had a great team, and I knew that we could go back to the Super Bowl. Bill could be our steely-eyed captain again, holding us on a steady course when adversity threatened to sink us.

He was going to become president of football operations, or something like that, but I never believed for one minute that he would be happy in that capacity. Bill is a hands-on type of person with a great creative mind. His competitive juices flow in the heat of competition, and I knew that he needed a challenge. Being a football executive and going over contracts and ordering helmets wasn't going to be enough of a challenge for him. Even in the draft, where he could be at his best, wheeling and dealing, is only two days out of the year, and that wasn't enough to satisfy his creative appetite.

I proved to be right, as four months later he quit to take the job with NBC sports as its chief pro football analyst. It was another challenge in another field, and it would satisfy his competitive nature for a while.

Why did he step down? I don't like to speculate on another person's reasons because those types of decisions are very personal. But I suppose that he felt that he was getting older and he wanted to stop and sniff the roses. He is a multifaceted person, and I guess he wanted to enjoy life. He also wanted to be in control of his own destiny. By walking away while his team was on top, he could do that. If San Francisco didn't win another Super Bowl, he would never get another opportunity to do it his way, playing by his own rules. I guess he could have tried to squeeze out one more season, but maybe he looked on that as being greedy. Perhaps contributing to his decision to step down were the rumors that Bill and Eddie weren't getting along that well.

Bill had an outstanding coaching career. He had taken a franchise that was in shambles ten years prior to his departure and built it into a dynasty. Not too many people in this world can claim that accomplishment. He had won three Super Bowls and was the architect of pro football's most envied organization. I think what was overlooked was the way he prepared the organization for his eventual departure. Nothing was left to chance. Everything had its proper niche. If he hadn't planned for when he left, the team wouldn't have gone back to the Super Bowl the following season. The team still carries Bill Walsh's spirit, even though not all of its management believes in what he believed in.

It appeared to be a smooth transition from Bill to George Seifert. George had worked under Bill since their days at Stanford, and he had incorporated a lot of Bill's ideas into his own philosophy. That's not to say that George isn't his own man, because he is. But Bill and Eddie worked together so there would be a smooth transition from one head coach to the next.

John McVay assumed some of Bill's executive duties, and when George moved up to be head coach, quarterback coach Mike Holmgren moved up to become offensive coordinator, and Bill McPherson went from linebacker coach to defensive coordinator, George's former position. Al Lavan was hired as running backs coach and Sherm Lewis moved to receivers coach. John Marshall was hired as defensive line coach. The rest of the coaching staff, including line coach Bobb McKittrick, remained the same. So we had continuity.

It bothered me a lot when some of the media and some of the players tried to bad-mouth Bill after he left. I don't know why they would do that, other than perhaps out of professional jealousy. Why would you criticize the man who made the organization a winner and put money in everybody's pockets? I knew I wasn't going to jump on the bandwagon just because he was gone. I respect the man from the bottom of my heart: he was my motivator. And Bill was a genius when it came to the passing game; I don't think you will find anybody who will argue that statement.

George is different than Bill in many ways. For one thing, he is a defensive coach, and he sees everything from the other side of the line. His psyche is geared to stop offenses. Bill was the opposite; he plotted to attack defenses. George did become more involved in the offense, but you can still see more of his influence in the team's defensive schemes.

That's not to say that Bill is better than George, or vice versa. Bill is the more outspoken type, while George is more reserved. But they are exactly the same in one regard; they both love to compete and will do whatever it takes to win.

◆

7. Reliving Childhood Memories

I couldn't wait for the 1989 training camp to open. I had slimmed down to 210 pounds by training on a hill with a two-thousand-foot vertical climb. We were coming in as the defending Super Bowl champions. Of course, there were a lot of question marks. We had a new coach in George Seifert. Jesse Sapolu had been moved from left guard to center, replacing the retired Randy Cross. We knew that every other NFL team would be gunning for us.

George got off on the right foot when he announced the first day of camp that Joe Montana was his starting quarterback. That was an extremely good move, because the year before I think Joe had been distracted by the fact that he wasn't given the starting job in training camp.

George said that as long as Joe was healthy, he was the guy. It was no reflection on Steve Young, who is a good quarterback. The coach said that if Montana was hurt, then Young would get the call, but as soon as Montana was well enough to play again, the job was his. It sounded fair to me. That's the way it should be. A starter should never lose his job when he's well enough to come back from an injury. Even Joe admitted that Bill's announcement at the previous season's training camp that there was an "open competition" for the starting quarterback job was "unsettling."

Another reason I was so excited was that my childhood buddy and best friend Jamie Williams had been signed by the 49ers as a Plan B player during the off-season. This was a dream come true.

We used to lived a couple of blocks from each other in Davenport, Iowa, and as youngsters we would sit on the porch of my house in the

77

evenings and dream about playing on the same team together. During summer vacation we would run in the hills behind Ninth Street. We were inseparable pals, like brothers.

We attended Jefferson Elementary School and J. B. Young Junior High together and played football together at Davenport Central High. Jamie is a real crowd-pleaser, more of a free spirit than I am. He was a great basketball player at Davenport. He was so cool out on the court. We used to call him "the Ice Man" in high school.

Our neighborhood was very poor, and it wasn't the most encouraging environment, but Jamie and I were full of dreams, and dreams don't know anything about boundaries. The focal points of our life were school and sports. The guys who played at our high school before us, like my brother Curtis and Jamie's brother Dennis left a rich sports legacy, which we were expected to fulfill.

Jamie and I would play imaginary games at Harrington Park, complete with crowds and everything. He would be Billy Joe Dupree of the Dallas Cowboys and I would be Archie Griffin of the Bengals or O. J. Simpson of the Bills. We would pretend we were in the Super Bowl, making great runs and great catches, taking our bows before an imaginary crowd. Every once in a while there would be a real serious football game between the older kids behind the hill at Goose Hollow, and Jamie and I would be invited to play.

Our parents worked hard to get us the things we wanted, but it was an impossible situation, because half of the student body at Davenport Central came from affluent families. As kids, you want the same things other kids have, and you very seldom understand why you can't have them. I don't think we ever had any middle-class kids at Davenport High, just the haves and the have-nots.

Jamie and I took our athletic talents seriously and tried to advance them another step. Many of our peers would make fun of us and our workout regimen, but we didn't let that bother us. Some kids went to the small local colleges, but our dream was to go to a major college like Nebraska. When Curtis went to Nebraska, he showed Jamie and me that it could be done, and that gave us renewed energy.

I broke my leg in the opening game my junior year of high school and missed the rest of the season. I remember how depressed I was. Jamie, who is about five months older than I am and was a year ahead of me, was being recruited by various colleges and universities, and I can recall how envious I was. But Jamie kept my dream alive. He kept telling me, "Roger, I told them about you, so you have to really work hard. They're going to be back to look at you next year, and you have to be ready."

I was just like I am now; I couldn't stand to go through rehabilitation. I just wanted to cut the cast off, throw the crutches away, and start training again. I saw how contented Jamie was at Nebraska, and I didn't want to be left behind. When those recruiters came around my senior year, I wanted to dazzle them. In addition to playing football, I also ran the hurdles on the track team and wrestled. The inactivity was killing me.

I wouldn't have minded going to Iowa, but I guess they weren't that interested in me. My coach called them and told them all I had done, but they didn't display any interest in me until the last week of recruiting. Even then, it was just a phone call. None of the Iowa coaches came out to visit me. I had already made up my mind to go to Nebraska, anyway, because they showed the most interest and because of Curtis and Jamie.

Jamie redshirted that first year at Nebraska and when I accepted a scholarship there the following season, we became roommates. The two best friends from Davenport on the same football team, just like we used to talk about. We had to pinch ourselves to make sure that we weren't dreaming.

We played on the same college team for four years, and by then we were extending our dreams to the pros. We were both pretty certain that we would be drafted by the time we were seniors, and we used to think, wouldn't it be something if we landed on the same team together.

That really is the impossible dream. Two buddies ending up on the same professional team thousands of miles from their home just isn't realistic.

So it wasn't surprising that our lives took different paths following our senior year at Nebraska. The 49ers visited our campus and looked at both Jamie and myself, but they didn't have many draft choices that year. They had traded away their first-round pick and they only had four selections in the first six rounds. I was drafted by San Francisco in the second round of the 1983 draft, the forty-ninth player selected and the sixth running back taken behind Eric Dickerson, Curt Warner, Michael Haddix, James Jones, and Gary Anderson.

The New York Giants took Jamie in the third round, the sixty-third pick overall. So we were going to be playing at opposite ends of the country. However, Jamie didn't fare too well with the Giants, and he was cut at the end of training camp. He then signed with the St. Louis Cardinals, but they waived him after four games. He used to call me and tell me that he was down in the dumps, but I kept encouraging him to hang in there, to stay in shape and keep trying. We had worked too hard and come too far for him to turn back now.

He made one more stop his rookie season, playing briefly with Tampa Bay, but he sat out the rest of the season home in Davenport. I was having a lot of fun my rookie year—we went all the way to the NFC Championship Game that year, losing to the Redskins 24–21—and I kept phoning him to keep his spirits up. When the 1984 season rolled around, he went to camp with the Houston Oilers and signed a contract. It appeared that he had finally found a home, as he averaged 40 catches and nearly 500 yards during his first two seasons with the Oilers.

After we went to the Super Bowl for the first time in 1985, I went back to Davenport and showed Jamie my Super Bowl ring. I saw his eyes light up and watched the smile pass across his face when he slipped it on. I could tell that he was envious, but at the same time I could see that look of determination on his face. It said, "By God, I'm going to get one of these rings before I quit or else."

But when Warren Moon arrived in Houston from Canada, Jamie's production fell off. He was used mainly for blocking as the team went to a four–wide receiver set. You might say that he was one of the first victims of the run-and-shoot offense. In Houston's current scheme, they don't have a tight end on the roster. The only time they use a tight end is for blocking, and they can line up a guard or tackle to perform that task.

We used to talk on the phone, and I would tell him about the thrills of playing in the Super Bowl. He would say that if he could only play one play in the Super Bowl, he would be the happiest man ever to walk the streets of Davenport. I told him that that wasn't quite true; there was a guy in town who had two Super Bowl rings.

Two other former Davenport High athletes made the NFL, but neither was ever on a team that won the Super Bowl. In 1970, Jim Hester played for the Chicago Bears, who lost to the Rams in the playoffs, and Jim Jensen played for Dallas in 1976, and in 1977 he played for Denver against the Cowboys in Super Bowl XII, but the Broncos lost to the Cowboys 27–10. Jensen also played two seasons for Green Bay.

But even though Jamie had started every game for the Oilers since 1984, Houston failed to protect him during the 1989 Plan B period, and the 49ers snatched him away. I don't understand how a team doesn't need at least one tight end, but their loss was our gain. We had lost John Frank to medical school and his backup, Ron Heller, to Atlanta in another Plan B move, so we definitely were in the market for a tight end. And Jamie is one of the best around, with good hands and a devastating blocker.

So when we reported to training camp in Rocklin, I had Jamie to pal around with once again. Who would have ever guessed that we would be teammates on a team headed for the Super Bowl?

We were starting training camp without a controversy—well, I guess that's not quite true. Our top two draft choices, Keith DeLong and Wesley Walls, still hadn't signed, plus we had a few veterans who were holding out for better contracts. That group included defensive backs Jeff Fuller, Tim McKyer, and Don Griffin, defensive linemen Larry Roberts and Kevin Fagan, offensive linemen Steve Wallace and Guy McIntyre, and linebacker Charles Haley.

I really wasn't too happy that Wallace and McIntyre were out. They were two of my guys and two of the major reasons I'd rushed for 1,502 yards the previous season. But that was their business and I wished them the best.

Because of the absence of those players, the team had gone out and signed a bunch of free-agent hopefuls and has-beens to fill out the training camp roster. Most of them were guys who had been in training camps before and were hoping for just one more shot at the brass ring.

I heard some of the coaches refer to them as "training camp fodder." I know that is not a very complimentary term, but I think it's closer to the truth than any other name you could give them. I'm sure that none of these free agents figured heavily in the 49ers' plans that season. Still, you never know. Harry Sydney, our special teams captain, came in as a free agent and he's still there. He was out of football and sent the 49ers a résumé, and they invited him to training camp. So every once in a while someone catches a piece of the dream, and it's nice to see.

One of our free agents was a likeable tight end named Mark Gehring who had been kicking around NFL training camps since 1986, when he had a tryout with the Vikings. He had played for Calgary of the Canadian Football League, came back to play for Houston during the 1987 NFL players' strike, and had been in the Redskins camp the previous season.

He told me that all he wanted was to have the opportunity to give the Niners coaches a reason to keep him. It's tough once the preseason games start because the free agents don't get the reps that the veterans do. "I've been close, but I've never gotten the cigar," he told me one night.

Mark wasn't some brainless kid whose only skills were football. He had a degree in business administration from Eastern Washington University. He also had a wife and two little boys. I felt like telling him to give up his dream and get back to the real world, but I didn't have the heart. Besides, who was I to say how his story would turn out?

But honestly, the odds were stacked against him. I think he was the fourth or fifth tight end on the depth chart, listed behind Jamie, Brent Jones, the rookie Walls, and another free agent named Rod Jones. He needed a big break to even think about making it past the first cut.

He got a small one, literally, when Jamie got his hand tangled in a jersey during a blocking drill and broke his finger. It had to be surgically repaired, which meant he would miss the first four or five games of the season. So Gehring stuck around until the final cut-down day, and then he was gone. I felt sorry for him, but in another way it was good that he found out when he did. He was going to get cut when Jamie came back anyway, and this way he could start plotting his future sooner.

After opening the season with a 30–24 road win against Indianapolis, we had a very interesting week as we prepared for Tampa Bay. The 49ers brought former Raider great Matt Millen in for a tryout. The middle linebacker had been dumped because Raider owner Al Davis figured that he had outlived his usefulness.

However, as we were to find out, Davis made a major mistake. Millen not only wasn't over the hill, he had a lot of good football left in him. We outbid the Rams for him, and it proved to be a prudent move on the 49ers' part in the run for a second straight Super Bowl. I think that the Rams actually offered Matt more money, but he felt more comfortable in Northern California, having played for the Raiders in their final year in Oakland. Plus he was tailor-made for our defense.

Through the ensuing weeks we came to depend on Matt in our defense, just as we depended on Ronnie Lott and Michael Carter and Charles Haley. Matt became one of our team leaders, constantly giving advice to the younger players and becoming a perfect role model for them with his dedication and work ethic. For the time being he would play backup to inside linebackers Jim Fahnhorst and Mike Walter. Our incumbent middle linebacker, Riki Ellison, was on injured reserve for the entire year.

We flew down to Tampa on Friday and dispatched the Bucs, 20–16, on Sunday; Joe ran the ball in from four yards out with only forty seconds left for the winning touchdown. Matt saw his first duty as a 49er, playing on some special teams and logging a couple of downs in our goal line defense.

If it's September, it must be the road, and the following week we had to crisscross the country once again, this time to Philadelphia. During the week somebody had taken a Buddy Ryan mask off a soda carton, made a bunch of reprints on a copy machine, attached some disparaging quotes by Ryan, and hung the prints on our lockers. It might have seemed cute to some players, but it pissed me off because it cluttered up my locker. So I just ripped it off and tossed it away.

I don't need anything like a replica of a coach's face to get me ready. What did get me fired up, though, were Ryan's comments all week that Randall Cunningham was the best quarterback in the NFL. I don't know how he could make a statement like that and treat it as fact. I'm not taking anything away from Randall, but he has to go some before he comes even close to Joe Montana.

The flight into Philadelphia was the bumpiest in my seven-year career with the 49ers. We were riding the tail of Hurricane Hugo, which had cut a path of death and destruction through the Carolinas before moving inland. The winds buffeted our plane around as we started our final descent into Philadelphia, and suddenly the plane must have dropped about five hundred feet and the lights dimmed. At that point,

I would have agreed with Buddy Ryan that Cunningham was the best quarterback if only Randall would have landed our plane safely.

But everything turned out well and we made it safely to the ground. I guess most of the gridiron experts must have agreed with Ryan, because they picked the Eagles to beat us. And they probably would have, had we not had Montana. We'd fallen behind 21–10 in the fourth period when Joe started putting on a passing clinic. Joe threw four fourth-quarter touchdowns as we won going away, 38–28. He ended up with 25 completions in 34 attempts for 428 yards and five touchdown passes.

Poor Randall. Some of his invincibility was stripped away by our defense; he completed only 19 of 38 attempts for 192 yards and one touchdown. The stunned Eagles crowd sat in silence through most of the final period as Joe deftly cut through their defense like some sort of robosurgeon. Heading home with a 3–0 record, we figured that our Super Bowl Repeat Express was right on schedule.

We would have to share our home field with the San Francisco Giants for a little while longer as the Giants were playing for the National League pennant. But on Sunday, October 1, the Giants were out of town, and we were in Candlestick Park playing the Rams. The next two weeks would be crucial ones for us as we faced back-to-back NFC West opponents, first the Rams and then the Saints in New Orleans.

Although we outgained Los Angeles, 367 yards to 287, and out–first-downed them 21–10, our offense just never got untracked. Placekicker Mike Cofer was our only offense, kicking four field goals as we headed into the shadows of the fourth quarter.

It appeared, though, that we were going to win the game as we mounted a drive that went all the way down to the Rams' 22 yard line. But on second down Tom Rathman fumbled the ball, and the Rams recovered. They then marched down the field and placekicker Mike Lansford kicked a 26-yard field goal with two seconds left to give them a 13–12 victory.

Afterward in the locker room I really felt sorry for Tom. He was taking full blame for losing the game, which was wrong. Just as there are team wins, there are team losses. We had 152 yards rushing, but no one could punch it into the end zone. And in the end, when our defense had to stop their final drive cold, it couldn't. So Tom had no reason to blame himself. I tried to explain that to him, but he just looked up at me with those sad eyes that only those guys from Grand Island, Nebraska, seem to have. He said it was only the second fumble of his pro career and he couldn't understand why it had to happen when it did.

After that fiasco at home, none of us were too heartbroken to hit the road again, even though it would have been nice not to have to get onto an airplane again so soon. Actually, we were supposed to play

New Orleans at home. But the San Francisco Giants had made the National League playoffs, and they preempted us. So the NFL flopped our home-and-home series, with us traveling to New Orleans for the October 8 game and New Orleans coming to San Francisco for a Monday night game on November 6. Their fans were hopping mad because they were cheated out of their first-ever ABC-TV Monday Night Football game. Still, any game with the Saints, home or away, is a war. They had, and still have, perhaps the best set of linebackers in the league, and I always came away from playing them feeling like I had been wrestling a Cuisinart.

I really have a lot of respect for the linebackers of the Saints, Falcons, and Bears. They play for the love of the game, and they play clean professional football. My favorite is Bears linebacker Mike Singletary. He plays defense just like I play offense, and you have to respect that.

Singletary's off-field demeanor belies his trade. If you saw him sitting at a counter having a cup of coffee, you'd never guess that he played football for a living. He's the nicest man you would ever want to meet, a mellow, down-to-earth type of guy. A real class act. But on the football field, look out. He's like a cornered wolverine coming out of his hole after you. When you see him coming with those wide-set eyes ablazing, you just want to find someplace to hide.

But while the Saints linebackers had a good time limiting me to 70 yards on 18 carries, Joe Montana was having a field day, connecting on 21 of 29 passes for 282 yards and three touchdowns. Jerry Rice burned the Saints with a 60-yard touchdown reception from Montana with six minutes remaining in the third quarter. As Rice ran into the end zone he appeared to spike the football before he crossed the goal line. The Saints protested vehemently, but the touchdown stood. The last touchdown pass, a 32-yarder to John Taylor, came in the fourth quarter and rallied us from a 20–17 deficit to a 24–20 win.

Next were the Dallas Cowboys, and we dispatched them 31–14.

So we came home to face the Patriots at Candlestick Park with a 5–1 record. The season was far from over, but we had a good rhythm going, and we felt very good about our chances. While it's sacrilegious to mention anyone except the next opponent, in the back of our minds we were starting to think Super Bowl. Each of us would walk around the locker room talking up the next game, secretly thinking about another Super Bowl ring. Of course, none of the players would admit this out loud, including me. It was like our locker room was sheltering the world's largest secret.

Compounding our anxiety was the fact that New England wasn't a very good football team—just the type of team that can jump up and bite you. Our Monday team meeting was semiserious as we watched

I love playing football and can't wait to get out on the field. (*All photographs by Michael Zagaris*)

Some scenes from my pregame ritual:
Studying the playbook.

Taking acupuncture to relieve minor pains.

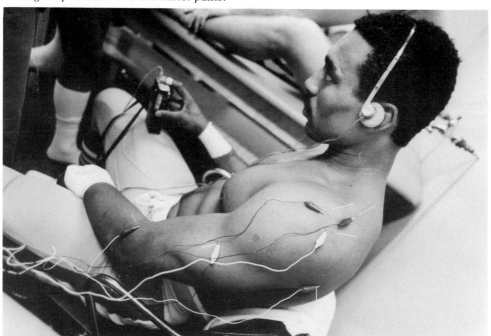

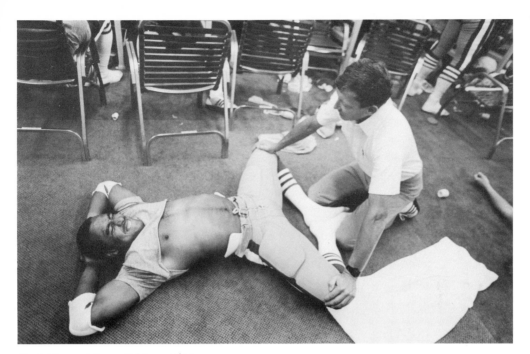

Stretching out those tight muscles.

Finally, a brief period of meditation in the shower helps me to focus my mind on the game.

High-stepping against Seattle in a 1985
Monday night game.

With my trademark wide eyes I watch the
49ers line make some great blocks against
the tough New Orleans defense.

Coming out of the backfield to catch a pass from Joe Montana.

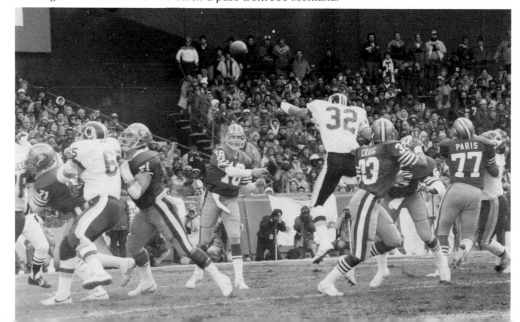

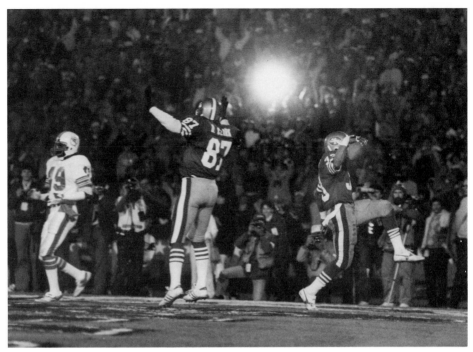

Celebrating my third touchdown in Super Bowl XIX—a Super Bowl scoring record that I share with my friend Jerry Rice.

Skying over tacklers against our arch-rivals, the Rams, in a 1987 win.

You have to be able to make the tough yards, too. Here I'm diving in against the Kansas City goal line defense, and (below) bulling to a touchdown against Dallas.

In the locker room with coach Bill Walsh and 49er owner Eddie DeBartolo in 1987, after our 41–0 blowout of the Chicago Bears.

In Tokyo for a 1989 exhibition with new 49er coach George Seifert.

Visiting with Jerry Rice in the locker room.

On the sideline with my backfield partner and University of Nebraska buddy Tom Rathman.

films of our victory over the Saints. There were a few guffaws and laughs as mistakes were pointed out by the coaches, but it was all good-natured kidding.

During the regular season the players usually have Tuesdays off. We all look forward to that day because it's the only one during the week that we can really spend with our families. Most of us run around trying to do chores and mend fences with our loved ones.

There was a World Series game between the Giants—they'd finally won the National League pennant—and the Oakland A's at Candlestick Park Tuesday night, and many of the players were planning on attending. Harris Barton was an old schoolmate of A's shortstop Walt Weiss, and he got some tickets and was planning to go with Steve Young, Mike Walter, and some of the guys.

Myself, I had a lot of chores to do, and I wanted to spend some time with the family. We had been on the road for four of our first five games, and I'm sure they felt a little neglected; I know I felt guilty for not spending more time with them.

I was looking forward to it being a perfect Tuesday.

◆

8. A Tragic Reminder

On Tuesday, October 17, 1989, at about 5:04 P.M., an earthquake that registered 7.1 on the Richter scale rumbled through Northern California, leaving in its wake devastation and death. The whole world knew about the calamity because the World Series game between the Oakland A's and the San Francisco Giants was just about to start at Candlestick Park, and much of the nation's sports media were assembled at Candlestick for the game, which of course was to be televised nationally.

For the next forty-eight hours news of the tragedy was relayed to the rest of the nation. Some apartment houses in the Marina district of San Francisco, a quaint neighborhood out by the Bay, collapsed and burned, a portion of the upper deck of the Bay Bridge broke off and fell onto the lower deck, and in the worst disaster of all, the upper deck of a freeway in the East Bay near Cypress Street collapsed onto the lower deck, crushing rush hour commuters. There were widespread death and damage in other communities as well, including Watsonville and Santa Cruz and San Jose. Fortunately, the homes and lives of our team's families were spared. I think there was some structural damage to Bubba Paris's home in San Jose, but for the rest of us it was just minor things like fallen pictures and broken vases.

I had gone shopping with my wife and son and we were in San Carlos, a small town on the Peninsula where we used to live before we moved to Portola Valley. I was inside a frame shop picking up a picture frame when all of a sudden the walls started shaking. I thought at first that a big truck had gone by. Some truck.

Then the ground started rumbling, and the floor started pitching and things started falling, and it got stronger. I said to myself, "Wow, I'm in an earthquake." Glass was shattering all around me, and people were screaming. I ran outside and saw Vernessia and Rogdrick in the van, and it was bouncing up and down on the street. It was an extremely frightening moment because I felt so helpless.

But my fears were far from over. I immediately started worrying about my two daughters, who were still in school, and I was concerned about the welfare of our live-in housekeeper and wondered what sort of shape our house was in. It seemed like it took forever to get home, but everyone was safe, thank God. Some of the interior walls in the house had cracked and some glass objects were broken, but there was no major damage and nothing valuable was lost.

That night all of the power was out and the gas was shut off, and we had to use candles and flashlights. I barbecued chicken outside because we couldn't use the stove. It was like we were camping, and the kids got a kick out of that.

Even more frightening than the earthquake, though, were the aftershocks. They would rumble through every hour or so, and when each one came we thought it was the start of another big one. We'd jump up and run outside. We were being held hostage by Mother Nature. That night none of us could sleep.

The next day it was practice as usual as we prepared for the New England Patriots. Even though there was devastation and tragedy all around us, we kept our minds on our job. It shows you just how focused the team was.

Friends and relatives began calling from the Midwest and asking us when we were moving back. They couldn't believe that we wanted to stay in a part of the country where such disastrous phenomena as earthquakes could strike without warning. But that's part of life. Heck, there're tornadoes in my hometown of Davenport, and there are hurricanes in the Carolinas and Florida.

There are elements of nature you can't control, and earthquakes are one of them. If something is going to happen to me, it was meant to be. Wherever you go, Mother Nature is going to be there, and she's going to have some challenge for you. But California is where I chose to make my permanent home. The weather is great, the schools are good for my children, and I feel a part of the local fabric. I love Northern California.

Meanwhile the stricken communities were struggling to get back on their feet. Little did the 49ers know that we would have to deal with our own team tragedy before the week was out.

Everything in the Bay Area was put on hold for the next several days while we held our collective breaths after each foreboding aftershock and dug ourselves out from the rubble. Candlestick Park, which had more than 56,000 fans in the stands for the World Series game, suffered some structural damage, but miraculously everyone was evacuated without incident.

When the World Series resumed across the Bay in Oakland, the A's made quick work of the Giants, so the question of where to hold the Giants' home games was moot. However, our game with the Patriots was still up in the air. Politicians argued back and forth as to whether the game should be played at Candlestick Park. Some said that it was sacrilegious to hold the game at all and that we should continue our period of mourning. But to tell you the truth, the Bay Area was mourned out.

Eddie D. flew a couple of his top engineers out from Youngstown, Ohio, and they went over Candlestick with a fine-tooth comb. He told the media that if he didn't consider the stadium safe for his own family, he wouldn't let anyone else's family attend a game there. That sounded fair to me. I certainly wasn't planning on letting Vernessia and the children go to the game. The NFL was brought in, and as we continued to experience aftershocks from the quake, the big honchos pondered the fate of our football game. Every swami and prognosticator and clairvoyant in the world jumped on the publicity bandwagon, predicting instant doom for the Bay Area. Some even predicted that the whole land mass would break off at the end of the bay and tumble into the ocean.

Personally, I thought we should play the game, and I didn't care where. I was anxious to get my mind on other matters. All the tears that could be shed had been shed. We were in danger of becoming mired in a grief, and it was time that we snapped back to life. I thought that a football game would be a good diversion.

Finally, on Wednesday they announced that Candlestick needed too much repair work to bring it back up to safety standards in such a short period of time. It wasn't so much what had happened to it as what might happen to it if there was another quake of similar magnitude with 64,000 fans in the stands.

Now they—Eddie D., the politicians, and the NFL—had to decide where to play the game. The NFL mentioned switching the game to Foxboro, where the Patriots play, while the 49ers explored the possibility of holding the game at Stanford Stadium, where Super Bowl XIX was played. There seemed to be no easy solution. Television was putting the pressure on all parties, demanding to know immediately where the game was going to be played. Foxboro didn't sound too bad to me. We were 5–0 on the road, and besides, we were used to packing up and leaving home every Friday.

But on Thursday the San Francisco mayor's office announced that the game would be played at Stanford Stadium. That was all right with me too. In Super Bowl XIX against Miami, I set a Super Bowl record for most points (18) and most touchdowns (3) by an individual. I also accounted for 135 yards in our 38–16 victory. So you can see that Stanford holds a special place in my heart.

On game day we bused down the Peninsula to Stanford. My home is only about four miles away in Portola Valley, so it was actually a much more convenient location than Candlestick. Or Foxboro.

We stepped off the bus and right into a college atmosphere. It was a beautiful, sunny fall day and the mood reflected the weather. You could smell the aromas from the barbecues people were firing up under the big trees that line the campus. It was a very festive crowd and reminded me of my college days at Nebraska. People had been living with the earthquake for five days, and I think they were just happy to get away from all of the sad stories and dire predictions of gloom and doom. I know I was. It was depressing to watch television and see and listen to all of the stricken survivors. It was time for the Bay Area to get on with its life, and this was as good a place as any to start. There was a crowd of nearly 70,000 in the stands when the game started, which is about 6,000 more than could fit into Candlestick.

It happened on the second play from scrimmage. New England running back John Stephens took a pitch and started right. Jim Fahnhorst, our inside linebacker, grabbed Stephens by the legs, and Jeff Fuller, our safety, dived into Stephens at about the New England 22, hitting him head on. There was a sickening *whack,* then silence. Everyone on the 49ers bench looked out at the field. We knew it was serious. Stephens finally struggled to his feet, but Jeff never moved. Our trainers and doctors rushed to Jeff's side, but it was obvious that it was a serious injury. They finally called for an ambulance and strapped Jeff to a stretcher so his head and neck were immobilized. He could move his legs, but not his arms.

The ambulance took Jeff to Stanford Hospital, right on campus, and play resumed, but we knew that Jeff was badly injured and it was hard to focus on the game. It got worse. Backup fullback and special teams cocaptain Harry Sydney broke his left forearm, and then Joe went out with a sprained knee just before the half. Finally, Fahnhorst suffered a stress fracture in his left foot. It was proving to be one of the costliest games we'd ever played.

We ended up winning 37–20 as Steve Young threw three second-half touchdowns and I scored a touchdown on a two-yard run. We had to make a lot of adjustments, but we won.

However, there was little to celebrate in the locker room after the game. All of us were more concerned about Jeff than the win. The first reports were that he had suffered compressed vertebrae. Dr. Michael Dillingham, our team's orthopedic specialist, explained that the nerve endings between his neck and right arm had been pulled apart. He was in the intensive care unit at Stanford Medical Center, and the prognosis was not good. We all bowed our heads in the locker room and prayed for Jeff's recovery.

George Seifert was very solemn when he addressed the club. I'm sure that when he accepted the head coaching job, this kind of heartbreak wasn't included in the job description. He told us that he was proud of us and that we'd played a good game, and that he was sorry that none of us would be able to enjoy this victory.

It was too bad because it could have been a great afternoon. We had provided the Bay Area with something else to think about besides the earthquake. But we also lost a comrade and a good friend. A bunch of us went over to the hospital to see Jeff after the game, but he wasn't much up for visitors.

The next morning when I woke up it seemed like a bad nightmare, but then I picked up the papers and knew that it had all actually happened. Jeff was still in intensive care, and the doctors were saying that he probably would never play again. Something about the nerves being unable to regenerate themselves.

I tried to put myself in Jeff's place, but I couldn't. I couldn't imagine not being able to play football again. I was too upbeat to even contemplate it. One second Jeff was one of the best safeties in all of pro football, and in the blink of an eye it was all over. It showed just how fleeting and fragile a career can be. Or a life, for that matter.

It's strange, but when you're out there on the field and the adrenaline is pumping through your veins as you dodge a defender, you never think it will end. You feel like you can run right through infinity.

Harry Sydney was scheduled to have surgery and a plate was to be inserted in his broken arm. Joe was still listed as doubtful for the following week's game against the Jets, and Jim Fahnhorst was out indefinitely with his foot injury.

There was a piece of good news that week—though I'm not sure that's the way management looked at it. Tim McKyer, our outspoken cornerback, was reinstated on Tuesday after serving a month suspension without pay. That had to hurt, because I think that the four missed games cost Tim more than $160,000.

I honestly don't have anything against Tim, but I didn't understand him at times. He complained a lot that management didn't understand him and was insensitive to his problems. But I believed at the time that San Francisco was the best place to play in the NFL, and I could never understand why Tim didn't think the same. He would find out what it was like before the next season started. Meanwhile, we were all glad to see Tim back. For one thing, the wide-angle smile he brought with him brightened up our locker room. And, with Jeff gone and Ronnie Lott still hobbled by a right ankle sprain suffered against Philadelphia in week three, we were extremely thin in our defensive backfield. Tim is a great cover man and would be a welcome addition to the overworked defense.

But we were 6–1 and ready to hit the road again, headed for New Jersey to play the Jets. In light of everything that had happened in the past couple of weeks, I think it was good that we were getting out of town for the game.

Steve Young was scheduled to start, as Joe still had a banged-up knee and had been declared unfit to play by the team doctors. I was really looking forward to Sunday, as all week long in practice we had put special emphasis on the running game. Offensive coordinator Mike Holmgren had detected a vulnerability in the Jets' defense which could be exploited by the run.

I had been struggling, and it was beginning to bother me—though not as much as it was bothering other people, especially the media. The Jets were *really* struggling, and I guess that the New York media and the fans were calling for coach Joe Walton's job.

We left on a Friday and had a brief practice Saturday outside the Meadowlands on a vacant field because we showed up at the same time the New York Giants were preparing for a Monday night game against the Vikings. It kind of ticked us off, because the Giants could have let us use half the field, but coach Bill Parcells said no even though we had permission to practice inside the stadium. No big deal, though. It just meant that we got more of the afternoon off.

On Sunday it was just like Mike had said it would be, and eight of our first fifteen scripted plays were runs. Only I wasn't the main guy, Tom Rathman was. At the half I had 42 yards on nine carries while Tom had 45 yards on seven carries, and we had a comfortable 20–7 lead. Midway through the second quarter, though, our collective hearts stopped when Steve was bent backward with his legs pinned under him. It was George's worst nightmare, with Joe already inactive for the game. The only one who had any sense of humor about it was Young, who quipped as he was being helped off the field that he heard something snap and that hopefully it was a spare part that he didn't need.

With Steve out, our other Steve came in: Steve Bono. He was an interesting study. Bono was one of those free agents who wasn't supposed to make the team, but he beat out former Dallas quarterback Kevin Sweeney, a Plan B free agent, in the preseason. Even coach Seifert admitted that he had considered waiving Bono and keeping Sweeney. The Minnesota Vikings sixth-round draft pick in 1985, Bono had bounced around the league for five seasons. In that time, he had only played in seven games and completed 46 passes.

So we weren't sure what to expect. But he turned our heads in his brief appearance, though his afternoon started out shaky. It was third and seven when he came in, and the first call was a quick pass to me. I got the ball, but someone hit me from the side and I fumbled. Jets safety Erik McMillan scooped up the ball and ran it back 45 yards for a Jets touchdown.

So Bono was one for one—and the other team had seven more points than when he came in. On our ensuing series, he first passed to John Taylor for seven. Following a seven-yard gain by Rathman, Bono hit J.T. over the middle for a nine-yard gain. Then on second and one, we ran a play-action that sucked McMillan up, and Steve aired it out to Jerry for a 45-yard touchdown.

Young came back the next series, but Bono returned later to finish the game off. He ended the day with four completions in five attempts for 62 yards and a touchdown. Not bad for a third-string quarterback. More important, though, he gave us confidence that we could depend on him if something happened to both Joe and Steve.

We went on to win 23–10; I got 78 of our team's 159 yards rushing on 17 carries, and we were now 7–1 as we headed west towards the fading sun. This victory belonged to the coaches, as they were able to script the game plan that took advantage of the Jets' weaknesses. It went just like they had told us in the meetings. Unfortunately, they hadn't figured on the injury to nose tackle Michael Carter. He injured his right foot, and the prognosis was not good. The doctors were talking about his being out a minimum of four weeks.

When we arrived home, we once again were confronted with a dilemma as to where to play our home game against the Saints. It would be difficult playing this one at Stanford because it was a Monday night game and Stanford has no lights. Art Agnos, the new mayor of San Francisco, showed Eddie reports that Candlestick was safe. But Eddie wanted some more inspections done. It was finally determined that we would play the game at Candlestick Park, though several of the players said they wouldn't let their wives go to the game because they didn't trust the stadium.

This was an important game for us for two reasons: the Saints were in our division, and the season was already half over and we still hadn't won a game at Candlestick. We didn't want a repeat of the strike-shortened 1982 season. That year also the 49ers were coming off a Super Bowl season; they went 3–6, with all three of the victories coming on the road.

George told us at Monday's team meeting that Joe would start the game. We were pretty sure it wasn't going to be Steve Young, because he showed up Monday at camp on crutches. Fahnhorst underwent surgery Tuesday to repair a broken bone in his foot and was placed on injured reserve.

This was proving to be an interesting week as we prepared for our second go-round with the Saints. First, New Orleans was still ticked off about the Jerry Rice touchdown, which they claimed was a nontouchdown. They were also unhappy that they had had to flipflop dates with us and had therefore missed out having a Monday night nationally televised game in the Superdome.

The fact that the Saints appeared to have righted themselves after an abysmal 1–4 start didn't help matters, from our point of view. They had won their last three games, including two straight over NFC West rivals, a 40–21 thrashing of the Los Angeles Rams and a 20–13 win over the Atlanta Falcons. I figured that it was going to be like running into a hornet's nest Monday night.

In addition to that, we were entering the most difficult part of our schedule. We had just come off the cream puff part, scoring wins over New England, Dallas, and the Jets. Their combined record was 4–20. We were now going to have to deal with the Saints, Atlanta, Green Bay, and the Giants. Combined record: 17–15. This stretch would tell us if we were bona fide Super Bowl contenders.

The strangest thing that occurred was our signing of former New York Giants nose tackle Jim Burt on Wednesday of that week. I say strange because he was the last person in the world I thought the San Francisco 49ers would sign. The Giants had given up on him and convinced him to retire. But Michael Carter was going to be lost to us for an undetermined amount of time, and Burt was signed to fill the void.

To get some perspective on Burt, you have to go back to the first half of a game on January 4, 1987, on a chilly afternoon at the Meadowlands in New Jersey. We were playing the Giants in an NFC playoff game, and it was still a a close contest. Just before the half, Joe dropped back to pass, and Burt, then the Giants nose tackle, came crashing through and leveled Joe with a bone-crushing slam. It wasn't a dirty play, but still the velocity of his hit was questionable. The entire stadium went quiet as Joe's crumpled form lay still on the green carpet.

I remember how he looked so vulnerable and childlike while the doctors were tending him. Finally Joe was removed to the locker room on a stretcher just before the half, and an ambulance was called, and he was rushed to a New York hospital with a severe concussion. It was an eerie second half, as we didn't know what had happened to our quarterback, our team leader. The Giants went on to crush us 49–3, and we went home with our tails between our legs.

That was the first time that I had heard of Jim Burt, but I remembered him well. And now he was on our team, wearing a 49ers uniform. It just seemed so weird, like some surrealistic dream where we signed the Devil up to play for us. Jim Burt, all kind of frumpy and wadded up, his jersey stretched back so it looked like he was wearing two single-digit numbers, in a San Francisco uniform, rooting for the quarterback he had tried to behead. But that's football. Never unpack your bags and never burn any bridges. If you send the cleaning out, make sure to leave a forwarding address.

In a way, it bolstered our spirits. It showed us that our owner would go to any lengths to get somebody who could help us get to the Super Bowl. There was no animosity toward Jim. Actually he was just doing what we all try to do every Sunday, and that's win a football game.

Even Joe didn't harbor any hard feelings. They kind of joked about it, and later Joe poured some water on Jim. Burt told us that he just wanted one more grab at the gold ring. He also was pissed off the way the Giants had convinced him that he was no longer in their plans and that it was in his best interests not to play football again because of his chronic sore back.

George didn't have to tell us in the locker room that night that this was a pretty big game. You could feel it all around the room. Ronnie was his usual sullen self, and there was not much chatter. Everybody was focusing in on this game early. I went around and gave everyone a shot of encouragement. "You can do it, babe. You can do it," I said as I went along the offensive line's lockers. "Everybody is going to see how good we are tonight. We have to be at our best because all of our mamas are watching us tonight."

We charged out of the locker room and onto the field. A huge roar rose from the crowd. Surprisingly, there weren't too many empty seats, even though this was Candlestick's first audience since they'd evacuated the World Series crowd on October 17. It was a charged atmosphere, and you could sense the electricity in the air.

We blew the Saints away, 31–13. It was a total team victory, and it was important in more ways than one. First, the victory gave us a three-game cushion over the Los Angeles Rams in the battle for the NFC West. With seven games remaining, the Rams were running out of time.

Second, it left the Saints reeling with a 4–5 mark, out of the conference race for the second straight year, for all intents and purposes. Third, it brought us one step closer cementing our reputation as the "team of the decade."

But, more important, it gave us a clear run at the playoffs and a chance to repeat as Super Bowl champions. If I had to pick a hero in this one, it would have to be Joe. He showed no signs of his knee injury, nimbly scrambling when he had to and picking up secondary receivers. With the entire nation watching, there was no doubt as to who was the best quarterback in the NFL. Randall Cunningham and John Elway, eat your hearts out.

We got on the board first when Joe hit Jerry on a sideline route and Jerry ran it in for a 22-yard touchdown. But the Saints came back to tie it up, and I thought to myself that I was going to be right about this one going right down to the wire. But I wasn't. Joe came right back and capped an 85-yard drive with another touchdown toss to Jerry, this one for two yards.

Later in the first half, Joe and John Taylor hooked up for a 25-yard touchdown, and we left the field at the half with a 21–10 advantage. At halftime the coaches were still after us to play better, and they kept pointing out our mistakes. It was almost like we were behind. We still held a 24–13 lead going into the final quarter. It was nice that we were in front, but still I didn't feel comfortable. Not against the Saints.

Finally, we got down to the Saints' 3 yard line. It was third and goal, and Joe called a slant to Jerry; if he was covered, Joe was going to hit me circling out of the backfield on a delay. But the corner and safety bracketed Jerry, and linebacker Rickey Jackson dragged me down before I could get into my pattern—so Joe improvised and ran it in for the touchdown. George accused Joe of purposely calling that play so he could run the ball. But I could tell that Coach was kidding, or at least half kidding.

Joe finished the evening with 22 completions out of 31 attempts for 302 yards and three touchdowns. I had another so-so game, struggling for 51 yards on 17 carries for a paltry 3.0 yard average.

But the credit must go to the defense. They kept the pressure on Saints quarterback Bobby Hebert the entire way. At the end of the game you could hear him at field level hollering and swearing at his offensive linemen. That's something that Joe Montana would never do. The big difference might have been that Ronnie Lott was back. Ronnie hadn't played since week three against Philadelphia, but now he was in the starting lineup and you could almost see those receivers looking back over their shoulders as they were venturing across the middle.

I know that Ronnie breaks up passes now and then, but sometimes I wonder how many he breaks up just by his mere presence. If a receiver knows that Ronnie is lying in wait somewhere out there in no-man's land, he probably has second thoughts about catching the ball. He might hear Ronnie's footsteps or even imagine he hears the steps, and he might bring his arms back in before the ball gets to him. Or he just might forget to run his route correctly. Someday I would like to have some statistics person figure out how many balls were dropped or missed because of intimidation. I bet you that in Ronnie's case it would be an NFL record.

You'd think that with an 8–1 record and a three-game lead in the NFC West, the media would have plenty to write about the 49ers. But that wasn't the case. They had been keeping close tabs on my rushing statistics, or in this case, my lack of rushing statistics.

Honestly, it didn't bother me as much as it did other people. Through nine games that season I had run for 573 yards on 158 carries for a

3.6-yard average; at the same point the previous season I'd had 851 yards on 165 carries for a 5.1-yard average. But now we were 8–1, and the year before through nine games we'd been 6–3.

I was doing whatever it took to win, and I didn't care what people were saying or writing about me. I read where writers said that I'd lost a step, but I honestly didn't believe that was true.

What was true was that teams were keying on me after the year I'd had in 1988. They would be foolish not to key on me. If they respected our run, then we must have been doing something right, because even so we had a better record than we'd had the year before. I was more of a decoy now; I'd open up Jerry and Tom and Brent Jones. My job wasn't to catch the star and take curtain calls, it was to play hard every play and to do whatever it took to win. Sometimes I was called to make a play-action fake, and other times I cleared out two or three guys with a bogus pass route so someone else could make the catch.

There were games when the linebackers just keyed on me, like that Sunday against the Saints. Linebacker Vaughan Johnson followed me all over the field. He was my personal valet for that game. Next week it would be Atlanta's Jessie Tuggle. They hit me, tackled me, knocked me down before I could get into my rhythm. But I didn't get frustrated. Naturally, I would like to have made the big runs; that's every running back's goal. But if I could open up Tom for passes, then I was happy. The year before I had a great year individually, very productive—and we were 6–5 and nearly eliminated from the playoffs.

So I answered my critics by telling them that I'll be the one to pass judgment on Roger Craig, not them. I'll know when it's time to give up the game, not them. Believe me, the way I train I know my body.

Sometimes you can do less obvious things that give you just as much personal satisfaction as a long run. For instance, I made a key block on a touchdown pass and I felt very much a part of the score.

We were passing the ball more this year because of the development of Brent and J.T. That just made our offense that much more potent. When teams keyed on me, they were making a big mistake. Besides, the media was making a big deal out of nothing. Our running game was ranked fourth in the NFC, which isn't too shabby.

In 1988 our running game set up our passing game, and this year it was the opposite. Our passing game would eventually set up our running game. Like I said, I wasn't worried.

Some of the reporters asked me if I had complained to George about not carrying the ball more. I told them, "You've got the wrong guy. I never complain." Look at it this way: we were spreading the ball around more, and that was making more people happy.

Actually, George agreed with my assessment of the situation. He told the media at his Monday press conference that week that my production was down from 1988 because "teams are keying on him. Just as we gang up on good runners like Eric Dickerson, teams are ganging up on Roger. He attracts a great deal of attention."

It was nice to have George seeing it my way. He also told the media that the team was trying to break me loose for a big day, so now we'd see how I did in my next game. I was confident, but then I go into every game thinking I'm going to gain 200 yards and score six or seven touchdowns.

We were scheduled to play the Falcons on November 12 at Candlestick. If we won that one, it would make it pretty tough for the Rams to catch us. After that game, we would have only two NFC West games left, and barring a major collapse, we'd have the inside track in the race for the conference title.

George told the team that he was concerned that we would get complacent because we had such a substantial cushion over the Rams. He told us that everything we had accomplished up to that point didn't mean a thing unless we kept on winning.

The Falcons had beaten us at home the year before, 34–17, and that was with Jeff Fuller and Michael Carter, neither of whom would play in this game.

So we were on our toes when we took the field Sunday against the Falcons. George made his appeal to us that we not get complacent, but I was sure that wasn't going to happen. We were all pretty intense in the locker room before the game. During the pregame introductions everyone was charged. When Rathman was introduced, he practically mugged Joe.

This was the Sunday we had been waiting for. This was the Sunday that we put it all together. Offense, defense, and special teams. It was the kind of game that you can look back on with a great deal of personal satisfaction.

I broke out of my slump with my second century game of the season, gaining 109 yards on 17 carries for a 6.4-yard average. Our 234 yards rushing and 515 yards total offense were season highs, as we throttled the Falcons, 45–3.

The only guy who wasn't happy in the locker room was Ronnie. He thought that we'd made too many mistakes to be able to consider it a great effort. But that's Ronnie for you. He's the most critical person I know. He'd make a great movie critic for some newspaper. All I know is that we put 45 points on the board and our defense held Atlanta to a field goal. Linebacker Matt Millen, who had been released by the Raiders because they thought he was washed up, keyed our defense along with Ronnie.

We were now 9–1 and held a solid three-game lead over the Rams in the NFC West with six games to go. We'd showed people that when we put everything together, we could put teams away.

Our next opponent was the Green Bay Packers, who were enjoying a renaissance of sorts. The Packers, after stumbling around in the lower depths of the NFL for so long, were making a mild run at the NFC Central title. They were coming into Candlestick with a 5–5 record and trailed the conference-leading Vikings by only two games. A 5–5 record wouldn't sound like much to 49er fans, but up in Green Bay it was cause for celebration. They were practically mentioning these Packers in the same breath as the fabled teams of Vince Lombardi.

I certainly didn't have much time to rest on my laurels. Terrence Flagler, my backup, and Keith Henderson, Tom's backup, had both been injured against the Falcons, and it didn't appear as if either would play. To compound matters, Rathman had a bruised shoulder. So when we resumed practice Wednesday, Spencer Tillman and myself were the only healthy running backs. I ran a couple of plays at fullback, but I was hoping that Tom's shoulder would come around by game time.

Football is a strange game. Here we were coming off a game where all facets of our team had finally jelled, and there almost seemed to be a letdown during the week. I can't put my finger on any particular reason, but this game worried me more than any of the others had that season. Certainly, the Packers had beaten some good teams, including the Rams in Anaheim, but they had lost to some bad teams, too.

They were an inconsistent team, and I think those are the most dangerous. Everybody was predicting that we had finally found our stride, and that the rest of the season would be a cakewalk for us, but the 49ers knew the truth: there is no such thing as a cakewalk in the National Football League.

My premonition proved right as the Packers came into Candlestick and beat us, 21–17. Or rather, we beat ourselves. We out–first-downed them 30–11, we outpassed them 289–139, and our 360 yards total offense was 112 yards more than the Packers got. But the scoreboard doesn't lie, and it showed that we'd been beaten. The loss not only snapped our six-game winning streak, it also shortened the distance between ourselves and the Los Angeles Rams in the race for the NFC West title.

Eventually the 49ers would get to the Super Bowl and play the Denver Broncos. I believe the final five regular-season games left in 1989 helped us hone our skills for the playoffs. Three of the opponents were playoff teams and I credit them with getting us prepared. The hard part was getting there. Beating Denver was the easy part.

◆
9. Bring on the Gumbo

Every time I think of the Denver Broncos in Super Bowl XXIV, I get pissed off. We were expecting a dogfight in the pits; instead we had a stroll through Golden Gate Park on a mild Sunday afternoon.

For that, I'll never forgive the Broncos. I don't think any of the 1989 San Francisco 49ers will. It kind of pissed all of us off, because it was so easy.

Maybe it was exciting to the 49er fans, but for the rest of the country it stunk. The Super Bowl is supposed to be the ultimate game; it's where you throw all caution to the wind because there's no tomorrow. The season is over. It's not a time to play conservatively or wait for the other team to make mistakes. None of that Chris Evert baseline football. You just go to the net and attack your opponent's weaknesses. You take it to the guy across from you right from the git-go.

We were looking forward to a real challenge, like Cincinnati had given us the year before when we had to fight from behind to win it. That's the kind of Super Bowl that keeps everybody happy: the players, coaches, fans, viewers, and those TV sponsors who pay the megabucks. It would have been terrific if there'd been two great teams battling it out down to the final minutes—with San Francisco winning, of course.

But it didn't quite work out that way. Because of all the hype surrounding the game, the public expects a lot more, and I don't blame them. So do I. It's a championship game, and it shouldn't be lopsided. After all, theoretically, it features the two best football teams in the world. It's supposed to be like a great boxing match: Muhammad Ali versus Joe Frazier; Rocky Marciano against Joe Louis. You know, two combatants slugging it out round after round in the middle of the ring, first one landing a punch and the other, both bloodied but proud, and in the end only one team is left standing, barely. Something of that magnitude.

Instead Denver let us down. They let everybody down. This was like a one-round kayo. We held up our end of the bargain, but unfortunately, because we won so easily, people look on us as having spoiled everything. Don't get me wrong, winning 55–10 is a lot of fun—certainly a lot more than losing 55–10. But after that game I had a sour taste in my mouth. It wasn't like Super Bowl XXIII, where I dragged my weary body into the shower and played that final, winning drive over and over and over in my mind, savoring every second of it. I felt so fulfilled after that game, like I had really earned something special.

But after this game I couldn't dredge up any memories to savor. It just didn't seem like there were any high points or satisfying feelings of accomplishment. Denver had beaten us four straight times in the eighties, and I figured that would be a real confidence booster for them. I really expected a knock-down, drag-out contest.

I thought that the fact that they were 12-point underdogs would motivate the Broncos more, that the lopsided point spread would provoke their sense of pride. Usually you don't pay any attention to point spreads, because on any given day in the NFL any team can knock you off. And in a game of major importance, everyone seems to play over their heads.

But they didn't suck it up or come back regrouped after the half. They were probably the biggest disappointment in Super Bowl history. They have some real good fans up there in Denver, and I can just imagine how miserable they felt after their heroes lost the Super Bowl by 45 points.

Maybe I'm being too harsh on the Broncos. It probably was their game plan more than their personnel, anyway. I know they can be a determined team; I remember how they came back to beat us in overtime in a swirling wind during a regular-season game at Candlestick in 1988.

But I'm getting ahead of myself. After losing to the Packers, we got ready to host the Giants in a Monday night game at Candlestick Park. Let me tell you right now, we don't need any extra motivation for the New York Giants. Just mention their name and guys line up at the locker room door ready to dash on the field to do battle. I think it stems from the way they ruined our repeat mission during the 1985 season.

We had come into that season as the defending Super Bowl champions, and I think we figured we'd march right back to the conference title and then roll right over our AFC opponent. But our arrogance and the Giants got the best of us and sent us home for the remainder of the postseason. Then the following year they did the same thing, humiliating us 49–3.

So there was a special aura of excitement in the chilly Candlestick Park air on the night of November 27, 1989. Both teams came into the game 9–2 and leading their respective NFC divisions. The winner was expected to emerge as the favorite to be the NFC representative in the Super Bowl.

The Giants entered the game with a reputation as a running team, while we were known more for our passing prowess. Personally, I had been struggling, and I was hoping for a big game. Some of those stories about me losing a step had been dusted off and were making the media rounds. I wanted to show everyone that I was still the same old Roger.

Unfortunately, I had another subpar outing, gaining only 49 yards on 20 carries. But we won, 34–24, and now had a 10–2 record with four games left. Afterward I didn't feel so bad when I saw that the entire Giants team had rushed for only 52 yards, three more than I had. I can't say enough about our defense in that game; to hold the Giants to 52 yards was incredible.

Week thirteen we beat the Falcons in Atlanta, 23–10, and I had 97 yards rushing in 17 carries. The following week we could cinch the NFC West title and the home field advantage for the duration of the playoffs if we could beat the Rams in Anaheim.

I understand that every Tuesday, former Rams coach John Robinson used to go to lunch with owner Georgia Frontiere at the Beverly Hills Hotel. John just sat there, kind of embarrassed, while she waved to her friends and made certain that everyone saw her with her head coach.

Personally, I like John. After I ran for 190 yards against Los Angeles in a 1988 game, he called me the greatest running back in the National Football League. That was quite a compliment coming from a man who used to coach Marcus Allen at USC and who had Eric Dickerson with the Rams. He seems like an excellent coach, and I know that players who play for him tell me that he's a players' coach who will back his players with the media and management. I like that trait in a coach.

Just as when we played the Giants, we never needed any motivational speeches to get primed for the Rams. Both ends of the state always seem to be bickering over water rights or fog versus smog or politics, and the two football teams have a similar rivalry.

It was a Monday night game, and the Southern California fans were really vocal on a perfect evening. Rams placekicker Mike Lansford kicked a 22–yard field goal to start the fourth quarter, and we were down 27–10 with 13:34 to go. The fans were delirious with happiness. They were chanting "Super Bowl Pretenders" and "Super Bowl Chumps" at us. Georgia was inciting them even more by blowing kisses to the crowd and hugging and kissing her players on the sidelines.

I turned to one of our linemen and commented matter-of-factly, "They might be celebrating a little prematurely." We all knew that our team performed at its best when our backs were to the wall. When you have the greatest quarterback the game has ever seen, no lead is insurmountable.

Sure enough, we scored 20 points in the next ten minutes and fifteen seconds. I got the go-ahead points with a one-yard run with 3:42 left and we went onto win 30–27. After I scored I went to the sidelines and looked across the field to find Georgia. I wanted to wave to her and blow her a kiss, but she was nowhere to be found.

The following week we played the Buffalo Bills, who needed to win to stay in the playoffs. George rested some of the veterans, including Joe Montana and Ronnie Lott. But I convinced him that I didn't need any rest, and he let me play. I gained 105 yards and we won the game, 21–10. That gave me a total of 1,023 yards for the season, and I became the first 49er running back to rush for more than 1,000 yards in each of three straight seasons.

We now had a 13–2 record, matching our 1987 mark. The final regular-season game, on Christmas Eve, was against the Chicago Bears. Personally, I'd rather have been home with my family. We'd all rather have been home with our families. But you just don't call in sick in the NFL. So we all showed up, and we won 26–0, as our defense again rose to the occasion. I only carried the ball ten times for 31 yards, but I finished the regular season with 1,054 yards.

Our locker room was like Death Valley about a half hour after the game, as all of us dashed out to race home and be with our families. I was one of the first out the door, and some of the reporters were upset because I didn't stay around to chat, but most of them understood. Hell, they had families, too, and they wanted to finish their work and get out of there as much as we did.

The division winners are given an extra week off while the two divisional wild-card teams meet to decide which one will move on. George, our compassionate coach, gave us three straight days off. It almost seemed like a two-week vacation.

If the Rams upset the Eagles in the wild-card game, then we would play the Vikings, the winners of the NFC Central, because two teams from the same division can't meet in the first playoff game. That rule came out of either the Vatican or the NFL honchos on Park Avenue in New York, I can't recall which.

The Rams did beat the Eagles 19–13 in overtime to advance to the

NFC Championship Game, so we got the Vikings in the opening playoff game for the third straight year. Inwardly I'd been hoping that we'd play Minnesota again; it had been two years, but I still couldn't rid myself of that bitter taste they left us with. There were others on the team, like Jerry Rice, who felt the same way I did. Which was good, because we needed all of the motivation we could muster.

I watched game films of the Vikings defense all week long. Every free moment I got, I studied the way their defensive ends charged off the ball and made a beeline for the quarterback. I noticed that if you stepped inside them, you could pick up some pretty good chunks of ground. I also noticed that if you ran right at them, you could drive them back before they had chance to get set for the tackle. I honestly couldn't wait to get my hands on the ball.

We played on Saturday, and a record Candlestick Park crowd of 64,585 roared its approval during the introductions. The energy in the stadium was so intense that I couldn't stand still. I just bounced around until the opening kickoff. Minnesota took a 3–0 lead, but we came roaring back to secure a 20–3 lead at the half. I made a four-yard touchdown run in the final quarter and finished with 125 yards in 18 carries as we won going away, 41–13.

Guess who was coming to town next? If familiarity breeds contempt, and it does in this situation, we were in for a contempt-filled Sunday in the NFC Championship Game. Arch–division rival Los Angeles upset the New York Giants 19–13 in overtime for their second straight playoff victory and drew the honor of playing us for the NFC title, with the winner going to the Super Bowl.

Besides playing the Rams twice a year in the NFC West, we'd also played them in the American Bowl in Tokyo way back when the exhibition season began in August. They knew exactly what we were going to do and vice versa. When you've played each other as many times as the Rams and 49ers had, there aren't any secrets. The outcome would come down to which team executed the best and which one committed the fewest turnovers.

While I certainly respect John Robinson, I didn't mind beating his team at all.

It had rained on and off most of the night before, but the turf had been covered with a tarp, and the field was in surprisingly good shape. We had our second record crowd in a row, officially tabulated at 64,769, and they were even more vocal than the one the week before.

Los Angeles had scored first on a 23-yard Mike Lansford field goal, but then their offense suddenly went silent. Our defense dug in. Chet Brooks, our safety, pinned Jeff Fuller's jersey number 49 to the shoulder of his jersey. Chet said that way Fuller would be in on every tackle that

Brooks made. Jeff was undergoing therapy, but the prognosis was not good. He still didn't have use of his right arm and it appeared the nerve damage might be permanent.

Meanwhile, our offense came alive and we kept building on our lead, which reached 30–3 by the fourth quarter.

I was on the sidelines midway through the final quarter and I started chanting, "Bring on the gumbo, bring on the gumbo." We were going to New Orleans. We were going to our second straight Super Bowl.

♦

10. Way Down Yonder . . .

What I can't figure out is how come those oddsmakers in Las Vegas are so smart. I heard that they had made the 49ers 11½-point favorites to beat the Broncos even before the final gun of our NFC title game with the Rams.

The week in New Orleans begun routinely enough, but before it was over we had to chastise four young players for yielding to the lures of Bourbon Street and survive a national drug rumor that threatened to bring down our star player.

It had been business as usual as we left the San Jose Airport on Sunday morning, January 21, at around 11 A.M. There were about three hundred people on hand to see us off. I was glad we were leaving town. Although I knew I would miss my family immensely, I was sick and tired of playing ticket broker. It seemed like everyone I'd ever known was going to be in New Orleans for the Super Bowl, and they just happened to need tickets.

We were only allowed to purchase fifteen tickets each, and most of mine were going to my immediate family and my chiropractor, Nick Athens, and my masseur, Dr. Don Sanchez. The last two people are part of the team that keeps my body in alignment and running at an optimum level.

We were expecting warm weather, but when we arrived in New Orleans it was cool and there was a brisk breeze blowing off the Mississippi River, which was right next to our hotel, the Hilton Riverfront Towers.

Jerry Rice and I went to dinner that night at the New Orleans Hard Rock Cafe. We figured it would be a good night because most of the fans hadn't hit town yet, and we could dine in relative anonymity. We were all looking forward to Thursday, when our wives, children, and girlfriends would be arriving. Jerry and I returned to the hotel early to get a good night's sleep. We knew we needed our endurance for the next day, when we'd be descended upon by the national media for the first time. Our patience would be tested during a week in which our lives would be gone over with a fine-tooth comb.

But four of our young eligible bachelors got caught up in the Mardi Gras revelry, which hangs out on every street corner in New Orleans. I guess they met a few ladies and completely lost track of time. Our curfew for the first night was originally set for one A.M., but coach Seifert extended it to two right after we arrived. However, that still wasn't enough time for safeties Chet Brooks and Johnnie Jackson and wide receivers Terry Greer and John Taylor. They didn't roll in until the wee hours. They soon found out just how expensive succumbing to the temptations of the Crescent City can be. They were each fined $1,000. In addition, they were redressed at a team meeting the next day.

First coach Seifert spoke to the team, reminding us that this was a business trip. He said that he hoped there would be no more incidents like that. Then Joe Montana and Ronnie Lott got up and addressed us. They put on their most serious faces and reminded everyone that our mission was not to party but to beat the Broncos. They pointed out that the curfews were there for a very important reason, and that this would be the last time that any violators would be let off quite so easy.

In a way, I think it was good that it happened when it did. It was early in the week, and I think that it served as a good lesson, not only for the culprits but also for any other young player who might have been similarly tempted.

Tuesday night Jerry and I again went to dinner, to a hole-in-the-wall joint for some soul food. We chowed down on seafood gumbo, fried chicken, collard greens, and corn bread. Man, it was scrumptious. That's the great thing about New Orleans. You can walk into almost any dive and get great food, especially spicy Cajun food. This was going to be my last night away from the hotel for dinner, because the streets were starting to fill with the crazy fans, and soon it would be impossible to get more than a few minutes' privacy.

Following Tuesday's practice, we all gathered around Coach Seifert and sang "Happy Birthday" to him. He walked away mumbling something about how he didn't even want to talk about being, as he put it, "a half century old." I could tell that he felt embarrassed.

The next morning at George's press conference, in front of the national media, Ronnie Lott, Joe, and myself got this huge birthday cake and walked up to the podium with it just as George was making his closing remarks. He had this big grin on his face, but I could tell that he would have been a lot happier if we had saved this birthday presentation until the team dinner that night. The photographers were having a field day with it.

There had been a bug circulating among our team, and that night I started feeling a little woozy and my stomach began doing the funky chicken. At first I tried to attribute it to nerves, but I knew I was coming down with the stomach flu.

I went to practice Wednesday, but by now I was really feeling bad. I couldn't keep anything down, and I was as weak as a newborn kitten. Every movement I made was a struggle. George noticed that I wasn't myself, that I appeared tired and pale. So he sent me back to the hotel, where I stocked my room with PowerBurst and some bottled water. While I enjoyed the New Orleans food, I really didn't trust the water.

But as poor as I felt, I wasn't feeling half as bad as Joe was. Some Washington, D.C., TV reporter from a small cable station had gone on the air late Wednesday night with a story linking four starting quarterbacks to cocaine use. Naturally, because the story broke during Super Bowl week and because Joe had had to call a press conference once before during his career to refute drug rumors, the media started assuming he was one of the four.

Although I still wasn't feeling that chipper, I did attend the mandatory Thursday morning press conference, which was the final one the players had to participate in before the game. We were led through the kitchen and along the back corridors of the hotel to a huge ballroom. From behind the doors we could peak out and see the huge assemblage surrounding the podium where Joe was supposed to speak. He didn't hear about the drug rumors until just before we were supposed to enter the main room to meet with the media.

I have to give Joe credit, though. He could have insisted that what had happened wasn't fair and asked to be excused from the press conference. But that's not Joe. He likes to meet everything head-on, whether it be a 280-pound defensive end or slanderous innuendo. He walked out and faced his inquisitors, who by now were twenty deep.

I believe that there was a conspiracy to bring down our team. Someone who for whatever reasons wanted us to lose, or who would benefit from us losing purposely planted that story, hoping it would have an adverse effect on our play, that it would throw our concentration off. But you know what? It had the exact opposite effect on our team.

That 49er team was like a family, and adversity just drew us that much closer. Our hearts beat as one, and an attack based on innuendo and rumor against any of us was an attack on all of us. Honestly, our team was real loving and cared about one another, which probably separated us from other teams across the league. We worked hard together and just tried to be the best that we possibly could. There was no way that we would let one another down.

After the media session was over, Joe got up and spoke to the team about the rumor, saying it was completely false. He was followed by Ronnie. We all started throwing things and hollering that we weren't going to let this bother us.

What the rumor did was make Joe hungrier. It pissed him off and made his concentration for the game that much more focused. Now he had something to prove. If some outsider insinuated something negative about us, we were going to retaliate on the football field. We'd turn that negative into a positive. That's why we were a team of destiny.

Later that week, nothing came of the report. CBS picked up on it and speculated, without any evidence whatsoever, that Montana was going to be one of the four quarterbacks named the next day. But it all sort of died down just as quickly as it appeared. The Washington TV station said it was going to release the names Friday, but it never did. All of a sudden, it was like it never happened.

It bothered me that there were no retractions or public apologies to Joe. It doesn't seem fair that someone can make a totally false accusation like that and not suffer consequences. I just hope that the irresponsible person who started that unsubstantiated rumor took the points and bet a lot of money on Denver. That would be justice.

Anyway, because of the virus, I missed Eddie D.'s gala party for the team and guests Thursday night at the indoor shopping mall that he owns next to the Superdome. I remained weak all the way up to game time Sunday. I couldn't keep anything in my stomach, and I really felt dehydrated. Between Wednesday and Sunday's late afternoon kickoff, I lost nine pounds. I was down to 203 pounds when I took the field for the pregame warm-ups.

I know some readers won't believe me, but I knew the day before our game with Denver that we were going to win Super Bowl XXIV. I'm not talking about listening to oddsmakers or being overcome with confidence. I mean plain, cold, outright knowledge based on a sixth sense, the kind you have when you're a child and you know that you're going to get a surprise or that someone close to you is going to become very ill. It's a sense that you possess, and it's irrefutable.

We were going through our final drills in the Superdome on Saturday, sort of a dress rehearsal. Usually there are a few rough spots, as players' minds wander ahead to the game and they make those small mental errors that drive coaches out of their minds.

But that day there was none of that. We had a picture-perfect practice. We didn't make any mistakes, not even in the warm-ups. It was like the quiet before the storm. Everyone was really focused, more so than I had ever seen before in practice.

When the practice was over, I had to stop and think about what had just transpired. I said, "Wow, I can't believe that we didn't make a mistake. That's never happened before." I knew in my heart right then and there that the 49ers were going to win the Super Bowl. It was that simple.

Of course, I didn't know it was going to be as easy as it was. The way the game turned out it was sort of anticlimactic. We could tell by the intensity we were playing with in the first quarter that it was going to be a much easier game than we figured, and the Broncos weren't bringing the heat that we expected. We thought they would map an all-out assault on Joe Montana, but they were more interested in trying to bump us out of our pass routes than they were in blitzing the quarterback. We had all of these elaborate blocking schemes involving the backs and the tight ends in our game plan, but we never needed them.

When we looked across the line of scrimmage, we could see that defeated look in the Broncos' eyes; they had that dull look your eyes get when you're dancing with someone you don't like and you can't wait for the song to be over. After the first few series I think they realized that this wasn't going to be their day. It was almost like they were waiting for the inevitable. If the officials had told us that we could go pick up our Super Bowl checks then if we didn't feel like playing anymore, the Broncos would have been the first in line.

On our first series I got the ball three or four times, and I thought I was going to die. I took a handoff on the second play of our offensive series and skirted around left end before being driven out of bounds by Denver cornerback Wymon Henderson, but not before I gained 18 yards.

Man, I could really feel it. On the third play Joe again called my number, this time on a short swing pass. But I was so winded that I couldn't quite get to the ball. On the fourth play, I again got the handoff and gained a yard. It was extremely hot inside the dome, and I felt woozy and weak. To add to my woes, I'd sprained my ankle slightly and it was throbbing.

So I had all of these negative elements working around me, but I never considered taking myself out of the game. I had worked too hard to get where I was to call it quits. I just had to suck it up and turn it up a notch. That wasn't so hard to accomplish, because I'd been doing it since I first touched a football.

I remember when I was at Nebraska, my running backs coach Mike Corrigan impressed upon me that one of the first things you learn about football is how to play with pain. He told me that if I couldn't play with pain, I couldn't play for him. I wanted to play football, so it was an easy decision.

I think most football players learn to play with pain or play hurt. It's an acquired art, just like catching passes. One of the reasons I never missed a game until the 1990 season is that I've learned how to play with pain and I've learned how to take care of my body. People criticize me for going to a chiropractor, saying chiropractors are quacks. But I believe in them. I know that I'm going to get banged up, and that's why I have my people waiting for me after games. If my hip joint gets knocked out of alignment, I have somebody who can put it back in place.

My grandmother is eighty-two years old, and she's been seeing a chiropractor for more than twenty years. And you wouldn't believe how healthy she is. I believe that the reason players get arthritic is that they don't take care of their bodies after their playing days are over. They figure, "I'm done with everything, so I don't have to run anymore, I'm never going to work out again."

So I stayed in the game because I knew that my chiropractor and my masseur were both there to minister to my body when it was over. By halftime I felt a lot better, and I was breathing normally.

The fact that we took a 27–3 lead off the field at the half probably had more to do with my recovery than any other factor. Our last touchdown drive had only taken five plays, and Tom Rathman picked up the slack for me. Joe found Jerry behind the Bronco defense and applied the coup de grace with a perfect 38-yard scoring spiral, so that series gave me the opportunity to catch my wind and have my ankle retaped.

There wasn't much to say in the locker room at halftime, except to tell one another not to let up and keep playing 49er football. Even the coaches seemed a little relaxed. Usually they are more uptight than the players. They reminded us to take it one play at a time and to hold on to the ball. They said not to worry about the big play but to keep the chains moving.

I don't know what the Broncos coaches were telling their players, but I don't think it would have mattered if Knute Rockne had risen from the grave and given them their halftime talk. We knew they were beat, they knew they were beat—heck, the whole world knew they were beat. There was nothing they could have done to come from that far back. Not against that 49er team. Not on that Sunday, anyway.

What was nice for our team about this Super Bowl was that everyone got to contribute. We spread the wealth around. Joe, Ronnie, and myself were the cocaptains for the game. As for the scoring, Jerry Rice led the way with three touchdown catches from Joe, while my old Nebraska buddy Tom Rathman ran for a pair of scores and John Taylor caught two touchdown passes. I finally got my opportunity with 13:47 left in the game when I scored our final touchdown on a one-yard run.

I also took a record away from one of those fabled Pittsburgh Steeler greats. The six-yard pass I caught from Joe with 3:11 left in the third period was my seventeenth catch in a Super Bowl game, breaking Pittsburgh wide receiver Lynn Swann's previous record of sixteen catches.

Jerry's first touchdown was a thing of beauty, like it was scripted for a Hollywood movie. Joe spotted Jerry breaking clear across the middle at just about the same moment that Denver free safety Steve Atwater figured out what was happening. Atwater came up and really blasted Jerry as he made the catch, but Jerry just spun off the hit and streaked into the end zone to complete a 20-yard scoring play. I don't think the Denver defense ever recovered.

I believed the key to our victory was our relentless defense. The defensive players never gave Bronco quarterback John Elway the opportunity to figure out what they were doing. If he read we were in man-to-man coverage, we were in a zone, and vice versa. For those schooled in the fine points of football, our defense played mainly a three-deep zone with the free safety rotating toward the weak side.

I actually felt sorry for Elway because he was really confused out there, not to mention harassed by our pass rush. He ended up completing only ten of 26 passes for 108 yards, and it was only because of his pure athletic ability that he was able to complete that many. Linebacker Michael Walter and our young strong safety Chet Brooks each had interceptions. And Brooks, along with defensive end Danny Stubbs, recovered Bronco fumbles.

At least Elway acknowledged that the 49ers were the best team. Afterward, he commented that the Broncos "had lost to a better football team." He added that he just didn't understand the why of it.

That's probably because he never got the opportunity to stop for a second and clear his brain. Our defense kept him on the run and limited the Denver ground game to just 64 yards. Bobby Humphrey, their hot-shot rookie, had 61 of those yards.

I was thrilled for two throwbacks to the old school of football, nose tackle Jim Burt and inside linebacker Matt Millen. Burt, who had been a member of the 1986 Giants team that won Super Bowl XXI, also against the bridesmaid Broncos, was like a little child after the game. Millen, an ex-Raider, was winning his third Super Bowl ring, having been a member of the winning Raider teams in Super Bowl XIV and XVIII. They were wandering around the locker room talking to anyone who would listen to their mumbling monologues. I also was very happy for nose tackle Pete Kugler, who had announced earlier in the week that this would be his last game. He was retiring to the corporate world in, of all places, Denver. Or so we thought.

I had a pretty fair day myself, outrushing the entire Bronco offense with 69 yards on 20 carries. Tom added another 38 yards rushing. Joe, as usual, was super, bowling through the Bronco defensive tenpins like Earl Anthony. He completed 22 of 29 attempts for 297 yards and five touchdowns. For his efforts, he was accorded the Super Bowl MVP award. I figured they just ought to award it to him permanently, because it was his third one. He's the only player in NFL history to win it three times.

Bronco Hinek, our equipment manager, should be credited with an assist on Joe's award. Before Joe arrived at the Stadium, Bronco had thrown a couple of towels, along with some football pants, in the cubicle next to Joe's. He then hung a jersey with the very familiar number 87 on it in the locker. That number used to belong to Joe's best buddy and former favorite target, Dwight Clark, who had retired the year before.

Bronco also hung a photograph of Joe's wife Jennifer with his daughters Alexandra and Elizabeth, each wearing one of Joe's Super Bowl rings, and his new son Nathaniel, wearing a towel with number 16 on it and Joe's third Super Bowl ring pinned to it. Under the picture was engraved, DADDY, THE NEXT RING IS YOURS.

Joe is a very loving and caring father. Though I'm quite jealous of him because of his influence on my little son, Rodgrick. A couple of nights before I left home for New Orleans I asked Rodgrick what number he was going to wear on his jersey when he grows up and becomes a football player. He answered, without any hesitation, "Number sixteen." It broke my heart. My son is a bigger fan of Joe Montana than he is of his own daddy.

Midway through the third quarter, right after John Taylor caught a 35-yard touchdown pass from Joe to put us up 41–3, making it obvious that the game was out of hand, I put my arms around Jeff Fuller and gave him a big hug. "We did this for you, baby," I told him. "We won Super Bowl XXIV Jeff Fuller."

Jeff forced a smile and congratulated me. I saw a tear roll down his cheek, but I didn't say anything. I continued to embrace him, all the while aware of his lifeless right arm. It didn't matter that he would never play football again. Jeff, whose arm was paralyzed making that tackle in the game against the Patriots back on October 22, was as much a part of our Super Bowl victory as any active squad member.

Still, I knew it must have been hard for him to stand on the sidelines, in the role of spectator, witnessing his teammates taking the Denver Broncos apart. It must have been extremely difficult on him emotionally knowing that he would never play football again, never be a part of the special camaraderie.

And it is something exceptional; don't let anyone try to tell you it's not. It's difficult to put into words, but there is this warm tingling feeling that starts down in your toes and moves up through your body. You look around and you see all of your teammates and you know that together you've accomplished something special, something that other people only dream about doing.

During that moment, while that warm sensation is enveloping your body, you want to reach out and touch every one of your teammates and thank them individually. From that magical moment on, their faces are indelibly etched in your memory. No matter how old you get or what course your life takes, whenever you call up that memory you will see their smiling faces again and again and again.

I had made a solemn promise to Jeff that Monday night we had come back to beat the Rams in Anaheim back on December 11 that we were going to bring the ring home for him. I kept my word.

I'm sincere when I say that Jeff's contribution had as much to do with us winning as anyone's. His sense of humor and dedication through what proved to be a career-ending injury served as an inspiration for all of us. He easily could have slipped into a shell and become bitter and turned his back on his teammates. But he didn't. He stuck with us through all of his painful adversity. I have no way of knowing what kind of emotional trauma Jeff has endured since he was injured, but I know he must be strong to keep it from getting him down, from just throwing in the towel and saying to hell with life.

Maybe it's our love of the game that allows us to take these serious risks. Jeff knew when he became a football player that the possibility of injury, even of career-ending injury, would be constant reality. Of course, when you're young you always believe "It won't happen to me." You read those stories about Patriots wide receiver Darryl Stingley, and you tell yourself, "Hey, that was the other guy."

But the truth is that football, especially pro football, is a violent business. We're modern-day gladiators, knights who fight to the death. In Mexico and Spain they have bullfights, and people point to their cultures and accuse them of being uncivilized. Yet playing pro football isn't much different than that.

When you stop and think about it, every hit you take can be the last. When he ran that crossing pattern, Darryl Stingley never figured that the hit Jack Tatum put on him would be the last one he ever took. Neither did Jeff Fuller think his head-on tackle of John Stephens would be his last.

But you really can't let those thoughts enter your mind when you're out on the playing field. Because once you do, you start playing tentatively, and you might as well turn in your uniform.

When we watch the game films, on Monday afternoons during team meetings, I sometimes wince when I see some of the hits I take. I'm actually surprised that I get up after some of them. When I do get up, there are times I can't remember where I am, or even who I am. You can laugh about it later, but at the time it's pretty frightening.

I remember an incident two weeks prior in the NFC Championship Game against the Rams at Candlestick Park. The whistle had blown, and I was waiting for the tackler to get off so I could get up and get back to the huddle. I relaxed for a moment, and all of a sudden this guy spears me and nearly breaks my neck. I staggered off the field, with no idea where I was. It was really scary. I was so disoriented that I even forgot who it was who speared me after the whistle. I had to watch the game films Monday to see it was safety Michael Stewart.

I recall during the 1986 season, when I dislocated my hip and kept playing, that I came up with what I thought was the stomach flu. I had this constant burning sensation in my stomach, and I was always feeling terrible.

At first I thought I could tough it out, but between my stomach and my hip I was forever in painful misery. I went to the doctor, and he ran some tests and discovered that I had an ulcer. He attributed it to prednisone, the powerful anti-inflammatory drug I was taking to diminish the swelling around my hip joint. I switched medications and my stomach calmed down.

But those are the kinds of things you can't think about when you step out on the field. You can't think about something like Jeff's injury or the spears or the cheap shots on any of the other grim consequences. When you do start thinking about them, it's time to find another occupation.

After the Super Bowl was over, we were standing on the sidelines mugging it up for the television cameras when some of the guys started chanting "Three in a row, three in a row. Back to back." I was trying to think of something clever, and all of a sudden I started hollering "Three-peat, three-peat." Soon my teammates took up the cry, and we were all chanting it. It would have made a nice title for this book, but later someone told me that Pat Riley had coined it after he coached the Los Angeles Lakers to two straight NBA titles, and that he owned the rights to it and that it couldn't be used commercially. Oh well, I made my point.

Anticipating another championship turned out to be definitely better than beating Denver. Right after a game of that magnitude there always seems to be a letdown. You work so hard for what seems like a lifetime and you get so pumped up, then all of a sudden it's over. The final gun goes off and suddenly there's nothing left to work for, to focus on. You grab on to the bar tightly and prepare for that emotional roller coaster ride to the cellar. I've been through it before, but I knew that some of the rookies and younger players were going to have a rough time dealing with it.

As pissed off as I am at Denver, I have to give them some credit for their comments after the game. This was the third time they had been to the dance and sent the Lombardi Trophy home in somebody else's car. It must have really bothered them. In addition to making $18,000 less per man than we did, they had to put up with the questions and criticism through the entire off-season.

When you lose a game like the Super Bowl, it's almost like losing your manhood. At least that's the way some people—mostly fans and the media—perceive it. They forget that you worked just as hard as the other guy to get there, and that twenty-six other teams didn't make it that far.

Bronco wide receiver Mike Young, who was shut down without a catch, said that we were "the greatest team to ever have played the game" and that "Joe Montana is the greatest quarterback to ever have played the game." I figured I could learn to like this guy, though I didn't know how he was going to explain the latter comment to his quarterback, John Elway, when the next season rolled around.

Our locker room was a madhouse after the game. They took us out to an interview area, but after we had talked for a half hour we were escorted back to the locker room and it was opened to the media. I think everyone except Walter Cronkite was there, and the atmosphere was oppressive.

I weary of answering the same questions over and over and over again. Every once in a while some reporter will come up with an original query, but for the most part it's repetition. "Hey Roger, tell us about your hill running again." "Hey Roger, how many more years do you want to play?" "Hey Roger, how do you feel?" The truth is, I feel sticky, hot, tired, grumpy, and I would like to take a shower, guys.

But cooperating with the media is all part of the job, and most of the time I enjoy it. It's just that it had been a long week, I hadn't felt well, the game had been too one-sided, and my family was all at Eddie D.'s party waiting for me to arrive.

I wanted to savor the third Super Bowl victory as much as I could because we had an early flight the next morning, and soon it would be nothing but a memory.

At the party I joined my family and the rest of my teammates and drank a toast and made a speech to some 49er fans, pledging them we would be back the next year. I told them to book their hotels and make reservations for the trip to Tampa right then.

Our motivation now was that we wanted to make football history. We wanted to become the only team ever to win three straight Super Bowls. The San Francisco 49ers wanted to be the charter member of a very exclusive club.

I was exhausted when I finally hit the sack. The enormity of the whole week had finally caught up with me. Sleep came fast; I was in the middle of thinking what an interesting year 1990 would be when it overtook me.

◆

11. Practice
Makes Perfect

After the Pro Bowl in February, I got started on my other professions. The life of a football player, when measured against other careers, is extremely short. Most of the time it ends before you've had a chance to plan for the future, like Jeff Fuller's did. So I've made some contingency plans and set some real goals.

I didn't wait for people to come knocking at my door. I went out and hired New York publicist Milt Kahn, and another agent, Charles Stearns, in addition to my regular agent, Jim Steiner. Together they formed Team Roger. I wanted to project my wholesome image to the media and to my fans.

First there were my endorsements for 1990. I had a modeling contract with Macy's, a contract with PowerBurst, and a contract with Mizuno. I also had product endorsement contracts with Pro Heat, Pro Line (NFL Products), Wilson Sporting Goods, and Calvin Klein. I've made a fitness video, *Turn It Up A Notch,* and signed a contract to host a weekly sports show on Pacific Sports Network. I've also cohosted KPIX's "Evening Magazine Show" and performed in a movie called *Dark Obsession.*

And just to show that I'm a multidimensional individual, I joined teammates Joe Montana, Ronnie Lott, Keena Turner, Tom Rathman, Michael Walter, and former player Dwight Clark to sing background harmony on a song entitled "A Couple of Days Off" on Huey Lewis and The News' album *Hard at Play.*

I guess the two most exciting things that have happened to me outside of football, though, were the movie and the Calvin Klein underwater ad I did for Macy's.

In 1989 at a party I met actor Danny Glover, who makes his home

116

in San Francisco. After I was introduced to him, we naturally struck up a conversation. He's a sports fan, and we got along very well. Danny is a guy I really look up to in the acting world because he worked hard and opened his own doors and became a smashing success. I confided in him my desire to someday have a movie career. He encouraged me to try it. When I asked him what I should do, what were the proper steps to take, he referred me to Jean Shelton, the woman with whom he first studied acting. During the off-season, I would drive up to San Francisco once a week for acting lessons with Ms. Shelton. When football season started, I didn't get up there quite as often, but I still studied and practiced my diction. Sometimes I read scripts aloud while riding an exercise bike in our training room down at Santa Clara. Some of the newer players looked at me like I was some sort of kook. I guess they'd led sheltered lives and had never seen a budding thespian in the locker room before.

One day, Milt Kahn, my publicist, introduced me to director Roger Corman, who later cast me in *Dark Obsession,* a movie. Corman makes about a movie a month, and the opportunity to work with him during the early stages of my acting career was very important to me.

I considered myself fortunate to be under his guidance because he provided Jack Nicholson, Robert De Niro, and Sylvester Stallone their first movie roles. *Dark Obsession* is one of those high-action films with a lot of killing. To prepare for my role, I watched a lot of crime movies like *Lethal Weapon* and *48 Hours.*

I was playing a rather surly man with a gruff demeanor, which is out of character for me. Every time I would find myself slipping into my regular nice-guy personality, I would think about those linebackers trying to poke my eyes out, and then I would turn mean again.

In the movie, which came out in fall of 1990, I'm an undercover cop named Ludlow and I actually get blown up when a bomb goes off in my car. Even though I didn't have too many lines, it was an arduous task. I took my role very seriously and tried to memorize my lines and go over the script every chance I could. I'll tell you one thing: it's not easy acting in a movie. The hours are long—most days we worked twelve hours—and tedium becomes a constant companion as take after take is shot. Mentally, it drains you.

But I think I was able to handle it because I'm a very organized person. That's how I found time to study my lines, check over the script, and get in a nice run now and then to stay in shape.

In many ways, being part of a movie production is like being part of a football team. Acting involves teamwork. The timing has to be there. You deliver and then the next person delivers. On the football field, the offensive line opens the holes for me; playing a scene, the other actors' lines also create my openings. The crew, the director, the actors—everybody works together. And the better the teamwork, the better the movie.

The director is like the coach. If you sense that he knows what he is doing, you have the confidence to perform well. The actor's biggest fear is that he will clash with his director. You have to know exactly how he wants you to interpret your character. Roger wasn't uptight and the crew felt comfortable, so it brought out the best in everyone.

Sure there's pressure, pressure to get the film done in time, because time means money—lots of it. Sometimes you might not feel good, or it may have been an especially exhausting day and your mind begins to play tricks on you. But you have to suck it up. You can't waste time—there isn't any to waste. At the end of the day I usually went right from the set to my hotel room and crashed.

The stars were William Katt, who played the lead role on the television series "The Great American Hero" and Rick Dean, who has a long list of credits. The only real tense moment on the set was when Dean and I were doing a fight scene in an alley. We were throwing punches as close to each other as possible without landing them, but one of my punches got a little too close and I accidentally hit him in the chest and bruised his sternum pretty badly. I had to keep reminding myself that we weren't wearing pads.

My most visible off-season activity, though, turned out to be an ad I did for Macy's, modeling Calvin Klein underwear. I must admit, the underwear ad was a big departure from my chaste upbringing. When the idea was first presented to me, I balked. I was kind of skeptical, because I didn't know how the fans were going to react to a family man with a clean image modeling underwear. I'd been modeling for six years, mostly business suits and dress shirts and athletic wear, but this was a whole new world, and I needed some time to think about it.

My best friend in life is my wife, Vernessia. She has a very objective outlook and sometimes she sees issues much less emotionally than I do. This was one of those times. We took a full day and discussed the pros and cons of the venture. Would she object to other women seeing my body clad only in underwear? Would something like that have a harmful effect on the children? What would the public think of me? I've always had a squeaky-clean image, and I didn't want to jeopardize it. Part of my success is due to the way I've projected myself. It would be silly of me to tear down my image over one modeling assignment.

But at the same time, Vernessia and I both felt excited over the project. It would break new ground. Former Orioles pitcher Jim Palmer had been modeling underwear for a few years, but as far as I know I was the first black athlete featured in a national campaign of this nature.

We made a few inquires with the modeling agency and decided that I would go ahead with the ad if it was done tastefully and artistically. That was a big part of the deal.

So I made an appointment to go to Studio 71 in San Francisco, where the photographs would be shot. On this particular day we did six different segments, and it took about five hours. Once I got on the set, I immediately became less self-conscious. They had music playing, and all of the people on the set went out of their way to put me at ease.

Still, there is a lot of work involved in modeling. I have to make certain that I stay cool and don't perspire. Then there is the makeup and the posing part. It takes a lot of concentration to come up with the different looks that the photographer and director want. I tried to give the ad my best wide-eyed, high-cheekboned look.

I could tell by the agency's excitement that the shoot had gone well, but not in my wildest dreams did I realize just how well. The morning it came out, I picked up the paper and said, "Oh, no." I hadn't known that it was going to be a full-page ad. At first it was frightening, and I thought about running around the neighborhood and taking papers off people's doorsteps before it was too late and they were opening them up over their morning coffee. But after my second glance, I realized how tastefully done it was.

As soon as the ads hit the papers, I began receiving calls from television shows requesting guest appearances. Locally, I did "People Are Talking" and "Evening Magazine." Nationally, I did segments with "Entertainment Tonight" and "Lifestyles of the Rich and Famous."

I also received many letters, ninety-nine percent of which were positive. The only negative ones were from jealous boyfriends or husbands, who were mad because their girlfriends or wives had made a pinup out of the ad. You're always going to get some feedback from people who don't agree with you or have negative thoughts. Macy's jumped on the bandwagon and had posters made, which they gave away with the purchase of Calvin Klein underwear.

I did get a few letters from women who protested that my body was being exploited. But when you think about it, all models' bodies are exploited. I consider myself a model, so I guess that's just an occupational hazard that I'll have to live with.

The amazing part was that I received letters from as far away as France and Germany. I got more attention from a single underwear ad than I did when I became the exclusive member of the thousand-thousand club in 1987, having gained a thousand yards rushing and a thousand yards receiving. Nothing I had ever done in football had brought me this much notoriety.

I've heard that John Madden never got any credit when he coached the Oakland Raiders; it wasn't until he started making commercials that people found out who he was. Little old ladies still think he's the Ace Hardware man who sells mops and brooms. They don't know that he was a very successful football coach. There's a whole world out there made up of little old ladies and other people who didn't know Roger Craig from Roger Rabbit until they saw that underwear ad.

I can be a consistent player and set NFL records and help my team to the Super Bowl, and never really raise any eyebrows. But then I do something different, totally unrelated to athletics, and people say, "Whoa, now let's look at this guy again."

Macy's printed up 35,000 posters of the ad and gave them to customers who purchased fifty dollars' worth of Calvin Klein merchandise. I also put out my own version of the poster and sold it for eight dollars, with part of the money going to Big Brothers and Sisters of the Peninsula.

I take pride of my work outside football. Now people are starting to recognize my talents away from the game. People are starting to see that I'm a multidimensional person who doesn't need a football in his hands all the time to make an impression. That's good. I like that, and I'm glad that I did the ad.

It seemed like the off-season was awfully short, but I guess that was because I had so much going on. The free agents and rookies reported to Rocklin on July 25, and the rest of the veterans reported three days later. I could have sworn that it was only a few days since we'd last been there.

I took a lot of ribbing from my teammates that first day of training camp. They gathered around my locker to see what kind of underwear I was wearing. One lineman told me that his wife told him that if Calvin Klein underwear could make his body look like mine, she would go out and buy him a whole trainload.

Camp seemed a bit slower than usual. Two of my offensive linemen, center Jesse Sapolu and guard Guy McIntyre, were holding out, and three other players—defensive linemen Charles Haley, Pierce Holt, and Kevin Fagan still didn't have contracts, so some of the chemistry was missing.

Two other players from our Super Bowl XXIII and XXIV teams had demanded to be traded to "greener pastures," and the 49ers had accommodated them. My backup, Terrence Flagler, was exiled to Dallas, along with defensive end Danny Stubbs, a second-round draft pick in 1988, and our rather loquacious cornerback, Sir Timothy McKyer, Esq., was practically given away to the Miami Dolphins.

I was really disappointed that Terrence felt the way he did. A number-one pick out of Clemson in 1988, Terrence had a lot of talent. But what he had in ability, he lacked in patience. He wanted to play at my position—*right now*. I used to take him aside and tell him, "Terrence, be patient. Your day will come. Just hang in there and learn all that you can." Have you ever told someone something for their own good and they wouldn't listen? That's the way Terrence was.

I was lucky my rookie year because the 49ers really didn't have a fullback who could run, catch, and block. I carried the ball 176 times for 725 yards and scored 12 touchdowns. But that was a matter of being in the right place at the right time. Another time, another team, and I might have sat for two or three years like Terrence.

My last advice to him was, "if you get impatient, bad things can happen." But no amount of cajoling could get Flagler to change his mind. Earlier in the season he had skipped a couple of practices to protest his lack of playing time. He appeared sullen and unhappy in the locker room. But the ultimate slap in the face to the organization was when he missed the Super Bowl parade to honor us.

Finally, I guess the 49ers had had enough, and they traded both him and Stubbs to Dallas. But that wasn't the end of Terrence's unhappiness. He also whined with Dallas and complained that he was hurt. In San Francisco he was assured of a backup role, and if anything happened to me he was the man. But down there he was thrust into the middle of a competitive atmosphere and had to battle for a roster spot.

Terrence eventually lost the battle on the day the final cut was made, and the Cowboys waived him. I could only think, What a waste of talent. He hooked up with Phoenix in week four, but his future was already cast. Eventually, they waived him. Terrence will forever be one of those players that teams call on in an emergency, and as soon as they don't need him anymore he'll be cast aside.

McKyer is an entirely different story. Two straight years Tim had not reported to camp over a contract conflict. The first time he and Don Griffin wanted their contracts renegotiated and held out in tandem. In 1989 Tim stayed away because he and management couldn't agree on a contract.

Basically, Tim is a nice guy and a very talented player, but he can't keep his mouth shut, and I think that it eventually gets him in trouble. Last season when we played Indianapolis in the opener, Tim failed to touch a player who had fallen in front of him after catching a pass. The coaches hollered at him for his mistake, and I guess he doesn't function well when he's criticized. Anyway, he claimed he had an injured hamstring and that he would never play another game while he was injured.

He missed the next three games, but the Saturday prior to our October 8 game against the Saints in New Orleans, the doctors cleared Tim to play. He met with Coach Seifert after the morning practice in the Superdome and was told that he was needed for the nickel defense because we were shorthanded.

Tim balked at the suggestion, saying that his hamstring was still sore. George argued that the medical staff said he was well enough to play. But Tim was stubborn and finally I guess George had heard enough. He suspended Tim for insubordination and put him on the next flight back to San Francisco.

Tim came back that year to play against the Jets and helped us win the title. But too many things had happened, and too many things had been said. I still don't understand why he acted the way he did. He's a really talented cornerback and can do so many things, but he was always complaining to anyone who would listen that he deserved to be in the Pro Bowl. I guess he wasn't getting enough attention, and he wanted to be the Ronnie Lott of our secondary. But we already had a Ronnie Lott.

To get selected to the Pro Bowl by your peers is an extremely high honor. It means other players respect the way you play. You don't force the issue. You play and let people know who you are; you make it on the strength of what you've accomplished out on the field. You have to pay your dues. Now, I'm not taking anything away from Tim, but really it's out of your control. You don't make it by bragging or talking about it. The best advice I could have given Tim was to go out and enjoy the game.

Another thing I couldn't understand is why Terrence and Tim would want to leave the 49ers. If NFL commissioner Paul Tagliabue suddenly announced that there was total free agency, NFL players would be lined up around the block wanting to sign with the 49ers.

So we opened up our 1990 camp without two players who had helped us to a pair of Super Bowl championships, and without five others who stayed away because of contractual reasons.

There were a few others missing, too. Defensive back Tom Holmoe had retired after the Super Bowl and was going back to school at Brigham Young to get his masters in sports administration and help coach the BYU defensive backfield. Tom was a very bright guy and a real team player. And Pete Kugler had announced his retirement after the game and already had a job lined up as an accountant in Denver.

We also lost veteran starter Riki Ellison and reserve wide receiver Terry Greer. Neither was protected during the Plan B period, during which teams are allowed to protect only thirty-seven of the players on their roster, and other teams made better offers.

Riki's case was unusual because he had played all seven seasons of his pro career with San Francisco and was thinking of running for public office in San Mateo County. But he'd told a couple of other players that he felt snubbed by the 49ers because they offered him a contract with half of his salary made up in incentive bonuses. Riki had missed all of the 1989 season with a broken arm and thirteen games in 1987, also with a broken arm. I guess the club felt that he was getting near the end of his career, even though he had always been a starter when he was healthy.

The Raiders reportedly offered him a three-year deal worth $1.7 million if he made the team with no other strings attached, which was considerably more than he would have made with the 49ers.

So I don't blame Riki for jumping to the Raiders. The bottom line is that you have to think of your family and yourself first. What's best for all of you? And Riki felt that going to the Raiders was best for him and his family. Ironically, our first preseason game would be against the Raiders. It was going to seem strange seeing Riki on the other side of the field. Both of us are from the class of 1983; I was drafted in the second round, and he was drafted in the fifth round.

Greer I didn't know that well. He had played for us on the 1987 strike replacement team and had stuck with the team after the labor dispute was settled. He had been a big star up in Canada, making All-CFL four times with the Toronto Argonauts. He mostly played on special teams for us, though I do remember one big catch he made against the Rams in 1988 that kept a drive alive and enabled us to beat them.

But there were plenty of rookies and young free agents who were more than willing to take their places. We had a fairly good draft, and rookies always bring that fresh enthusiasm that a team needs. Most rookies are right out of college and probably would play for nothing. To have the opportunity to make the roster of the defending world champion and get paid, too—well, that's pretty heady stuff for a youngster.

Our first exhibition game was August 11 against the Raiders at Candlestick Park. But even before the game, Jeff "Big Daddy" Bregel pulled his usual I'm-leaving-the-team routine. I call it a routine because he had done the same thing the past two training camps.

Jeff was a talented offensive lineman and he had started the first three games of the 1989 season at right guard. He was also very intelligent, being a USC Academic All-American and all. But in games he seemed to get flustered and lacked practical common sense. In 1989 he nearly got Joe killed during the Philadelphia game by missing his blocking assignments. After that game, it was back to the bench for Big Daddy, as Bruce Collie and Terry Tausch split the duties at right guard.

This time the team called his bluff. The 49ers announced that they had waived Bregel. I heard that he called back a couple of days later saying that he'd had a change of heart and wanted to rejoin the team, but George said thanks but no thanks.

Jeff had made the mistake of becoming a distraction, and there's no room for distractions in this game, because time is so valuable. You play, lick your wounds, and then get ready for the next Sunday. The coaches and staff don't have time to stop and figure out what's bothering a player. They'll do everything possible to get you prepared and on the field, but they're not going to play your mind games with you if you keep jerking them around.

So we went into our first exhibition game without another of our players from the Super Bowl XXIV team. Maybe we missed Jeff Fuller. Maybe we missed all of them, I don't know. After the Raiders beat us 23–13, we knew that we had a lot of work to do, and that we were in for a long week.

The practices were long, it was hot, and tempers began to flare. It looked like linebacker Bill Romanowski ran into the back of Jerry Rice after the whistle had already been blown during a Monday scrimmage. Jerry and Bill had gotten into it the previous year during training camp, and maybe this was just a continuation of that feud. Jerry took a swing at Romo, and the two tumbled to the ground, fists flailing. Romanowski claimed he didn't see Rice and that Rice tried to hit him and then dived at his knees.

Sometimes I think things like this are good for a team. They kind of fire you up and shake out the cobwebs that tend to form during the monotonous two-a-days. Of course there is always the chance that that sort of outburst could end up in injury, and you certainly don't want that. Later veteran nose tackle Jim Burt and rookie free agent offensive lineman Brett Wiese scuffled, as did offensive guard Bruce Collie and defensive lineman Pierce Holt.

Me? I stayed clear of all that stuff. It's not going to enhance my movie career if I have to put a handkerchief up to my ear to blow my nose.

We didn't have to play again until the following Monday night, when we were to meet the Broncos at Mile High Stadium in Denver. So we had ten days to prepare for the team that we beat 55–10 in Super Bowl XXIV. As it turned out, we were going to need all of that and more.

It was a war, which was what I'd predicted, and without an alert play by rookie defensive lineman Dennis Brown, they would have beaten us. The game was tied 24 all and Denver had the ball, second and five at their own 27. A pass bounced off the pads of Bronco fullback Melvin Bratton, and Dennis snatched it out of the air and ran it back to the Bronco 4. Mike Cofer then kicked a 22-yard field goal to win the game, 27–24.

For a moment, I got a little jealous of Dennis, especially when his eyes got large and round like mine do. He looked like a big, high-steppin' halfback on that play.

Actually, the game was a harbinger of what we were going to be in for all of 1990: we were pro football's marked team.

Midway through the second quarter, I took a handoff and was stopped cold after a couple of yards by half the Bronco defense. I kept wondering when the officials were going to blow the whistle. I couldn't believe they were letting the play go on. I waited for what seemed like an eternity and guys kept teeing off on me. Finally somebody body-slammed me, and I heard the whistle.

When I got up, I was livid. I don't usually lose my cool, but I felt this was uncalled for. I threw the ball down and screamed at the official, asking him why he had that stupid whistle growing out of his mouth if he wasn't going to use it. I could have been seriously injured on that play—hell, any one of us in that pile could have been injured.

The official didn't answer me. But he knew that I was plenty ticked off. I thought they were slow on their whistles. Denver was hitting late, punching and taunting all night long. The Broncos probably are one of my least favorite teams. I'm glad we kicked the stuffing out of them in the Super Bowl.

I had to laugh at the stories that appeared the next morning in the Denver papers. To read them, you'd think that the Broncos had beaten us soundly. According to one front-page story, "John Elway can finally say that he moved the ball against a Super Bowl champion, that he outshined a football god in Joe Montana." The story also said that Elway "put on an exhibition of revenge last night at Mile High Stadium," and that Joe "had to step off his throne for one night and made mistakes that Elway hadn't made since his days at Granada Hills High School."

Hey guys, the 49ers won the game, not the Broncos. And Joe played only the first half, while Elway was in for most of the game. And it was just an exhibition game, not part II of Super Bowl XXIV. Maybe those Denver writers were watching some old reruns of Denver-Cleveland games. I guess the smaller the town, the more provincial the writers. Sometimes I wish the media on the West Coast were like that.

This time the team had a short week. We didn't get back to the Sacramento Airport until the wee hours of the morning. Luckily we had Tuesday off and didn't have to report until dinner at six o'clock. But we had only Wednesday, Thursday, and Friday to get ready to play the Chargers on Saturday night in San Diego.

And the week was fraught with distractions. On Tuesday, the San Francisco *Examiner* carried a small article about how Steve Wallace was being sued by his parents because he'd reneged on a promise to make their house payments. The following day the San Francisco *Chronicle* picked up on the story, and without talking to Wallace, they ran a big article with quotes from his parents implying that Steve was less than a devoted son.

After the Wednesday morning practice, we chased the coaches away and gathered at the center of the field for a team meeting. Offensive guard Bruce Collie called for everyone's attention and suggested that we boycott both the *Examiner* and *Chronicle* reporters for one day. A couple of players, who shall remain anonymous, shouted out "make it all season." Then someone suggested to Bruce that we make it all of the media, not just the two papers, and maybe that through peer pressure their colleagues would make sure that nothing like what had happened to Steve would happen again.

Ordinarily, I wouldn't take it out on the media. I have a great rapport with most of them. But in this case, I wasn't about to go against my offensive line. I'm a team man first. If my team votes to go one way, then I'm the first one headed in that direction.

So as we came off the field, the reporters sauntered over to us, as they usually do, and started asking questions. All they got were a bunch of "no comments" and blank stares. Someone finally told one of the reporters that we had voted to boycott the media because of the Wallace incident.

I think the whole thing got blown out of proportion. For one thing, I personally didn't like the fact that the stories were attacking Steve for something that had absolutely nothing to do with football. I don't think the media should expose something like that to the public, because it's none of their business. At that time of the year, I think that the sportswriters should write about football. That's what the fans really want to read about.

At the same time, I can understand their position. If one paper gets a story and the other paper doesn't have it, then the writer who doesn't have it gets hollered at by his or her editor. Most of them are good guys and gals, and they're just trying to do a job. Times like this, we didn't make it any easier for them.

In all but a few instances I've enjoyed a good relationship with the media. I have a clean image, and you have to play off the media in certain instances. They help me and I help them. Most of the time I'm accessible in the locker room. I'm not a hermit like some of the other players. I believe that we all owe the general public information about a game and ourselves in the context of football. I'll answer questions as long as they don't breech private boundaries.

What does get me irritated are those writers who know little or nothing about football, like Glenn Dickey of the San Francisco *Chronicle*. They write articles about me and tell the public what is going on in my mind. Hell, they don't know what I'm thinking. When I switched positions from fullback to halfback, they said I would never make it.

Then in 1988, after I had a few poor games, these same critics wrote that I had reached old age and that it was time for me to quit. They didn't understand what the transition from fullback to halfback involved. I thought I handled it pretty well.

I don't want anyone telling me that I'm too old or I'm too slow or that it's time for me to quit. I'll know when it comes time to give it up. I don't need Glenn Dickey telling time for me. The 1990 season was my eighth season and I'd never missed a game yet.

We were talking to the press again by Friday, when we were supposed to break camp after lunch. But Coach Seifert threw the reporters a curve: instead of breaking camp after lunch, George held a short team meeting after breakfast and dismissed us. After being pent up in those dorm rooms and going through the two-a-days in the hot Rocklin weather for four weeks, we couldn't wait to get out of there. Most of us had packed our cars the night before and as soon as the meeting was over, we left. The parking lot was a cloud of dust and screeching tires as we headed for our homes, our own beds, and most of all, our loving families. I guess the media ended up interviewing each other that day.

After what seemed like an all-too-brief night at home, we reconvened at San Francisco Airport the next morning for a flight to San Diego for the preseason game with the San Diego Chargers.

We've always been able to pretty much beat up on the Chargers, but not this time. We were supposed to be coming together as a team, and it wasn't happening. The Chargers ended up beating us, 29–28.

It was an ugly game. One thing was evident—Joe Montana had become a marked man, which we'd all suspected would happen. After Joe threw an interception, San Diego linebacker Leslie O'Neal blindsided him, even though the guy who intercepted the ball had already been tackled down near the goal line. Then later in the game Chargers defensive end Lee Williams slammed his helmet into Joe's shoulder after he had thrown a touchdown pass to Jerry Rice. Later Williams was quoted as saying, "I tried to bury Montana's butt. I thought he wasn't going to get up. I thought I had decapitated his shoulder, you know, like 'here's your arm right here . . . pick it up.'"

I think that's really sick. It's one thing to play hard; it's another to go out and try to take someone's livelihood away from them. When someone puts a good, clean lick on me, I usually congratulate him. But there was nothing clean about those hits. And I think that Williams pretty much described the Chargers' intent.

Some of us, including me, were becoming concerned. We still had one preseason game left, against Seattle the following Friday night at Candlestick Park.

They say that adversity builds character. If that's true, then we must have had a lot of character going into the 1990 regular season. Maybe it builds characters—we have plenty of them too.

The final preseason game is usually considered the final dress rehearsal. It's the game in which all of your key players assume their

actual roles and the coaches fine-tune the little things in preparation
for a smashing "opening night." If that was the case, then we were
going to be in for a long season, as the Seahawks throttled us, 30–10.
The only major player missing was Joe Montana, who was held out
with a bruised shoulder. Of course, that's like *Gone with the Wind* without Clark Gable.

We finished the preseason with a 1–3 record. We hadn't been that
dismal since the 1983 season, which we finished by losing to the Redskins in the NFC Championship Game. I didn't help matters by fumbling on our 17 yard line, setting up Seattle's third touchdown. I was
really disappointed with the fumble; I jumped over a guy and just forgot
to protect the ball. I broke the running back's first tenet: always cover
the ball.

We had wanted to have a nice clean game going into the regular-
season opener against New Orleans, but we just made too many errors.
Still, I thought there were some positive aspects, too. Some of the runs
we executed well. And that's what the preseason is for. I thought we'd
be able to clean up the mistakes we made and should just chalk this
game up as a learning experience.

Offensively, Seattle tried some run-and-shoot plays with four wide
receivers and no tight ends. Little did we realize that it was a sneak
preview of what many of our opponents were going to be doing during
the season.

Center Jesse Sapolu and guard Guy McIntyre were playing their first
game after holding out the entire time we were in Rocklin. I thought
our concentration was lacking, which was reflected by the fact that we
picked up nine penalties for 99 yards. It was a very embarrassing evening in front of the home crowd.

Still, it was probably good that it happened; it made us realize what
the entire year was going to be like. We were bent on a crusade to
make football history, and teams were going to be shooting for us.
Better we understood that then, because the next day all of us, including Seattle, we would all be 0–0 going into that first game even.

When we reported to practice Monday the newspapers were re-
porting that cornerback Eric Wright and linebacker Keena Turner had
been waived by the team. It was a real shocker, because both had been
members of the 1981 team, the team that won the first Super Bowl, and
were considered team leaders.

When I got to the meeting room Eric was there. It appeared that he
had outfoxed the team. According to him, the 49ers had offered him a
two-game injury settlement, which amounted to $35,000, if he would
announce his retirement. They said that his alternative was being
waived with no money. But Eric had a pulled hamstring, and I guess
he made some noise about being released injured, because the team
backed down at the last second and left him on the active roster.

Keena, along with punter Barry Helton and veteran linebacker Jim Fahnhorst and incumbent right guard Bruce Collie, were indeed waived. However, the team brought back both Keena and Helton the next day after they cleared waivers. Collie was picked up by the Eagles and Fahnhorst returned to the team a couple of weeks later when Mike Walter broke the ring finger on his left hand.

I had a few personal goals but I didn't mention them to anybody, because I don't believe that your personal goals should be made public. Public statements should be reserved for team goals. But there were a couple things I had in mind.

I had 483 receptions going into the season, and Walter Payton held the all-time record for receptions by a running back, with 492 catches. So I only needed ten catches to become the all-time leader. I didn't put any timetable on breaking Walter's record, but I thought it would be nice to break it at home.

♦

12. And Away
We Go

My body starts aching every time I think about playing against New Orleans, especially in the Superdome. The Saints linebackers are about the hardest-hitting in pro football.

We opened the Monday Night Football season, so we had ten days in which to forget about the Seattle game and get ready for the opener. And, as it turned out, we needed every minute of those ten days for preparation.

Because my preseason production was low, there was some concern that I was doing too much or that I was playing too light. Coach Seifert didn't seem concerned. He told the media that some people take a vacation and read a book, but I wasn't one of them; he said others take a vacation and go climb a mountain, and that was my type of character.

But I wasn't too sure myself. I had trained harder than ever during the off-season. I had intended to come into camp at about 210 pounds and let the heat and two-a-days take me down to about 205. Instead I came in at 205 and now I had trouble maintaining my weight at 200.

Michael Carter, our nose tackle, had undergone arthroscopic surgery on his knee and was going to be lost for a couple of weeks. In the interim, George coaxed defensive lineman Pete Kugler out of retirement. I don't think it was too hard. Pete was working in Denver as an accountant, and I doubt they make quite as much money as the $400,000 the 49ers paid him. Besides, when those Denver people found out that he used to play for San Francisco, they probably switched accounting firms.

I told everyone, especially the new players, to expect a rumble when

130

we got to New Orleans. I don't know if those damn southern teams are still fighting the Civil War or what, but we always seemed to run into battles when we got to both New Orleans and Atlanta.

The Saints didn't disappoint us. They came swarming at us like killer bees. It seemed that every time I got the ball, there would be at least six or seven Saints right there to dive on me. My body was taking a terrific beating, and the team wasn't doing that well, either. We trailed 12–10 until Mike Cofer connected on a 38-yard field goal with 12 seconds left in the game to lift us to a dramatic 13–12 victory over the stunned Saints.

I'm afraid that I didn't have a lot to do with the victory. Their linebackers strung out my runs pretty good, and I couldn't find much daylight down inside.

The hour belonged to veteran Ronnie Lott, who played like a man possessed. The Saints were leading and had the ball with three minutes to go when Ronnie hit Saints running back Dalton Hilliard so hard that the ball popped loose. Safety Chet Brooks recovered on the Saints 35-yard line to stop what could have been the drive that sealed our doom. Later, with about four seconds left, Ronnie intercepted John Fourcade's Hail Mary pass to end the game and preserve the victory.

Of course, none of this would have been possible if Saints coach Jim Mora had not called a pass play on third and five with 1:47 left in the game and the 49ers out of time-outs. None of us believed it when he called it. Had he called another running play, even if they hadn't made the first down, there would have been precious few seconds left when they turned the ball over to us. As it was, we got the ball back with ninety seconds still left in the game, and that was all Joe Montana needed as he drove us down to the New Orleans 21, where Cofer hit a 38-yard field goal to send the Saints fans off to Bourbon Street grumbling.

I thought it was an odd call, but I'll never criticize a coach because you never know when you might be playing for him. A couple of our players, including Ronnie, defended Mora's call. "If they get the first down, the game is over," said Lott. True, but they didn't get it, and they didn't win.

Eddie D. was waiting for us at the locker room door after the game was over. Even though we were sweaty and probably smelled like wet rats, he grabbed us and gave us big hugs as we came in. I'd seen Eddie emotional lots of times, but never this emotional.

Even though I'm no longer a 49er, I still stand by my statement that Eddie is a generous team owner. I've already told you the story about the $50,000 fine and the Super Bowl ring ceremony on Kauai. During my tenure with the team, we had a close relationship.

Most of us players considered Eddie to be one of the team. Just his mere presence gave us an added boost, because he cared so much about us individually. If he could suit up, he would. We probably should have dressed him in a jersey and put him on our bench for every game. Except I'm afraid he would have run out on the field and tackled somebody. Eddie D. is very intense, and he's not a phony. Those emotions are real, because he wants to win.

Following a particularly bitter 9–3 loss to the Los Angeles Raiders in 1988, we came into the locker room after the game and there was glass all over the place, and the glass door to our soft drink locker was missing. One of the other players told me that Eddie was so upset about the loss that he kicked in the door of the soft drink locker.

Ted Walsh, one of our equipment guys, told the media that he, Ted, had accidently broken it. Actually, I felt like breaking it myself. Eddie is so intense and such a winner that he took out his frustration on the soft drink locker. Better on the locker than on me.

He didn't mind spending money, as long as we were winning. And he would do whatever it took to build a winner. Unfortunately, it's impossible to stay at the top year after year. Injuries, age, and the NFL's constant quest for parity make it extremely difficult to have dynasties in this day and age. I don't know if Eddie understood that. Still, the 49ers were like heaven and there was no way I ever wanted to leave the team, even when the owner insisted on hugging and kissing you after a particularly close victory against the Saints.

Not that the victory wasn't costly. Saints linebacker Sam Mills ripped my arm with his helmet, and I had to go to the sidelines to have twenty stitches taken in it. He had done the same thing to me the previous year. I went up to him after the game and said, "Hey, Sam. What do you do? Carry a switchblade knife when you play us?" We both laughed about it, but the truth was I was hurting, and not just from the laceration. On the same play, someone laid a helmet right on my hipbone and gave me a painful hip pointer.

I could barely walk Monday morning, but I knew that I would be all right by game time the following Sunday. We were scheduled to play the Redskins at Candlestick Park, so that gave me nearly six days to get the hip well again. I wasn't worried, because I pride myself on my conditioning. The fact that I am in such good condition probably made the injury less serious.

My worst injury in football occurred in 1986 against Miami in the Orange Bowl. My hip was knocked out of the socket, and whenever I tried to run on it, it would just give out on me. The muscles and tendons around the hip were stretched, and consequently my hip didn't have any stability. I should have had it X-rayed, but I never did. I was afraid they would tell me not to play, and I wanted to keep playing. And I did, for twelve more games. Finally, in a 1987 wild-card playoff game against the New York Giants at the Meadowlands, I took myself out in the third quarter. My hip hurt, my ribs hurt, and I had a sore knee. We lost that game 49–3.

*   *   *

I woke up in the team hotel the morning of the Washington game with this feeling of keen anticipation. My stomach was a little queasy as I went over my pregame preparations. Usually, I try to visualize my run on certain plays. I run this little film through my mind that shows me cutting one way and then the other, always escaping the clutches of some hellbent-for-leather linebacker. I honestly believe that it helps me out on the field during the game. I kind of follow my instincts through the holes, because they've already been honed before the kickoff.

So the feelings of anxiety were a good sign. I felt exhilarated, and I couldn't wait to step out onto the field. I believed I was going to have a big game against the Redskins. So much of the running game is mental, and getting in a particular rhythm is important. I can usually sense that rhythm before the game, usually even before I'm getting taped. It's hard to explain, except that every movement I make seems to have a purpose, and my stride seems very loose.

In the 49ers system, then and now, once you get your running game going, the passing game follows. And when you get both going hand-in-hand, it's a thing of beauty; there was not a team in professional football who could stop us when we had both clicking.

I had a good afternoon, just as I figured I would. The offensive coaches told us at the meetings during the week that we should be able to run on Washington, and they proved to be right. It was a productive day at the office, as they say. I gained 82 yards on 22 carries, and my hip hardly bothered me at all.

But the important this is that we won, 26–13, against a team that was expected to vie for the NFC East crown. Our rushing game was able to take some of the pressure off the passing game, which in turn bought Joe the extra time he needed to spot the open receivers.

The offensive line was superb, opening the holes for me and keeping the Redskin defense off Joe's back, and more important, keeping Joe off his own back.

Steve Wallace had a particularly good game. He pitched a shutout against Redskin defensive end Charles Mann. It was retribution for all of the bad things that had been happening to Steve. First there was that thing with his folks, which the media blew out of proportion. Then he took the brunt of the media criticism after the Saints game because he was penalized four times for false starts.

The two men went at it pretty good. I could see Mann hollering at Steve, and later I asked Steve what he was saying. He told me that they weren't very nice words. He said Mann kept trying to bury his helmet in Steve's throat. Steve said that he hit him in the face mask a few times to slow him down, and that only served to enrage Mann further.

So I was very happy for Steve. As I've mentioned countless times, we were like a family, and it bothers you when one of your family is struggling. I also felt sorry for linebacker Mike Walter. Mike was like me, an iron man. He had broken the ring finger on his left hand in the opener against New Orleans, and he'd had two screws inserted in it so he could play against the Redskins. But during the game, he rebroke the finger, and the two screws were torn right out. There was nothing left but shredded bone. He had to undergo surgery again to try and repair the original break, and this time he would go on injured reserve and would miss at least four weeks. We were now 2–0, and we had the Atlanta Falcons to face next—without Walter, our leading tackler for the past two seasons.

Ordinarily, back in 1990, you count on beating the Falcons. They'd been the doormat of the NFC West for as many years as I could remember. But this year was different. Not only had the Falcons made a dynamite deal with the Colts, receiving tackle Chris Hinton and wide receiver Andre Rison in return for their first pick in this year's NFL draft, but they hired Jerry Glanville as their new coach.

Glanville had a strange reputation. You either liked him or you hated him. He had a reputation for reprimanding players in front of their peers, and not always for the right reasons. If he thought you were dogging it or feigning an injury to get out of practice, he'd cut you in front of the entire squad.

Jamie Williams and Spencer Tillman had played for him at Houston, and both had liked him, up to a point. But Glanville had this thing about Elvis Presley. He'd tell the media that Elvis was still alive, and then Glanville would leave a pair of tickets at Will-Call in Presley's name. They said his ongoing road show about Elvis being alive and all of that other crap sometimes proved a distraction to the team.

That week during a conference call with the 49er media, Glanville dogged Jamie. Jamie used to wear dreadlocks, which he was quite proud of. Glanville said, "I love dreadlocks, but that really isn't hair. Jamie found that hanging off some old horse's butt."

Now that didn't sit too well with Jamie. Neither did the comments about Glanville "making Jamie Williams." He told the media that Jamie owed him, Glanville, a million bucks because he had been cut by every team in the league until "we took him and made him into something."

Jamie's locker was just a few down from mine, and I overheard him telling the media that he was going to try and set up a block near the Houston bench so he could run out of bounds and hurl his body into Glanville.

Jerry also poked a little fun at Tillman, who, like Jamie, came to the 49ers as a Plan B free agent from the Oilers. Glanville accused Spencer of playing both sides of the fence.

"When it looked like they were going to fire me at Houston and hire

Jackie Sherrill, Spencer immediately wrote Sherrill a letter and told him how much he liked him. Spencer always was on top of things," Glanville told the 49er media.

Of course, he has some likeable qualities. How could you not like a free-spirited coach who drives a Harley-Davidson to practice and admits that he "leads America in making mistakes"? Most coaches never admit that they make mistakes.

Glanville has a way of getting a team fired up for a game, which worried our coaching staff. His players usually performed over their heads because of emotion. A team can do that for a while, but it will eventually catch up with you if you don't start winning. When a team loses, players will believe in a coach's unorthodox tactics for only so long before they start questioning them. Glanville's teams lost their share of games and he was second-guessed a lot by his own players.

On Wednesday night I got a telephone call at home from a friend who told me that Walter Payton was quoted in the paper as saying if someone was going to break his receiving record, he was glad it would be me. I admit that Walter is one of my idols, and he's the one who originally got me interested in off-season workout programs.

I grew up in the Midwest, and my hometown of Davenport was only about three hours from Chicago, so I was a Bears fan at a very tender age. And I idolized Walter.

I finally met him at the Pro Bowl in my third professional year. I still can't believe it, but we started in the same backfield. I spent the whole week with him. He left me with some good advice about how to better prepare myself for the season. He told me that I was going on natural ability, and that if I worked out I would protect and enhance that ability. Walter also told me always to think positive, even when you're injured. He said that if you bring positive thoughts to your mind when you are injured, it will help your body heal more quickly. I've always believed that, and I can show you documentation of how it's worked for me.

Walter is a first-class individual, a legend among NFL running backs. I don't know of any other running back who ever commanded the respect that Walter did. He would send me his workouts from time to time so I could adapt some of his training regimen to mine.

So breaking one of his records would be something I could cherish for the rest of my life. To be able to think that I was in the same class as Walter Payton would definitely be a thrill for me. After reading about his comments, I decided to call him.

He said, "Roger, go for it. The record is there. Out of all the backs in the league, I'm glad it's you." He had recently told a reporter that I was the best running back in the league. Again, it meant a lot to me coming from him. I just hope that I have as much dignity and humility when someone comes along and breaks my thousand-thousand record.

Pass receiving is something I take a lot of pride in because I learned that part of football after I left college. At Nebraska we didn't throw the ball much; I think I caught five passes my entire college career. But when I came to the 49ers, Bill Walsh told me that all of the 49er running backs had to know how to catch the ball.

So it was something that I developed through a lot of hard work. After practice I would ask people like teammate Tom Rathman to stay late and throw me ball after ball after ball. Now all of that extra time and perseverance was paying off.

I don't care how much talent you have, it takes a lot of hard work to become a good pass receiver, and it doesn't come overnight. There are a lot of talented backs who can do many things, but the question is, are you willing to pay the price over the years and take care of yourself in the off-season? When you take that pounding during the regular season, all you want to do when the season is over is lay out on some beach somewhere for five months and let your body heal.

But it doesn't work that way. You have to prepare yourself for the next season's beatings, and you have to be consistent in your work habits. You can take a week or two off, but that's it. You have to work just as hard in the off-season as you do during the season.

Just as Walter passed on his work ethic and formula for success to me, I'm going to pass it on to the younger guys that I come in contact with. In 1990 my project was Dexter Carter. I was trying to pump up his confidence and convince him that he'd be able to read the capricious winds of Candlestick Park on kickoff returns. Some day Dexter will be breaking my records.

Someone mentioned that when I broke Walter's record I should ask the officials to stop the game, but I vetoed that. What if we were driving for a touchdown and my selfish antics took us out of sync? When you're in the middle of a long drive, you develop a rhythm, and you resent anyone's doing anything to take you out of that rhythm.

I remember when I established the thousand-thousand club and team officials wanted to stop the game and award me the game ball. We had a nice little drive going, and we were on the verge of scoring. I protested loudly, telling them that I didn't want the ball right then. What would I do with a football in the middle of a game anyway? I said, "Let's celebrate after the game. Let's get this touchdown now."

I went into week three against the Falcons needing only three catches to break Walter's magnificent record. I caught one for four yards during the first drive and figured it was going to be my afternoon. But it turned out to be a very long and unproductive afternoon in more ways than one.

For one thing, I didn't get the record. I caught one more pass for no yards to tie it. Imagine, tying the great Payton's record with a pass for no yards. I had a chance to break the record when Joe threw me a short pass just after the start of the third quarter, but it sort of bounced off my hands. Joe had a little too much muscle on the ball for me to handle.

But the way my afternoon was going, I wasn't too surprised that I couldn't come up with it. I rushed 18 times for only 26 yards, a 1.4 yard average. I'd never had an afternoon where I've been so unproductive. Every time I looked for daylight, there was a huge Falcon linebacker ready to pounce on me. I honestly think they were playing with fifteen or sixteen guys on defense, but the damn officials just wouldn't throw a flag. Maybe they were intimidated by Glanville.

That meant I would have to wait two weeks before I could break Payton's record, because we had a bye the following week. The bye week is one of those ingenious plots thought up by television executives to squeeze more money out of commercials. By adding an extra week to the season, they get a seventeen-week season instead of a sixteen-week season. They also added another team to the playoff format in each conference; that gave them an extra playoff game, and one more week of prime-time football.

The fact that I didn't get the record against Atlanta meant that I would probably get it against the Oilers in Houston two weeks later. I would rather have done it at home; that way our enthusiastic fans could feel a part of football history too.

I also had my sights set on another record. This one I didn't mention very much, but it had been on my mind since the start of the 1988 season. The great Jim Brown, whom I consider the most durable back ever to play the game, never missed a contest during his nine-year career. He played in 118 straight games, an almost unheard of feat by a running back.

I very quietly came into the 1990 season with my own unblemished record. I had played in 110 straight games since joining the 49ers as a rookie in 1983. The Houston game would be my 114th, and if things went right for me—knock on wood—I would set a NFL record on November 4 in Green Bay against the Packers. That would be my 119th straight game, and it would eclipse Brown's mark. How very fitting, too, that I would do it on the hallowed ground where some of the greatest legends of football played, at Curly Lambeau Field in Green Bay. I could visualize Jim Brown on a muddy afternoon at Lambeau Field, running over the Packer defenders, breaking tackles. Just the mere thought of breaking the record in Green Bay resurrected in my mind the ghosts of football past.

But that was looking too far ahead, and I don't like to do that. Bill Walsh had instilled in us the discipline of thinking only as far as the next game, and I consider it bad luck to look beyond that. I hoped that I would be forgiven for that slight transgression of thinking about the game in Green Bay.

The good news was that we defeated the Falcons, 19–13, and now had a two-game lead in the NFC West with a 3–0 record. In a way, I guess the bye would help us get well again. John Taylor had suffered bruised vertebrae against the Redskins and was forced to miss the Atlanta game. Had we played again in a week, he would have had to miss that one too. The doctors said that there would be a chance he could be ready for the Houston game, and that would really give our offense a big boost.

The Falcon linebackers had left some good-sized bruises on me too. My body is never pretty after playing the Falcons. I think they enjoy laying the helmets on me. The other plus was that we were going to get a couple of extra days off over the next two weeks. That would give me some time to catch up on some personal business and get ready for a fashion show I was going to do at Fort Mason to benefit AIDS research.

13. The Nightmare

Remember what I said about looking too far down the road, how it's bad luck and all?

We left Friday afternoon from San Francisco International Airport for Houston. I was looking forward to playing in the Astrodome again. I had played there once before, in 1984, my second year, and I'd had a pretty fair day. I led our team in receptions with seven catches for 61 yards, and I also rushed for a touchdown.

I hadn't done much my first three games in 1990. I gained 82 yards rushing against the Redskins, but the Falcons had held me to 26 yards on 18 carries. They were putting eight men on the line of scrimmage and blitzing the hell out of Joe, so there weren't any gaps up the middle, and when I tried to get outside, the safety was waiting.

The fans are a pretty fickle lot. It doesn't matter what you did last week or what you might do next week, you're judged on what you do right now, and I didn't do much. The media sort of acts like the voice of the fans, and now those whispers that I'd lost a step, that I was through were coming back. It bothers me a lot when people make judgments on my ability or lack of it, or on my physical prowess. I knew that Houston didn't gamble like Atlanta and that I would be facing a more conventional defense, which would help our running game.

And I had gained back the five pounds I lost in training camp. Something had been missing; I hadn't felt I was as punishing a runner as I'd been the season before, when I weighed 210. So now I was back to nearly 210, and I felt strong.

I got taped early and trotted out on the field under the dome. My shoes felt all right on the surface. I did a few cuts, and then warmed

139

up with the rest of the team. I was excited, anxious for the game to get under way. I've usually done well on artificial surfaces—my best day the previous season had been 131 yards on 24 carries against the Colts in the Hoosier Dome—and I was looking forward to breaking Walter's receiving record.

The Oilers took the kickoff and went 65 yards on their opening drive for the score, which didn't portend well for our running game or for me. We took possession after the kick, but Joe threw an interception on third down. Oiler quarterback Warren Moon needed just one down to pass 30 yards to wide receiver Drew Hill, and we were down 14–zip before the first quarter was half over.

But our coaches didn't scrap the game plan; I guess they figured it was too early to give up on it. That was one thing about our team: we rarely panicked and we never gave up. Joe called my number on the third play of our next possession and I picked up three yards on a sweep, but the drive stalled.

We got the ball right back to start the second quarter. On first down, I ran six yards up the middle on a trap play. I was starting to feel a rhythm, and I knew this was going to be a productive day. On second down, Joe read my mind and called a short pass play to me. I circled out of the backfield, took the pass, and gained five yards. I entered football history with that short pass; it was the 493rd reception of my career, the most by a running back in the history of the NFL. One better than the great Walter Payton. Now I was really pumped.

Joe tabbed my number again on the next play. This was getting to be fun. It was a trap, and left tackle Bubba Paris laid a perfect trap block for me and I broke 13 yards up the middle. It really felt great to get past the line and break into the secondary.

I had planted my right leg and was starting to cut back to my left when I heard the pop. It was unmistakable. No one had even touched me. My whole body was surging left as I pushed off with my right foot, but my cleats had caught in the Astroturf.

I felt a dull ache in my right knee as I came back to the huddle. I looked over to the sideline, and the coaches signaled me out and sent in our rookie, Dexter Carter. The trainer and doctor took a cursory look at the knee, but I insisted that it wasn't hurting me. I didn't consider a dull throb major pain. Afterward someone told me that serious knee injuries never hurt until later.

I wanted to get back in and continue my good start; I had worked hard to prepare for this season and wanted to take advantage of every opportunity I got. Warming up on the sidelines, the knee felt pretty good. It was a little tight, but I figured that it would loosen up once I got back into the flow of the game. So I told them I was all right, and I went back in the game on our next series. I gained one yard in the middle on a carry, and the drive eventually stalled. By now I was look-ing forward to halftime, because my knee seemed to be getting more swollen and tighter.

I iced it down in the locker room and came out ready for the second half. On the second play of the half, I gained four yards and a first down, but the rhythm I had felt early in the first half was gone. I was like Miles Davis without his horn. I then tried a sweep left and ended up losing three yards. Still, I wanted to play. Later in the third period I gained ten yards on a delay. Two plays later Joe threw me a short pass on a curl pattern for eight yards, and I had my 494th reception.

But my knee continued to swell, and by the fourth period it was really beginning to hurt. Inside my mind I knew that I shouldn't be playing, but I couldn't convince my competitive nature that coming out was the best thing for me. I was wrestling with my own inner feelings. I had played injured before and had still been productive, but some-where there was this little voice telling me that maybe this was differ-ent, maybe I should heed what my body was trying to tell me and sit this one out. There'd be another game next week, and I wouldn't want to do anything to compromise my chances of playing in that one. What should I do?

In the interim, we ran the delay again, and this time when I tried to cut back, I had a hard time. I only gained one yard, and when I got up to go back to the huddle I was limping. I think that the coaches and I both decided at the same time that I should get the knee tended to. Dexter came back in, and I went to the sidelines. Little did I realize that it would be some time before I played football again.

By the time I showered and dressed and went to the training room for another examination, concern had replaced my initial optimism. The trainers and doctors looked at my knee and there was a lot of hmming and umming, but no one could give me an answer. Lindsy McLean, our trainer, handed me a pair of crutches, and I shuffled off for the bus. They told me that they would run an MRI, a magnetic reso-nance imaging test, on Monday at the doctor's office.

I went home after our charter landed in San Francisco that night, but I couldn't sleep. All kinds of horrible thoughts dashed through my mind. The next morning I went to the doctor's office and they con-ducted the test. They said that it showed two slight tears of my right posterior collateral cruciate ligament, and that it didn't appear to be too serious. The way it was explained to me was that the ligament is located behind the kneecap and provides stability and keeps the tibia bone of the lower leg from shifting backward inside the knee joint. Because it wasn't a complete tear, I figured that I would be ready to roll as soon as the swelling went down, which meant I could probably play the following Sunday against the Falcons down in Atlanta.

But at his weekly media luncheon, Coach Seifert told the press that I would probably miss a couple of games. He told them that there was a remote possibility that I would play, but that it was "extremely remote." But I didn't hear that part.

A couple of reporters stopped me in the locker room and asked me if I thought I could play Sunday against the Falcons. I looked at them like they were crazy. "How many games did I miss when I dislocated my hip?" I asked them. One reporter went to the head of my class when he correctly answered, "None." I was totally upbeat and optimistic when I left the locker room that afternoon. I did some work on the stationary bike and lifted a little bit. There was no doubt in my mind that I would play in my 115th straight game the following Sunday.

I went home, had dinner, played with the kids a little bit, and settled in my nice easy chair to watch Cleveland play Denver on Monday Night Football. At halftime Frank Gifford came on with a special report, and they quoted Coach Seifert as saying that the best-case scenario would have me playing again in "a couple of weeks." He then said that my return was "indefinite." He even said that there was the remote possibility that the injury could be career threatening.

Couple of weeks? Indefinite? Career threatening? No plans for surgery at this time? What kind of words were these? Where had this come from? He must have been referring to someone else on the team. That couldn't be Roger Craig he was talking about. I was going to play next Sunday, I was going to keep my consecutive game streak intact.

My hands were shaking as I quickly dialed Lindsy McLean's home phone number. What the trainer told me and what someone told George might be two entirely different stories.

Lindsy broke the news to me the best he could. The medical staff was of the opinion that I shouldn't play. The coaches had already penciled in rookie Dexter Carter to take my place. How could life be so cold? The body was still warm, and they already had a guy taking my place.

I had a difficult time sleeping that night. Tuesday morning I awoke with a new resolve. Just as I had intensely applied myself to fitness after the Vikings embarrassed us in the January 9, 1988, playoff game, I was going to dedicate the rest of the week to getting ready to play Sunday.

I started my rehab program Tuesday and then tended to some personal business. While driving home, I switched my radio to some sports show, and the announcer was talking about the 49ers trading for Marcus Allen of the Los Angeles Raiders. My heart dropped when I heard that.

I'm not a selfish person, but you have to wonder in this profession. I was certain that I was going to help my team win Sunday, and here my team was trying to make a deal for one of the premiere running backs in the league, and the week was only beginning.

And that wasn't the half of it. When I picked up my paper Wednesday morning before going to work, there was a story stating that the 49ers had brought in four running backs on Tuesday for tryouts. Included in the group was former New York Giants running back Joe Morris, who'd been a great back until he broke his foot early in 1989 and had had to miss the entire season. Questions kept whirling around in my mind. The events of the past twenty-four hours were making it hard to face the day.

Damn, the sky was falling on Chicken Little.

After a while, some of it made sense. The team probably would be bringing a lot of running backs through this week because of the uncertainty of my condition. That was their way of having an insurance policy. But in the back of my mind, I knew they were counting me out. That part of it I didn't much like.

But it was out of my control. It's a business, and the 49ers had to do what they had to do, even if it meant bringing in a replacement for me. They had to be able to feel comfortable going into the Atlanta game, and if they believed that I wasn't ready to play, then they were going to feel uncomfortable. I knew they had been talking to Marcus, but I couldn't concern myself with that part of it. I had to worry about my own well-being. What I had to do was just take care of myself, rehab my knee, and deal with the consequences when it was possible for me to come back.

The team knew what type of person I am. If they went out and got Marcus, it would help our team. He'd be a big asset to the organization, being the player he is. He can run, he can catch, and he's an excellent blocker.

When I'm healthy, I can deal with anything. But I wasn't healthy. Mentally, I was there, but physically I wasn't. If Marcus was a 49er when it was time for me to come back, or Eric Dickerson or whomever, I had to be ready to deal with that situation.

You feel a certain attachment to a position, like it's your own personal property. I guess it's because it has been drummed through your mind since you played Pop Warner football. If you compete for a position and you win out, then it's yours, and you take on all the benefits of proprietorship. I think any football player feels that way about his position. I'm no different than the next guy, and I wasn't ready to sign the deed over to a rookie or a former Raider.

But the reality is that a position belongs to no one. You play it for a while, and then circumstances change and somebody else moves into it. Now he is the proprietor. So when I did come back, I figured it would be wide open as far as my competing for a job again. I couldn't worry about whom the organization brought in. They'd bring people in, regardless of my wishes or feelings. What was I going to do? Go up to Eddie D., throw up my arms, and say, "You can't do that."

Deep down, though, I knew that they didn't need to bring in a new player on my account. I remembered how I hurt my hip against New Orleans in the first week and then came back the next Sunday to have a good game against the Redskins. I knew that my intense physical fitness program would pay off, and I would be ready to play against the Falcons Sunday. There was no doubt in my mind.

I honestly didn't understand it, though. Against the Oilers I was running the ball well, and then bam, a knee. It's like goddamn, a *knee*. It stinks. It really stinks. I trained my ass off to be prepared. I was physically and mentally at the top of my game that Sunday. I felt as though I was my old self; my rhythm was there, the line was blocking, and I was exploding off the ball.

Eddie D. called me at home Wednesday night, and we had a nice conversation. He was trying to talk me out of this idea I had about playing. He told me to take it real slow, not to rush Mother Nature. He said, "Listen to the doctor." He reminded me that it's a long season, and that my teammates would need me for the stretch drive.

The next day I went about my rehab program with the fervor of a zealot. I wanted to try and get the strength back in my leg to stabilize the knee. When you tear or stretch the posterior ligament, the bone at the back of the leg shifts because there is nothing to hold it in place. It's almost like you've hyperextended the knee. What the trainers were trying to do was strengthen the muscles so the bone was forced back to its normal position.

We had lost guys earlier that season to similar injuries, people like center Wayne Radloff and running back Keith Henderson, and they were still on injured reserve. But because I was in such good shape, I figured I could make it back by kickoff Sunday. I hadn't ruptured the entire ligament, it was just a couple of small tears.

So I was thinking positive all the time. I still felt there was nothing seriously wrong with me. I had to keep thinking that, because once I started thinking, I've got a bad knee, I've got a tear, then I'm dead. There would be no use in playing me for the rest of the year. I just wouldn't be the same. So it was important that I kept a positive frame of mind. My teammates were great. They kept telling me to take it easy and to make sure that I was still around for the end of the season, because they were really going to need me then.

But honestly, I couldn't think that far ahead. I've been programmed to think only as far as the next game, which was Sunday against the Falcons. We were going into the game on the offensive. None of that running sideline-to-sideline stuff, like we had the first time we met Atlanta; we were going to go straight at them between the tackles. Tom Rathman was going to destroy those linebackers and create big holes for the running backs to run through. I knew we were finally going to run some plays out of the I-formation, and I'd been lobbying for that for weeks. Damn, I wanted to play.

As the week progressed, I still held out hope. I did all of the rehab prescribed by the medical staff and then I went out and worked out on my own. We boarded the charter for Atlanta Friday afternoon, and I took my usual seat. I fell into a deep slumber, and I dreamed that I was running all over the field, through players and around players. I was having a great day.

Suddenly I saw Jim Brown in my dream, and he was scowling at me. I awoke with a start. I remembered my life-long goal to break his consecutive-game record. It was something that I'd worked extremely hard for. It would say a lot about me as a person and as a football player if I could accomplish that task.

To me Brown's mark exemplified excellence, diligence, and a complete dedication to your profession. I think only a running back can really appreciate that record, someone who's gotten up 118 Monday mornings with a swollen body that has been pounded and bruised by a thousand football helmets and said, "Let's do it again this week."

I knew then and there that if I didn't play, there would be no cameo appearance. Either I kept my streak alive honestly and played in my 115th consecutive game, or I didn't get in the game at all. Jim Brown worked hard to get to that plateau. Even though I was only four games short, I didn't want to cheapen the accomplishment, like George Brett had done when he pulled himself out of the lineup so he could win the 1990 American League batting title, or Franco Harris, when he tried to unretire in 1988 to go after Payton's rushing mark of 16,726 yards.

It would have been an insult to Jim Brown, because that's not the way he played. I made up my mind to tell George that I didn't want to go in for one or two plays just to keep my streak alive. If I couldn't help our team beat the Falcons, then I didn't want to play. I was sure Jim Brown would respect me more as a person for my decision.

On Saturday I went to practice, and I even ran a few plays. I was running well, cutting well, and I felt good. I convinced myself that my knee could take the pounding. I wanted to show the coaches that the knee was strong. But ultimately, the decision would lie with George, and I got the feeling he would rather I sit this one out. Still, there was one person who could overrule the coach, and that was Eddie D. When you own the team, you have a lot of clout.

So when we got back from practice, I stood in the lobby with Eddie making small talk, and he suggested we find a sports bar and watch some college football games. It sounded like a good idea to me. Hey, I was going to hang on to his coattails for the rest of the day and lobby my case.

Finally, after Stanford upset Eddie's alma mater, Notre Dame, we talked about my desire to play. I pleaded with him to let me play. He told me that he didn't want to risk losing me for a longer period. He was trying his best to convince me not to play without ordering me not to play. I really respected his concern, but I still wasn't totally convinced.

That evening, George pulled me out of the meeting and told me that he was going to deactivate me for the game so that he could activate cornerback Eric Wright. George said that he and Eddie met and discussed my wishes. But he pointed out that there were eleven games remaining. Then he looked at me and—I'll never forget those words—simply stated, "We're not going to play you." He was very diplomatic about it, but he said ultimately he had to do what was best for the team. Atlanta used that new run-and-shoot offense, and he told me that he was going to need all of the secondary help he could get on Sunday. He told me that he didn't want to jeopardize my career in a game he thought the team could win without me. He told me that if I went in for a couple of plays and got hurt, then he would have needlessly sacrificed a defensive player that the team could otherwise have used.

They were concerned about my career, which I respected. Then again, I'm the type of guy who can't sit down. I'm too impatient. On one hand I was dying to play to keep my record intact, on the other hand, if I took some crazy hit I could damage my knee for the rest of the season—or the rest of my career. Atlanta was the type of team that would have gone after my knee. They would have put some cheap shots on me. The who's who of running backs is made up of players whose careers were cut short by knee injuries.

That night, I tossed and turned. My mind geared up to play and I just couldn't sleep. I got up in the morning with a very empty feeling, knowing that I wasn't going to be out on the field with my teammates.

It was a gloomy feeling, like a gray day when it's getting ready to rain. I hate that dismal atmosphere. I like sunshine, because I'm full of sunshine. This day was depressing. There was an empty feeling in the pit of my stomach, and to tell you the truth, I didn't feel like watching the game. I felt like I was helpless, like I had my hands tied behind my back and people were beating me. It was like I was handicapped.

But I owed it to my teammates to help them any way possible. So I made up my mind that if I couldn't contribute on the field, I would contribute on the sidelines. I didn't want to just stand there and be a spectator. I went up to Dexter Carter in the locker room before the game and I could tell he had the jitters. I told him to relax. "Remember your best-ever college game, and make believe that you're playing in that game again," I said. I told him to let it flow and let it happen. When the game began I stood on the sidelines and shouted encouragement to my teammates.

Then it started to happen. Jerry Rice, my training partner, caught a touchdown pass, and then he caught another one. Soon he had caught three touchdown passes, and finally four. Jerry was doing a spectacular job, running plays and working very hard. My mind went back to the two of us in training, running those hills.

Pretty soon I got caught up in his success. When he'd come to the sidelines I'd rush over to him and tell him to relax and breathe easy. I could tell he was getting tired, but I kept encouraging him to keep going. I was in his ear constantly, prodding and coaxing him to push himself just a little bit more. I could see that he was thinking about records. I started hollering at him when he was out on the field. "C'mon Jerry, just two more. C'mon buddy, get another fifty yards." He started pumping himself up.

When it was all over, Jerry had tied an NFL record with five touchdown catches, receiving a career-high, club record 13 passes for 225 yards and reaching 6,938 yards in total receptions to surpass Dwight Clark's team career receiving record of 6,750 yards by nearly 200 yards. His 30 points were also a team record.

So it kind of worked out well for me, too. At least I felt like I contributed a little bit to our 45–35 victory over the Falcons, and my body wasn't bruised and battered like it usually is after a game.

Still, it was an extremely disappointing day for me personally. It was really important to me to break Brown's record. If I could have accomplished that task, it would have said a lot about me as a person. Not only did I relinquish my chance at the record, but I also had a streak of 61 regular-season games in which I had at least one reception, and I lost that too. But what can you do when they put a harness on you and hold you back? We flew home, and I called my masseur to come up to the house that night and give me a massage. It was more for my feelings than anything else. It certainly wasn't because my body had been banged around.

Back home I resumed my rehab, bound and determined to play the upcoming Sunday against the Pittsburgh Steelers. I did everything that the doctors and trainers told me to do. The Steelers play a lot of deep zone, and I figured it was a team that we could run on. Plus I was getting impatient; I'm not used to watching other people do my job. I loved Dexter and knew he was going to be a good football player and everything, but I was determined to get back in there.

Coach Seifert again put me on hold. I ran a few plays in practice that week, but for the most part I went through my rehab program and rested the leg. I was pretty certain by Friday that I wasn't going to play, because Dexter was taking all of the reps in practice. On Saturday, George and I had a long talk, and he told me that he was going to place me on the inactive list again. It was easier to accept this time because my streak wasn't involved. Still, I wanted to play.

On Sunday, just before the team went on the field against the Steelers, Ronnie Lott stood up in the locker room and called for the team's attention. He felt that our intensity level, for whatever reason, was not what it should be. There had also been some remarks made by the Steeler players about how they were going to take care of us.

Ronnie said that the Steelers didn't respect us, and he didn't take kindly to their remarks that they were going to come into our own back yard and kick our asses. He said we had to get our heads together and used the Oakland A's, who had just been swept in the World Series by the Cincinnati Reds, as an example of what could happen to a team that wasn't together. The A's believed what they read—that they were invincible—instead of executing and playing like the Oakland A's should play. He said that just because you're world champions doesn't mean you don't have to go out and perform. The A's had the better team, but the Reds were hungrier. If we didn't get our act together, Ronnie told us, the same thing would happen to us. Needless to say, our team left that locker room plenty jacked.

We beat the Steelers rather handily, 27–7, and Dexter had a big day, gaining 90 yards on 17 carries, as our team rushed for 150 yards. It was just as I'd figured: we could run on the Steelers.

After the game I told the media that I could have played except the coaches stole my uniform. I was sort of kidding on the sly.

We were now 6–0 with the lowly Cleveland Browns coming to town. They had been struggling, and there were rumors that their coach, Bud Carson, was on the brink of being fired. Some of the papers were saying that the only way he could save his job was to have his team upset the 49ers.

Wednesday after practice George told the media that I had been given the green light to return to practice, but that didn't necessarily mean I would play Sunday. On Thursday there was a horde of media surrounding my locker. I hadn't had so much attention since I scored three touchdowns against the Dolphins in Super Bowl XIX. I told them that I wasn't sure whether I would play much on Sunday or even whether I would play at all. I told them that I was going to run some plays in Thursday afternoon's practice and see how I felt.

After I ran about five plays, I looked at my watch and saw that it was time to check in to my rehab program with conditioning coach Jerry Attaway. I told running backs coach Al Lavan that I had to go in and lift weights, and he said, "Go ahead." I also told one of my teammates to tell Coach Seifert that I had to leave for treatment and to lift some weights. Somehow, in the translation, my message got lost. When George met the media after practice he told them that I left practice early because my knee was sore. That started the speculation all over again.

I felt great, and I wasn't afraid to cut. I could sense my confidence returning. The trainer suggested that I wear a knee brace for the game, but I quickly discarded that notion because it felt too restrictive. The ligament is in the rear of the knee, anyway, so there was really no way a brace could help stabilize it.

Milt Kahn, a publicist I had hired at the time, called me that night and perked me up. He told me that I had been offered another movie role in a film called *Married With Eight,* which was going to be shot in February. So the week was really looking upbeat. My leg *was* still a little sore, but I wasn't going to tell anyone about it. The swelling had gone down considerably, which was a good sign that I was well on the road to recovery. The main thing was to take it slow and not overwork myself.

Saturday night at the team hotel in Burlingame, George again called me aside and told me that I was going to be inactive Sunday against the Browns. My heart dropped. I had been looking good in practice, and I was confident that I would be able to contribute to the team. But he explained to me the more I rested the knee, the stronger it would be when they needed me.

He pointed to a stretch of games that included the Los Angeles Rams, New York Giants, and Cincinnati Bengals. He said that's when we would be trying to clinch the division title. I had to agree, though I still felt I could play.

So I watched in street clothes as we held on to beat the Browns, 20–17, on Mike Cofer's 45-yard field goal into the wind with nine seconds left. It was a sloppy game for us, with some drive-killing penalties and a couple of dropped passes.

I kept seeing things that I could have done to help the team. I found myself second-guessing Dexter on some of his runs, which really wasn't fair because you can always find better holes to run through after the play is over. But back-seat driving is one of the hazards of watching from the sidelines. I guess that's why the coaches holler at us after a play doesn't work.

George told everybody at his Monday press conference that, barring a major setback, I would be back in the starting lineup the following Sunday against the Packers in Green Bay. That was the greatest news I had heard in a long time. It was really tearing me up to sit, and I was difficult to live with—just ask Vernessia and the children. The hurt of losing my chance at Brown's record was still very fresh, and it seemed like ages since I'd carried the ball in a game. I knew that my timing would be off and I knew that I would be cautious until I took that first hit.

14. Back in the Saddle Again

I have a theory about what makes a team good: I believe that when you play with great players, it makes you a great player. By playing alongside Joe Montana and Jerry Rice, my talents are elevated, and I think the same applies to them. Jerry and I enable Joe to play better, and so on and so on. The cast feeds upon its own talents, and that's what made the 49ers such a good football team. There were twenty-two guys all pushing to make those around them play better, and it had a snowball effect. The more we pushed our teammates to excel, the more we were pushed to excel in return.

We were headed for Green Bay, and there was a whole cartload of ironies traveling with us. First of all, we were going for our sixteenth straight regular-season victory and our fifteenth straight on the road. The last team to beat us was the Packers, in week ten of the 1989 season. Second, if I hadn't been injured, this would have been the game in which I broke Jim Brown's record. Instead, it would be the game where I made my comeback.

Running backs coach Al Lavan told me that I was going to split time with Dexter, which was all right with me. The coaching staff didn't feel that I was quite ready for a full game, and I wasn't so sure I was either. I wanted to ease myself back into the action.

It was raining when we arrived in Green Bay late Friday night, and by Saturday the weather had turned cold. Lambeau Field, the cradle of football lore, was covered with a protective tarp, so we had to practice indoors at an adjoining pavilion. It proved to be nothing more than a light walk-through.

It was about 39 degrees Fahrenheit at kickoff, which didn't do a helluva lot for my injured knee, which had been outfitted with a support. It was a battle, just as we expected. Green Bay was struggling; a victory over us would have been a nice way for them to crawl back into the race for the NFC Central title.

Actually, the Packers probably should have beaten us, except for one major coaching error. After they had scored to take a 10–0 lead with thirty-two seconds left in the first half, they elected to squib-kick instead of kicking straightaway. They had us pinned down with bad field position all afternoon, so I don't know why all of a sudden they lost confidence in their defense.

Harry Sydney plucked the bouncer out of the air at the 22 and ran it back to our 41 yard line. So instead of running out the clock like we would have done had we been pinned back on the 20, we decided to see how far we could go and whether we could maybe get some points out of the deal. With Joe Montana as your quarterback, anything is possible.

First Joe passed seven yards to Tom Rathman, and we called a time-out with twenty-two seconds left in the half. On the next play, Joe found Jerry down the left sideline for a 29-yard gain. Now we had a first down on the Green Bay 23 and there were still sixteen seconds left. Joe can pull a dozen rabbits out of his hat with that much time left. On the third play of the drive, waiting patiently until John Taylor broke toward the middle of the end zone on a post pattern, Joe threw a perfect strike for the touchdown. There were still eleven seconds left in the half.

We went on to win the game, 24–20, for our eighth straight victory, as Joe passed for 411 yards to move to number five on the all-time list with 25,599 yards passing.

Joe is a unique team leader. People used to ask me what kind of guy he is, and I had a hard time describing him. He's not a rah-rah type. He usually lets his play speak for him. If I had to use one word to describe him, it would be shy. He's very quiet and keeps to himself off the field. He's very much the family man.

Around the locker room he might joke or say something sarcastic, but for the most part he stays to himself. Not that he's aloof or anything. If you have an opinion, you can bounce it off him. It's just that he doesn't go out of his way to make noise and draw attention to himself.

On the field, he's very assertive. In the huddle there's no arguing or talking over his commands. One sideways glance from those steely blue eyes, and you know who the boss is. But he's not one to yell at you, like some quarterbacks do. When it's time to go to war, you can count on him. I don't think there's ever been a better quarterback, especially in the clutch.

The world can be falling down around him, bodies flying every which way, but Joe remains the eye of the hurricane. He has that aura about him that makes you believe your team can surmount any obstacle that's placed in front of it.

I remember that 92-yard winning drive against Cincinnati in Super Bowl XXIII. He came into the huddle very relaxed, looking around, and simply said, "Let's go out and do it. Let's just concentrate on making first downs and not do anything foolish." And that was all there was to it. We all knew our roles, and we had confidence in our quarterback. And that makes all the difference in the world in football.

So that type of two-minute-drill drive against Green Bay was routine for us. Heck, we did it in practice every day, and we were used to executing it without thinking about the pressure involved. We just reminded ourselves to pull together as a team and keep the chains moving, keep two hands on the ball, and not take any major risks. We did it so much in practice that it was like second nature in the game. Especially for Joe.

What wasn't routine was the dismal rushing game we had against the Packers. Going in, their defense had been giving up more than 121 yards per game, so we figured we'd fatten up our running game, which was averaging just 88 yards per game. Unfortunately, the Packers stuffed our run, and we gained just 34 yards on 20 attempts. It was our lowest rushing output since 1980. I had just eight yards in five carries, but at least I was back. Truthfully, I couldn't stand the inactivity.

Even though I wasn't very productive, I felt good about myself. When I took that first hit and my knee stayed intact, I knew that the worst part of my ordeal was over. The next time I got the ball, I just buried my head into a big pile and kept driving with my legs.

In the third quarter, Coach Lavan pulled me aside and said that they wanted to rest me for a series or two because they were concerned my knee was getting stiff. I already had run the ball more than I was supposed to, so I said okay. Looking back, I think it was a wise decision, because my knee was getting pretty stiff. I could have gone back in, but it was getting colder by the minute, and I could have ripped something and really screwed my knee up. So I tried to keep warm on the sidelines as our little rookie got his feet a little wetter.

Monday afternoon we reported back to Santa Clara for a team meeting, a brief walk-through, and our weekly postmortem with those sage Monday-morning quarterbacks, the media.

Right away the talk was about our December 3 meeting with the New York Giants. Both teams were 8–0, and I guess it was the first time since 1934 that two teams had gone undefeated so long into the season.

The Giants were doing great, but I didn't want to look that far ahead. We had to think about Dallas first, and then Tampa Bay and the Rams after that. The Giants game? It seemed like it was in the next century.

But everybody was hyping that game, especially ABC, because it was a Monday night game. They were really hoping that both teams would come in undefeated and that their ratings would soar. But who cared about their ratings? I certainly didn't. Once you start looking ahead, you lose all sight of your goal. All I could focus on was Dallas, so I deferred all questions about the New York Giants to a later date. I already suffered the consequences of looking ahead. There's no room for that in this business; I think my knee injury proves that.

I was hoping, though, to have a big game against Dallas. Early in the week George announced that I would again be splitting duties with Dexter. Some starters might resent that strategy, but our coaches didn't feel that I was quite ready to play a full game, and I partially agreed with them. In addition, this game would be on artificial turf, and we all knew what had happened the last time I played on artificial turf. That had been in Texas, too. I hated the thought of playing on artificial turf, because my knee was still tender, and I didn't want to risk reinjuring it. And if it was going to benefit the team by giving Dallas a different look with Dexter coming in, that was fine.

I had already just about resigned myself to not making the Pro Bowl in Hawaii. I had made it three of my last four years, including the last two, and I had factored in that free trip to Hawaii on my vacation schedule. I had missed too many games to be a consideration.

When I picked up the San Francisco *Chronicle* Wednesday morning, there was a story by sportswriter Ira Miller implying that I had lost a couple of steps. He said, "Roger Craig, even before his injury, showed signs of slowing down. Craig doesn't break tackles like he used to, and his average per carry has dropped precipitously, from 4.8 yards in 1988 to 3.9 yards in 1989 to 2.7 this year."

By the time I got to my orange juice I was seething. Hell, if I lost as many steps as he implied, I would need a golf cart to get to the line of scrimmage. But I told myself that I wasn't going to give Ira the personal satisfaction of acknowledging what he wrote about me. Whatever Ira writes is a joke because he usually doesn't know what he's writing about.

He would find every little angle to distract us from our mission. But it never worked, because we didn't pay any attention to him. Ever since I went thousand-thousand he'd been writing that I had lost a step. After that year he said I was never an Earl Campbell and that I was washed up. Why couldn't he get it through his mind that his negative writing couldn't touch me? I'd like to suit him up and have him go one-on-one with me. Then I'd see if I could break any tackles.

When we reported for practice Wednesday, we found out that safety Chet Brooks was out. Wide receiver John Taylor was still hobbled by a sore knee and was not expected to play that much. But what else was new? Our leading tackler, linebacker Michael Walter, went back on injured reserve with stretched nerves in his arm; backup nose tackle Fred Smerlas had preceded him to IR a couple of weeks earlier. We also lost wide receiver Mike Sherrard to a broken ankle in the Cleveland game.

But that's the nature of football. A television announcer pointed to us and said the reason we were doing so well was because we had escaped the injuries that plagued other teams. I had to laugh. You could almost stock another franchise with our injured list.

As the week progressed, I was prepared to share duties with Dexter Carter. He was beginning to become a mainstay in our offense, and I was kind of proud of the way he'd stepped forward when I had my injury. That's the kind of dedication that you need. So many times a young player either is afraid or not motivated enough to take over a proven veteran's spot. But Dexter was doing quite well, and I almost felt like a proud parent.

I'm not one given to pregame speeches—I like to do all my talking by moving the chains on the field—but during pregame warm-ups at Texas Stadium, I sensed that we weren't quite focused for this game. It was true that Dallas had won only three games that season, but opposing teams are like wounded predators; they can sense when your guard is down, and that only causes them to come at you even harder. If we let the Cowboys know that we were taking them lightly, that we weren't really intense for the game, there was no doubt in my mind that they would come after us with a vengeance.

So when we returned to the locker room after the warm-ups, I stood on a chair and called the team together. I told the team just to go out and execute and have fun, that I felt we were getting too tense and trying too hard and that we had to bring the fun back to the game. I told them just to go out and play 49er football and not to worry about the hype or the tension. I ended my impromptu speech by telling them to enjoy their job and to love one another. Then we left the locker room and proceeded to beat the Cowboys, 24–6.

I rushed for 49 yards on 16 carries, and I felt really good about myself. The knee was a little stiff, but it held up despite the pounding on artificial turf. Poor Dexter only got to carry the ball twice. But I had gotten into a rhythm and really felt good. Coach Lavan told me that he was going to take me out for a series, but I told him, "No, I'm going too good now. Don't take me out." He agreed to let me keep playing. I didn't want to stop because once I did, the knee would really get stiff.

We ended up with 107 yards rushing. It wasn't going to make you forget about Woody Hayes, the late Ohio State football coach who felt the forward pass was the same as a mortal sin, but it was a start. Everyone thought it was vital that we get our running game untracked, but we were winning ballgames. We were 9–0, and it didn't seem to matter whether we ran the ball or not. But I agreed that we needed to improve on the ground if we wanted to succeed in the playoffs.

After the game, defensive end Kevin Fagan stopped by my locker and congratulated me. Then came Ronnie, Matt Millen, Jim Burt, and the rest. When the defensive guys start coming up to you to offer compliments, you know for sure you're back. I had earned their respect again, and it really felt good. The players, especially the defense, knew what I was going through.

Other guys drifted by and held out their hands to congratulate me. It was like I had been away on vacation or something, and no one was really sure if I was coming back. But that's the type of game football is. You constantly have to prove yourself. When you're injured, there's always that doubt whether you will make it back, especially when a running back has a knee injury.

There was genuine concern for my health, but there was also the reality of the sport: If I wasn't capable of carrying my weight, then the coaches would have to hurry up and get somebody else in there who was. In this game, a player who is a liability is taking food off the tables of the contributing players. So I was more than willing to accept the accolades. It meant that I had earned my way back into the 49er family again.

My right leg had been twisted in the game, but I didn't tell anybody. It got tight and a little swollen, but most of it had subsided by the time our chartered flight landed in San Francisco. It was hurting, but I've never let a little pain stop me. I knew that the leg was strong.

Because it had been a night game, I didn't get home until after 2 A.M. I was really beat by the time I crawled between the sheets. Even the throbbing pain in my knee couldn't keep away the waves of exhaustion. I felt good. I was on the road to recovery, and our team was now 9–0 and tied with the New York Giants for the best record in the NFL.

We were now home for three games, which was a great relief. Although we were the best road team in the history of the NFL, two straight weeks away from home takes its toll. There's nothing like sleeping between my own sheets and eating Vernessia's home cooking. And playing with the kids.

On Friday after a short practice, George let us off early. I took some quick treatment on my knee, hit the whirlpool for about twenty minutes, and then showered and hurried home to watch my daughters Damesha, eleven, and Rometra, eight, ride the horse I had bought them.

We live in Portola Valley, which is a very horsey suburb about thirty miles south of San Francisco. The town is made up of a lot of little farms and ranches, and horses are as common as automobiles. Last year Damesha had really become interested in horses, so I got her some riding lessons. In April she still showed an intense interest in riding, so I bought a horse, half thoroughbred, half quarter horse and we named him Buck. Buck has a real easy disposition and tempera- ment, and the girls just love riding him. It also gave them some respon- sibility as far as caring for and grooming the animal. We board him at Portola Valley Farms, and they have an arena where the girls can perform.

In the third week in October Damesha entered a junior horse show in Vallejo, and she took second in the jumping competition. Unfortu- nately, we played the Steelers that Sunday, and even though I was inac- tive I felt an obligation to be on the sidelines with my teammates to lend them moral support. But Vernessia videotaped Damesha's ride, so I did get to see it when I got home. The honor served to further inten- sify her desire to become an outstanding equestrienne. Her goal is to compete at the 1996 Olympics, and who knows, if she stays with it and doesn't get burned out, it's a possibility. These Craig people aren't eas- ily deterred by barriers, physical or otherwise.

My little daughter Rometra is the soccer queen. Her team made the playoffs in 1990, and if I got home early enough on Fridays I could catch some of her practices. Unfortunately, the games were on Satur- day, so I didn't get the opportunity to see them.

Rometra is fun to watch because she kind of reminds me of myself. She's intense, she hustles. And she's an excellent athlete, very fast, a take-charge player on the soccer field. She's also multifaceted like me: she plays the violin and the cello and takes part in the school plays. Her school, Ormondale School, recently put on *The Wizard of Oz*, and Rometra played Dorothy.

Rogdrick is Rogdrick. He's very mischievous and a lot of fun to be around. He's become my good pal. Joe Montana used to be his favorite football player, but I think he's coming around to my side. He would be five years old on the day after Christmas and still wasn't quite sure why his daddy had to spend so much time away from home.

On Saturday, while Rometra's team was in the playoffs, I had to re- port to Santa Clara for our team meetings and a short walk-through. We were scheduled to play Tampa Bay Sunday, and we figured that we'd finally be facing a team we could run on. The Bucs, after getting off to a quick start, had fallen on hard times, losing five of their last six games. They were also in the middle of a quarterback controversy, with coach Ray Perkins benching Vinny Testaverde in favor of Chris Chandler. There's nothing like a quarterback controversy to tear a team apart. We were not concerned about what they might do to us so much as what we might do to ourselves. We had to approach each game like it was a playoff. If we didn't we wouldn't stay undefeated very long.

However, while we'd struggled in past games against some rather mediocre opponents, there was no doubt about this one, right from the git-go. Our pass rush, which had been rather quiet for most of the season, ran a bunch of stunts, constantly harassing Chandler. Testaverde was probably chortling to himself on the sidelines in his clean uniform.

When the Bucs were forced to punt midway through the first quarter, Montana needed just eight plays to move us 64 yards to the end zone. I carried twice on the drive, picking up 12 yards. That drive sort of set the tone for the rest of the afternoon.

Our defensive line was awesome. At a time of year when most defensive linemen are worn down from the constant warfare in the pits, ours had taken their play to another level. Led by Charles Haley, Michael Carter, Kevin Fagan, and Pierce Holt, the line was playing better now than at any time that season.

I rushed for 44 yards on eight carries for a 5.5 yard average, my best of the season, as we won going away, 31–7. Tight end Brent Jones was our main offensive weapon, catching six passes for 74 yards and two touchdowns. I also tied Joe Perry's team record of 50 career rushing touchdowns. That was quite an honor, as Perry is a legend around San Francisco. It was my first touchdown of the season, and it felt as if a big load had been lifted from my shoulders.

This was Thanksgiving week, which meant that we got off a couple hours early on Thursday to be with our families. Pro football doesn't recognize holidays like the real world does. Rain, sleet, or snow, like the postman, we're making our daily rounds. But at least the postman gets Thanksgiving and Christmas and New Year's off. We work right through them. I don't mind working New Year's, though, because that means we're in the playoffs, and that's what playing this game is all about.

On the day before Thanksgiving, a few of the guys in the locker room set some of the rookies up for a few laughs. One of pro football's most storied hoaxes—I believe it's as old as the game itself—is duping the rookies into believing that they're entitled to a free Thanksgiving turkey at a local poultry market.

Usually, someone scrawls the name and address of a market on a chalkboard under the heading of FREE TURKEYS. I was a victim of this locker room scam when I was a rookie, and every year since, one or two rookies, or even more, get taken in.

Teddy Walsh, the 49ers assistant equipment manager, was in charge of perpetuating the turkey tradition on our team. It fit Teddy's personality, because he's kind of a wise-ass prankster anyway, in a nonvindictive sort of way.

Teddy added a few new twists to the prank, collaborating with the manager of a local sandwich shop where the players sometimes bought lunch. He and the sandwich shop manager made up an elaborate letter on company stationery, promising each player a free turkey if he would show up at the eatery and pose for a picture in an Indian headdress. He added that there were a limited number of turkeys and they would be given away on a first-come, first-serve basis. They even doctored a picture of offensive coordinator Mike Holmgren to make it look like he'd posed in an Indian warbonnet and posted it on the shop's bulletin board.

Walsh then distributed the letter to the rookies and sat back and waited for the fun to begin. Dexter Carter was the first player to come off the practice field and read the letter. He hurriedly showered and blew off a reporter who was in on the prank and was trying to stall Carter with questions. "I don't have time to talk now," replied Carter. "I have to hurry over to Togo's to get my picture taken and get my free turkey. This is a great deal—and I don't have a turkey yet for Thanksgiving."

The locker room veterans could hardly contain their guffaws as Dexter ran out the front door and hopped in his car.

But the prank nearly backfired on the store manager, and he called Teddy to tell him he wasn't going to participate in the scheme anymore. It seems that Dennis Brown, our big 300-plus-pound rookie defensive lineman, also fell for the prank. After he had his picture taken in the Indian garb, the manager explained to him that it was all a locker room joke and that there wasn't any turkey.

Brown failed to discover the humor in the explanation and started demanding his turkey. He then ripped up the picture and started to threaten the manager, who in turn phoned Walsh.

Needless to say, Teddy probably will be more careful the next time he pulls the prank, perhaps leaving out those mammoth, ill-tempered defensive linemen. But I hope they keep the tradition. Everyone had a few laughs over it, and it helped ease the locker room tension.

Jerry Rice and his wife Jackie had invited my family and me to their house for Thanksgiving Dinner. Jerry was one of my best friends on the team; I guess I would put him in the same category as Jamie Williams and Tom Rathman. They're like brothers to me. We do things outside of football together. So the Craigs spent the evening at the Rices and had a great time, not to mention a great meal. As Jerry and I gazed around at the smiling faces of our families, we realized we had a lot to be thankful for.

Most of the conversation wasn't about football. It was one of those evenings where you want to forget about the game for a few hours, to laugh and joke, and look at the lighter side of life. There aren't that many times during the course of a season when players can escape the pressure cooker of football, and this was one of them.

But the game did come up once or twice. Jerry was upset because teams were double- and triple-covering him. He said that defenses were taking the fun out of the game. He feels it is necessary for him to have an impact on every game he plays. I pointed out that when he tied up two or three defenders, it left other guys unaccounted for. He agreed, but I could tell he still felt he wasn't meeting the standards he set for himself.

Jerry is one of the classiest receivers in the NFL. I also happen to think that he is the best, and I get very few arguments on that statement. When he first came into the league, he was bashful and had a difficult time communicating with the media. He comes from Crawford, a small town in Mississippi, and attended Mississippi Valley State University, a small black college in Itta Bena. So Jerry led a sheltered existence until he got to the NFL.

He was unhappy with his first agent, an Oakland attorney. He came to me for some guidance, and now we both have the same agent, Jim Steiner. Jerry was beginning to realize his marketing potential and starting to make some commercials. He even modeled some underwear himself, was featured on the cover of *Peninsula* magazine, and now is seen nationally in Nike ads.

Jerry epitomizes the businesslike philosophy of the 49er organization. He quietly goes about his task of rewriting the NFL record book, while less talented receivers on other teams do war dances and have all sorts of celebrations in the end zone after they score a touchdown. But that's not the team's personality, and it's not Jerry's. That kind of styling is for the guys on teams who are staying home during the playoffs.

We were instructed that you have to be sensitive to your opponents' feelings. When Jerry caught those five touchdown passes against Atlanta's Charles Dimry, he didn't dance around the guy or point fingers in his face and taunt him. He very politely handed the ball to the official and trotted to the sidelines. Afterward, Jerry told me that he felt bad for Dimry. He told the media that Dimry just had an off day, and that he was a talented cornerback. Jerry felt he had to have some consideration for his opponent's feelings, and that's the way he is.

We're professionals, and we're taught to approach this wonderful game from a professional perspective. The 49ers had an aura of confidence and class about ourselves, and our emotions didn't require that we strut all of that egotistical stuff. Sometimes when individuals do indulge in that, it incites the other team. It makes them want to take their rivals' heads off, and sometimes they do.

*   *   *

On Friday Jerry and I waddled back to practice after stuffing ourselves with turkey and all the trimmings. We had a critical weekend ahead of us and we had to be ready for the Los Angeles Rams. Many people were referring to them as the "L.A. Lambs," because of their 3–7 record, but they always played us tough at Candlestick Park.

Already, much of the media's focus was on our scheduled Monday night, December 3, showdown with the New York Giants at Candlestick. Both the Giants and ourselves were undefeated going into week twelve, and the media already had concluded that both teams—the Giants would play the Eagles Sunday—were going to emerge unscathed. ABC, which was going to televise the game, was plugging it on their network as "The Titanic," while some of the other media was referring to it as "Super Bowl XXV½." So in addition to having the weekly pressures of trying to keep an unbeaten record intact, now people were trying to force us to go against our better judgment and look ahead, past an archrival who had always given us trouble. But we knew that if we peaked around the corner past that game even a little, we would be looking for trouble.

I honestly believe that Coach Seifert did a good job of keeping us focused on the Rams game. He pointed out that we would become a part of history if we won, and how much that would mean. In addition to keeping alive our chances for an unbeaten season, a victory over the Rams would also set a new NFL standard of nineteen straight victories, going back to the previous season. And we would take a step closer to our first goal for the season, which was to win the NFC West crown. The only team left with a chance of winning it was New Orleans. A win by us and a loss by them in any of the six remaining games would clinch the title for us.

We were constantly reminded by the coaching staff about everything that was at stake Sunday. I call this the danger zone, taking on a hungry team that has nothing to lose and which can make its season by knocking you off. The Rams had been reduced to playing for pride, and if they could beat us it would help ease the pain of not making the playoffs.

We knew they would come ready to play, because they always do. The Rams and 49ers are traditional rivals, like Muhammad Ali and Joe Frazier or Nebraska and Oklahoma. I was born into this rivalry when the 49ers drafted me. Wendell Tyler, a former Ram and my predecessor at running back, used to tell me to keep my head on a swivel when we played the Rams because you never knew what direction the next hit was coming from. Wendell sure knew how to give excellent advice.

I knew I would be pumped up for this game by Sunday morning. These games usually have playoff intensity, and won-lost records don't mean very much. People sometimes ask me if I hate opponents, and I have a difficult time explaining my feelings. I don't think that I've actually hated any person in my life, but before a game, I can hate what an opponent stands for. That's just the nature of this business. Does that make sense? So I guess I have the seeds of hate in my heart, but by the time the game is over all of my negative emotions are strewn all over the field of battle.

The Rams had lost to the Dallas Cowboys the previous week and were the overwhelming underdog. They might have been eliminated from the playoff race, but these were the same guys who played us for the NFC Championship the past January. Their personnel hadn't changed that much, so I could only guess as to why they were having so much trouble. It just goes to show you that it's not that far from the penthouse to the outhouse.

I ran a lot of different plays in practice that week, so it appeared as though we had a good running attack planned. That was fine with me because I was raring to go. The knee was still a little sore, but I felt much stronger than I had since I'd come back. It was going to be a very interesting Sunday.

15. All Good Things Must End

I believe that running the football is a state of mind. Coaches plot elaborate offenses designed to take advantage of another team's defensive weaknesses, and coaches plot elaborate defenses designed to shut down offenses. In a way game plans are a very intricate chess game, each side holding what it believes are keys to unlock the opposition's game plan. Often the matchups lead to temporary stalemates, in which case the game plan undergoes an on-field revision.

Plays do not unfold exactly as they are drawn up on the chalk board. A certain running play might have the guard blocking the outside linebacker. But when the play unfolds on the field, the linebacker might be in a different spot. Or maybe the guard takes one step too many, and overruns the linebacker. Sometimes you run a play four or five times for a minimal or no gain, and then on the sixth time the linemen block whom they are supposed to block and the runner follows the script exactly as he is supposed to, and it goes for big yards.

There aren't really that many new plays in football. NFL teams are still using many of the same plays that Amos Alonzo Stagg and other coaching greats of yesteryear devised. The success and failure of a play depends on when you use it, against what kind of defense, and the talents of your personnel. If you call a deep pass against an all-out blitz, it's not going to work and you might get your quarterback killed. But if you call a sweep or a quick screen to a back against a blitz, chances are it will go for big yardage. Timing is everything in football.

I mentioned earlier that I go over a game plan and visualize myself running through defenses. I make the same cut in my mind over and over so that it's perfect, and then when I'm in that situation in a game,

I automatically know what to do. I've talked with other great backs, like Walter Payton, and they agree with my theory. The art of running is a combination of mental and physical preparation. As a running back, you'd like to see your coaches call a minimum of forty runs per game. Ideally, I would like to run the ball at least twenty to twenty-five times a game. That's not a lot, compared to Jim Brown's thirty to thirty-five carries per game. A running back has got to get into a rhythm. With the 49ers, that was sometimes difficult because they are a passing team. With the Raiders it is also difficult, but for a different reason. Raider Coach Art Shell uses a committee at running back—Marcus Allen, rookie Nick Bell, and myself.

I need at least ten carries before I can even get into the flow of a game. It's really difficult to find your rhythm with only three or four carries. Sometimes coaches will go away from the run early because a couple fail, but I don't agree with that philosophy. You try a run three times and net only a total of five or six yards, but on the fourth attempt, all the pieces fall into place, and it goes for a big gainer of twenty or twenty-five yards. And after that it keeps on clicking.

A coach might get a little impatient and say, "Hey, the running game is not functioning." But it doesn't work that way. You have to get a feel for the defense, figure out which way they're stunting or running their line slants, where their strengths and weaknesses are. A running back out on the field is like a boxer: he has to feel out his opponent before he can go for the knockout.

Earlier in 1990 it had been difficult to run the ball very much because we kept playing teams with eight-man fronts. So we went away from the run and depended almost completely on the pass. But in order to go all the way to the Super Bowl, and to win it, I think you need a running game sooner or later, or else your opponents will just load up their pass rush to tee off on your quarterback.

A running attack also performs another function for the team: in addition to taking the heat off the quarterback, it also builds up the offensive line's confidence. Have you ever seen the wide-angle smile on a wide-bodied offensive lineman after a particularly good run? It speaks for itself. But that year there hadn't been many smiles, mostly just frowns.

Historically, though, the 49ers had been a passing team. Our team's offense was constructed in the image of Bill Walsh, and he is one of the greatest architects of the forward pass that the game has ever known. We led the league in running in 1987 and I set a team record with 1,502 yards rushing in 1988, but those were strictly aberrations, fluke years. If it came down to the final down, the 49ers would always rely on the pass.

I'm not saying that's wrong. Just look at our success ratio. In my eight years with San Francisco, we had never been a run-oriented team. Most of the time we'd had just enough running plays to keep our opponents honest.

But to tell you the truth, it's a frustrating offense for a running back. In 1990 we really didn't work extensively on the running game until after we secured the division title. Most of the offensive line's reps in practice each day were spent on pass-blocking drills.

There was no doubt in my mind that our running game could have improved to the level it was on in 1987 and 1988 if we had practiced running every day as much as we did passing. When the media criticized the team for our lack of a running game, I had to take the heat. The reporters came up to me and asked, "How come you can't run the ball?" Then they wrote that I was not running like I should or that I was too old or that I had lost a step.

I saw other teams' running backs, who weren't nearly as good as I was, carrying the ball twenty-five or thirty times a game and racking up the yardage. So naturally I got frustrated. But I couldn't let it get me down; I had to do what was best for the team.

I don't want to sound selfish. The bottom line is that we were undefeated, so we must have been doing something right. It's just that good running backs thrive on hard work. My all-time favorite, of course, is Walter Payton. Walter would have taken the ball every play if Bears coach Mike Ditka would have let him.

I like to think I pattern myself after Walter. We both set lofty goals and we both have a demanding work ethic. Another back whom I really admire is Walter's successor with the Bears, Neal Anderson. I think he sets the tone for the Chicago offense. He displays team leadership and is a hard worker. Plus he has a big heart and works for everything he gets.

He reminds me a lot of Payton, as far as running, blocking, and catching the ball. He's the complete back, and I think that he's a lot like me.

Another runner I think has plenty of talent is Tampa Bay's Gary Anderson. He also is an all-around back. It must be something in the name. He has really quick legs, and the moves he puts on guys are unreal. Gary reminds me of Gale Sayers. I never saw Sayers play—I was only five years old when he made rookie of the year for the Chicago Bears—but I've seen the films. He set twenty-three team records and seven NFL records during his seven-year tenure. Anderson is one of the most underrated backs in the league. Tampa Bay doesn't use him enough. If a team has an outstanding runner, then it should flaunt him.

Lots of people thought that former Raider Bo Jackson was the best running back in the league before he suffered his football career–ending hip injury. He got a lot of publicity, but I couldn't really rate him with the top backs. He came into the league every year when people were tired and already had eight games in. He came in with fresh football legs, and he hadn't taken a pounding, so it's really hard to say that he was one of the truly great ones.

Bo had a lot of talent. I'm not taking that away from him. But as far as being a full, complete running back, one who ran, caught, and blocked, I can't say that. Maybe it's because he's played two professional sports. Personally, I think that Marcus Allen is a better running back. Marcus runs extremely well, and I know that he can catch and block.

My opinions aside, we had the Los Angeles Rams coming into town in week twelve and I was excited because it finally looked like my frustrating afternoons would be at an end. The Rams had lost seven of their ten games, and the media said they were a team in disarray. Their coach, John Robinson, reportedly was on the hot seat, and some of the guys were starting to point fingers at each other. When the finger pointing starts on a team, that's usually the beginning of the end.

We put the game plan in on Wednesday, and there were lots of running plays. Lots of them. Our coaches felt that we could run on the Rams 3–4 defense, and I certainly wasn't going to argue.

As you can imagine, I was really excited going into this game. My knee was getting better by the hour, maybe even by the minute, and I was anxious to break loose for a big game and silence my critics, who were a growing crowd by now.

Sunday was one of those gloomy days, overcast and cool with ominous dark clouds. I remember thinking as I drove to the stadium that I hoped it wouldn't rain, because I wanted our running game to click. Not that I can't run on a wet field; it's just that the offensive linemen have better footing when the field is dry.

I felt pretty good warming up. My knee seemed looser than it had been, and I was excited because I knew that we had a lot of running plays in the game plan.

Our first series should have been taken as an omen. We gained nine yards on the first play and then, on second and one, we called two passes to the flat. Both were incomplete, and we ended up punting. Then the rains started to come, and the next twenty minutes were a nightmare. Tom Rathman fumbled, Jerry Rice fumbled, Joe Montana threw an interception. And when it was our turn to catch a break, the ball bounced the other way. On a third-down play Dave Waymer, who was filling in for Chet Brooks at strong safety, grabbed at an errant Jim Everett pass only to have the interception bounce out of his hands and into the hands of Flipper Anderson, who ran it for an eighteen-yard gain, keeping the Rams' drive alive. They scored three plays later to take a 14–0 lead.

I believe that the Rams outsmarted us in this one, both the 49er players and the coaching staff. They came out with a Navajo defense, a variation of Chicago 46 defense with an eight-man front, which is virtually impossible to run against. Then, as soon as they had us in the catch-up position, they switched to the nickel defense and dared us to run. The nickel features five or six defensive backs, usually playing a zone, and is designed to stop a team's passing attack. However, because the extra defensive backs replace linebackers, that type of defense is somewhat vulnerable to the run.

Unfortunately, for whatever reason, our coaching staff chose not to go back to the run. Even in the third quarter when we rallied and seemed to have the momentum, closing the gap to 21–17, our running game stayed in the garage. Of the sixty-seven plays we ran, only seventeen were designed runs. Two others were scrambles by Joe when he got in trouble. Now, for a team that was expected to run, seventeen running plays for an entire game isn't very much.

It rained throughout much of the game, but we couldn't use that as an excuse; it was just as wet on the Rams' side of the ball as it was on ours. We didn't execute well enough and made a lot of errors. If you have that many breakdowns, you're not going to win many ballgames. Even my reliable buddy Rathman couldn't hold on to the ball, fumbling for only the second time in three years. Ironically, the other one was against the Rams the previous season in their 13–12 win at Candlestick.

We went into the locker room at halftime trailing 21–7. Now, there was nothing unusual about us being behind at the half: we'd trailed at halftime in five of our previous ten games that season. But this one seemed different. We were making the errors, and we were the team, not the Rams, that seemed disorganized.

But we didn't panic. We talked about regrouping, and coaches Mike Holmgren and Bobb McKittrick went over the blocking assignments with the offensive line. The Rams were mixing up their defenses pretty well.

During the week we had prepared exclusively for the Rams' 3–4 defense, and now they were completely throwing us off with different fronts. They brought those two linebackers up and ran a lot of line stunts that we didn't expect. I have to admit they fooled us, and they fooled our coaching staff. They got the big plays when they needed them, and we didn't.

We told ourselves to regroup for the second half, and we came out strong, closing the gap to 21–17. It appeared that we had the momentum, and that Joe was going to rally us from the hole the way he usually did.

The most painful part of the game, and probably of our whole season, was the fourth quarter. We were poised to take the initiative, but it never happened. The Rams took over on their own 10 yard line just after the start of the fourth quarter. A penalty put them back on the 5, and it looked as if we were going to have good field position once we forced them to kick.

We were real excited on the sideline. We figured that our defense would hold them, we'd get the ball back, and then we'd march right down the field for the winning score. That formula had worked for us five times already during the 1990 season, and there was no doubt in our minds that all we had to do was get the ball in Joe Montana's hands.

But we kept waiting and waiting and waiting. The Rams offense kept moving and moving and moving, taking a yard here and two yards there and eight yards somewhere else. Whatever it took to get a first down and keep a drive going, they did. Hell, they reminded me of us. I can't ever recall a game where I was more frustrated.

Their offense held on to the ball for nearly eleven minutes. That's practically the entire fourth quarter. I couldn't believe that they could have possession that long. I thought our offense would get back on the field at least a couple more times, but by the time we got the ball back, it was filthy with Rams' fingerprints, and the milk cows had gone back to the barn. The shadows were ready to take over the stadium, and personally I was looking for a nice large one to slip behind.

The NFL record we had coveted so much, winning nineteen straight games, had literally slipped through our hands, as had the once-in-a-lifetime opportunity to put together an undefeated season. I heard they were cheering in Miami because Don Shula's 1972 team is the only one to make it through an entire season unscathed.

But it wasn't like they whipped us. We committed six turnovers and bumbled around the field like a bunch of sleepwalkers. I don't care how good a team you are, when you turn the ball over to the opposition that many times, you might as well go home and turn out the lights.

In the locker room afterward, the media tried to make us admit that we were looking ahead to the Giants. They kept asking me why we didn't run against L.A.'s nickel defense. To tell you the truth, that was exactly the question I was asking myself. They also wanted to know why we kept getting off to a slow start. In our eleven games that season we had scored only 27 points in the first quarter and found ourselves in an early hole almost every game. I told them that no team is going to lie down for us, just so we could score some early points. It's not like teams say, "Okay, we want the 49ers to score a ton of points in the first quarter." It would be nice to get off to a fast start, but it always doesn't work that way.

But let me make this clear; we did not overlook Los Angeles. The

Rams go to war with the 49ers two times every year. We knew them and they knew us as well as any two teams in the league knew each other. I don't know why it is, but they always played us well in Candlestick Park. They did an outstanding job of controlling the ball. They displayed that they had character, just the way we did.

The game against New York didn't even cross our minds, other than that we knew they were no longer undefeated when we took the field. The fact that they lost to Philadelphia, 31–13, should have served to motivate us. It's like the Rams had some kind of voodoo working against us at Candlestick Park.

We hadn't lost in such a long time, not since week eleven of the 1989 season, that it was a strange feeling. It really hurt inside, like someone close to us had died. I know that sounds silly, but we had built up so much confidence in ourselves that a loss had been pushed out of the realm of possibility. But as much as it hurt, I knew we could build on the experience. The true test of any football team is how it reacts following a loss. So it was vital that we understood the lesson, put it behind us, and put together a good week of practice the following week.

I had committed myself to do a guest appearance on *Sports Final* that night, a local sports news show featuring KRON's Gary Radnich. I'd figured that we would win the game, and that I would regale the television audience with my expertise on how invincible the 49ers were, maybe even discuss my first hundred-yard game of the season. Now I was left with the commitment, when all I wanted to do was go home and go to bed.

But I don't think it's very nice when you tell someone you will help them out and then you don't show up, so I told Dave Guingona, the producer, that I would be at the studio to tape the show around six thirty. By the time I got there I was in a little better mood, but something was still bothering me.

Gary and I talked about the game, he showed some highlights, and I made some inane comments. We laughed and told a few funnies, but to tell you the truth my heart really wasn't in it. After the taping, I took Vernessia and Rogdrick to have some pizza in the city. Then we went home and I stayed up until eleven thirty that night to watch the TV show. I wanted to see if my disappointment showed through as much as I thought it might. Fortunately, it didn't.

I tried to close my eyes and get some sleep. My left hip was burning. For the third time that season, I had taken a helmet on my hip, and it was really hurting. But that wasn't what was keeping me awake. I kept going over our game plan, and I kept wondering what had happened to those running plays. I'm not a complainer, but the reason we hadn't established a running game was because we didn't try to.

Naturally, Monday's newspapers focused on the fact that we didn't have a running game, and that old Roger Craig had lost a step. It was beginning to piss me off. The thing that frustrates me the most is when people say negative things about me when I'm hurt. I had a bad knee and I had a chronic hip pointer, and neither made me run better. So criticize me when I'm healthy, don't criticize me when I'm hurt. I'm a different back when I have all of the elements working for me. It's kind of difficult to develop a rhythm when you run two or three plays and then sit out two or three series. But you have to keep a positive attitude in this game. If you don't, you might as well call it a day.

My hip felt much better after treatment Monday afternoon; Tuesday was our day off, and I got some more treatment. This was the week that everyone had been waiting for, and I was trying to keep a low profile around town. I wanted to be totally focused on the Giants, without any distractions.

Of course, the more you plan something the worse it turns out. I was trying to keep interviews at a minimum, but I had promised one of our regular writers, Mike Silver of *The Santa Rosa Press-Democrat,* that I would give him five minutes.

Mike asked me how the team could improve its running game, and I guess that I was just tired of making excuses. So I told him that we needed to exercise the run more. I said that we couldn't expect to have a running game if we only ran sixteen or seventeen times a game. I told him that a running back gets cold sitting on the sidelines, and suggested that we go back to the two-back offense of Tom Rathman and myself. I noted that bringing different guys in and out the whole game hurt the team.

I told Silver that evidently the running game wasn't a big deal with the organization, or you would've seen Tom and me in there all the time. I guess I could have stopped there, but I didn't. Things I had been thinking privately for some time now were bubbling to the surface. "You wonder what they, the coaches, really want," I said to Silver. I wanted to help the team get its running game untracked, but I couldn't do it on the sidelines, and I couldn't do it running in and out of the game like some messenger.

Silver asked me about the Rams' nickel defense, and I told him that I thought we should have exploited it more. I told him that I thought I could have run for a hundred yards against the Rams. I'd gotten off to a good start, I was feeling warm and I was getting into a rhythm, when boom, they pulled me out. You can only do so much and then it's out of your control. I also thought I could have run for a hundred yards against Tampa Bay the previous week.

But I pointed out that if the bottom line is winning football games, then the coaches have to do what is best for the team. And the best way for that is to use everybody. And we were winning our division, so the coaches must know what they were doing.

I felt much better after I vented my frustrations. I thought about what I said, but I didn't think there would be any repercussions. Santa Rosa is a sleepy little town about forty miles north of the Bay Area, and I didn't figure any of the coaches read *The Press-Democrat.*

But how was I supposed to know that *The New York Times* owned the paper? The *Times* copyrighted the story and sent it out on its wire to all of their subscribers around the country. When I came off the field Friday afternoon, I was confronted with dozens of inquisitors wanting to know how I felt about the running game and the coaching staff. Because this was the week we prepared for our big showdown with the Giants, our training camp was crawling with national media. Chris Berman of ESPN watched our practice Friday, and Cris Collinsworth of HBO had been there earlier in the week.

A distraction over the running game was the last thing I needed during what had been one of my most focused weeks of the season. But things were starting to cloud up quickly. First there was my health. No, not my knee; that was getting stronger, and I found that I didn't have to wear the runner support anymore. It was my right hip that was really bothering me. The hip pointer I'd gotten the first week of the season against New Orleans had never quite cleared up. When it had just about healed, I would get hit there again. I got hit on the hip in the Tampa Bay game and again Sunday against the Rams.

I had this burning sensation that ran down my hip, and Dr. Dillingham said I had probably damaged the nerve called the hip flexor. It's really delicate, and experience told me that it wouldn't get any better until the season was over and I had a chance to rest it.

So in addition to the injury, now I had started a controversy over the running game. But I had made those statements, and now I had to stand by them. I told the media that, yes, I did say those things, and that I really wasn't complaining as much as I was venting off steam.

I had been frustrated by my injuries and frustrated about the way I was playing and frustrated about not getting the opportunity to run the ball more. I told them that I was just doing what the coaches told me to do. I would like to play every play, but we had to do what's best for the team. We couldn't do what was best for Roger Craig or worry about what he's thinking.

I felt like I was ready explode in a game, and that the coaches were holding me back. Once I got that first hundred-yard game, it would break the ice, and we could establish a rhythm with our running game.

And I wasn't the only one being affected by the criticism of the running game; the offensive linemen were also suffering because of it.

They were losing their confidence, just as I was. I don't think the coaching staff really understood what the running game meant to me and the linemen. By not utilizing the run, it was like they were taking something away from us. It was something we longed for, something we took pride in.

Mike Holmgren is a great offensive coach, and a great disciple of Bill Walsh football. I knew that he leaned heavily on the pass, because that's what he did as an assistant at Brigham Young, where they threw the ball fifty times a game. But he was looking for some kind of miracle from the running game, and it wasn't going to come unless we ran the ball more during practice and during the game. It wasn't going to happen until we got into a rhythm, and we really hadn't had much continuity, as we'd had the season before with Tom and me running the two-back offense.

I also knew that when you force the pass, sooner or later you're going to make mistakes. If teams had to respect our run, some of the defensive pressure would be taken off Joe. I think everyone agreed that we needed a viable running game by the time we reached the playoffs.

I managed to duck most of the media by doing a promotional spot for a pilot for a music video show. A friend, Dave Wilson, asked me if we could tape it at lunchtime, and I said yes. With all of the hype about the game going on, and with the media chasing after me now to confirm the Santa Rosa story, I welcomed the chance to escape the limelight for an hour or so.

That night we had a late team meeting. George was really taking this game seriously, and he had us go over every detail of our game plan. I hadn't run much that day, so I really felt fresh. After the meeting I hurried home and had a nice dinner with the family, took a nice, long time in the Jacuzzi, and then had Vernessia give me a massage. My body felt completely relaxed. Even the hip felt a lot better than it had.

I was ready to rock n' roll. I felt this game was going to be bigger than an earthquake. I was already getting keyed up, and it was only Friday night. Saturday we'd have a short walk-through and some meetings, and then Sunday we'd meet at our hotel in Burlingame and bus up to Candlestick Park for some practice under the lights. Then it was back to the hotel and, we hoped, a good night's sleep. But I was getting antsy. I knew I was going to have a difficult time sleeping Sunday night. Damn those Monday night games.

Pregame introductions tell you a lot. I don't know if you study them, but I do. First there is the crowd. If they are primed, there is a sense of electricity in the air, and you can feel the energy as a player. And if they are blasé and rather subdued, you can feel that also.

This crowd was really stoked. They were ready for some Monday

Night Football. They were already roaring during the pregame warm-ups, and I could feel that energy creeping into our locker room. Of course, the media had done its part by ballyhooing the game as the ultimate showdown between the NFL's two powerhouses.

I carried the ball only nine times for 21 yards, but we won the game 7–3. Now, I could look at this two ways. I could sulk and point to the fact that while I only got to carry the ball nine times, Dexter Carter carried it twelve times. I could stand in the corner next to my locker and pout, and bemoan the fact that I was virtually excluded from the game plan.

Or I could bask in the warm afterglow of a team victory. I could point to the fact that my third-down pass reception was the key play in our only scoring drive. We had third and six at our own 41 yard line, and I ran a delayed slant out of the backfield. Joe saw me and threw about a four-yard pass, and I took off crossfield, picking up blockers as I angled toward the left sideline. By the time Giants safety Greg Jackson ran me down, I had gained 31 yards to New York's 28. I then gained five more yards on a sweep, and then Joe passed 23 yards to John Taylor, who made a sliding grab in the end zone. And those were all the points that we needed as we also wrapped up our fifth consecutive NFC West title with four games still remaining.

Or I could shower, dress quickly, and slip out the side door without saying anything. This night belonged to our defense—actually both defenses—and I didn't want to say anything to take the spotlight away from them.

So I chose the latter course. By the time the media horde had descended on the locker room I was halfway to my car in the parking lot. The defense deserved every accolade it received. When the game was over, a record crowd of 66,413 stood and chanted "Defense, defense, defense," over and over again.

The Giants had come into the game with a reputation as a running team, and our defense limited their rushing game to just 75 yards. Phil Simms is known as a resourceful quarterback who takes what a defense gives him, but ours didn't give him much, and he finished with just 14 completions out of 32 attempts for 153 yards. All told, our defense limited the Giants to just 221 net yards.

Of course, their defense played nearly as flawlessly. We were only able to get 240 net yards against them, but 88 of those were rushing yards. Coach Seifert also tossed a few words of praise toward the running game, saying that we "ran the ball effectively and got the yardage when it counted." He was referring to our final possession, when we ran the ball the last seven plays.

I couldn't believe what some of the writers and electronic journalists had to say about the game. Many of them referred to it as "boring."

One columnist, who should have known better, said that our offense "was in a stupor." Even Dan Rather remarked on his national radio show that the game was a dud and that college games were much more exciting. Now you tell me, what does Dan Rather know about professional football to pass that kind of judgment? I guess he forgot that the Giants brought one of the best defenses in the NFL into Candlestick with them.

To me, it was an exciting game. It was one of those occasions when I would have loved to have been a fan. There was drama and high emotion on every play. I know that the true football fan understood what a classic matchup it turned out to be and knew it could very well be a preview of the NFC Championship Game. Either way, neither team deserved to be the loser in that one.

There wasn't very much time to savor the fruits of our labors. When we came back to work Wednesday, we only had three days in which to prepare for the Cincinnati Bengals, our Super Bowl archrivals. Our schedule called for us to work out briefly Friday afternoon and then head to the San Francisco airport for a five o'clock charter to Cincinnati.

We were on the road again, where we hadn't lost a regular-season game since November 6, 1988, when we'd been beaten by the Cardinals, in Tempe, Arizona. So in addition to our cold-weather gear we packed our ongoing NFL record of fifteen straight road victories. If you count the 1988 NFC title game in Chicago, Super Bowl XXIII, our 1989 postearthquake game played at Stanford, and Super Bowl XXIV, we had won nineteen straight games away from our Candlestick Park home.

The Giants game turned out to be a very expensive victory, though. Safety Ronnie Lott, our defensive leader and one of the major binding forces on the team, suffered two sprained knees in the game and was on crutches when we had our team meeting Wednesday. The irony is that his left knee, which was the worse one, was injured when he was standing next to a pile of players and teammate Kevin Fagan dived in and his helmet hit Ronnie's knee. Sort of like the jet pilot who flies a suicide mission and then gets run over by a Jeep back at the base.

Ronnie's injury made about as much sense as that. He is a team leader who leads by example. Every time he moves in for a tackle, he sacrifices part of his body. I don't think there has ever been another defensive player in all of football who plays with as much intensity as Lott.

One year he got his finger caught in an opposing player's face mask, and he ripped all the tendons in the finger and kind of mangled the bone. The doctors said they could repair the finger, but that the rehabilitation would take most of the season. Ronnie asked them what plan

B was, and they told him they could amputate the tip of his finger and he would be playing in two weeks. It didn't take him long to make up his mind—cut the fingertip off and get him back on the field.

Ronnie truly loves the game, and I imagine it will be very difficult for him to walk away from it when the time comes. He's already starting to show the wear and tear of eleven years of throwing his body around the field with complete abandon. The 49ers were certain that 1991 would be his last, or else they wouldn't have let him get away. But he had an outstanding season for the Raiders and led the NFL in interceptions for the second time in his career.

Going into the 1990 season with San Francisco, Ronnie said he wanted to play two more seasons. But after having such a sensational 1991 season with the Raiders, I don't know if he will want to make this one his last. His intensity really brought the Raiders secondary to new heights.

I always figured Ronnie would be a 49er to the end, just like I figured I would be. His name is synonymous with the success of that team. But I'm glad I'm still on the same team with him. I certainly wouldn't want to be playing across the line of scrimmage from him, not the way he hits.

He is a throwback to the old-time players who played the game for fun. The only agents they knew about were in the FBI. In a way, he's a lot like Hacksaw Reynolds was. No matter what the uniform, as with all great players who play the game with unbridled passion, they will have to drag Ronnie out of the locker room kicking and screaming when his time to leave the game comes.

Down the home stretch of the 1990 season we were going to miss Ronnie's presence on the field. Our defensive backfield had suffered a rash of injuries that season, and Lott was constantly quarterbacking new players like Dave Waymer who were filling in. Ronnie's departure meant that both of our safeties were out. Chet Brooks, who injured his knee in the Dallas game, had recently undergone arthroscopic surgery and his return before the season's end was questionable. Waymer, who had been filling in for Brooks, would move to Lott's spot at free safety, and Johnnie Jackson would come off the bench to fill Brooks's spot. But they both knew they were only minding the store for Ronnie, because he would find a way to get himself back in the starting lineup.

It was nippy in Cincinnati, and the smells and sounds of Christmas were in the air. It reminded me a lot of childhood Christmases at home in Iowa. Cincinnati is a typical Midwest city, and everywhere bundled-up people with smiles and bright faces were carrying Christmas packages. There was an outdoor ice rink right around the corner from our hotel, and there were skaters and children caroling. It gave me a very warm feeling. I guess that's why I love Christmastime, and the winter setting in Cincinnati really put me in the Christmas mood.

We had already sewed up the NFC West title and were on the verge of securing the home-field advantage for the playoffs. The Bengals had been an in-and-out team in 1990, at times dominating and at other times struggling.

When I awoke Sunday morning I had that edgy sensation that I usually get when I'm going to have a good day. My knee and hip felt pretty good, considering that they had taken quite a battering that season. I left for the stadium in the first bus because I couldn't stand sitting around my hotel room any longer. I wanted to get taped and get out on the field to start warming up.

Our game plan that week included a lot of running plays, but I figured I'd have to wait and see how many we actually used in the game. I had been in the same situation before and gotten my hopes up only to be let down. But they weren't kidding this time. I carried the ball twenty-one times, and even buddy Tom Rathman got it for twelve carries. It was the old two-back 49er offense, and he and I ultimately combined for 150 yards.

Mike Cofer kicked a 23-yard field goal with fifty-seven seconds left to tie the game at 17 all and send it into overtime. We won the overtime toss on a heads-up call by Spencer Tillman, our special teams captain for the day. Spencer called tails, and that's what it came up. He told us that he'd called tails on about nine other occasions, and every time but one it had come up tails. Hey, if that's what Spencer believed in—and it works—then I believed in it too. Tails it was from then on out.

We received the kick, marched downfield to the Bengals 6, called in Cofer for one more 23-yard kick, and went home with a 20–17 win. I gained 97 yards and would easily have topped the century mark for the first time that season had not one of my better runs been called back because of a penalty. All in all I considered it a very good day.

On the flight home, I leaned over to guard Guy McIntyre and kidded him that he looked a little skinny. I told him even though I hadn't gotten my hundred yards, 97 was close enough and that he should spread the word to the rest of the offensive line that I was taking them to dinner Tuesday night. The guys up front had made up their mind to get the job done, and we ended up running for more yards (202) than we gained passing (170).

I felt vindicated to a certain extent, because we stayed with our running game instead of switching to the pass. If you stay with the run enough times, you're going to have success sooner or later. I'm not saying that I specialize in telling coaches what to do, but in this case I think my point had been proved: the 49ers had a running game if we put our minds to it.

A lot of the credit for our rejuvenated ground game had to go to line coach Bobb McKittrick. Early in the game, the Bengals kept moving David Grant, their defensive tackle, down in the gap just before the snap, which made it difficult for Bubba Paris to block him. One time the guy came through untouched and nailed me in the backfield right after I took the handoff. We were lucky that he didn't get the handoff before I did. At halftime McKittrick made some adjustments on the offensive line, and I never saw the tackle again. Bobb is great at making adjustments; he's like a quarterback calling an audible.

Even though we won and were now 12–1, our critics were still dogging us. They said that we were lucky to get out of Cincinnati with a victory, and that we'd have to play a lot better if we expected to be a force in the playoffs.

I suppose you could've looked at it that way, but that's not the way I saw it. We were winners. We were used to winning, and I think that's what makes the difference in the close games. Our team had character, which had been constructed on a winning foundation. There were a lot of guys on that team who didn't know how to lose and would fight to the end. Good teams sometimes fold when the pressure increases, but great teams fight right through it and win. Great teams win the tough games.

Unfortunately, I got my knee twisted again in overtime, and it had swelled up by the time we got home. I knew that it would bother me until the season was over, I knew that I would have to fight through the pain. But that's part of football.

Tuesday was the players' day off, and I usually taped my *Evening Magazine* segment and tended to other business, but this Tuesday I drove to Berkeley to see John Steinke, who is an acupuncturist. I had been seeing him on and off for nearly six years, and I wasn't the only player who visited him. Ronnie, Darryl Pollard, Pierce Holt, and Charles Haley also went to him from time to time. What he did was stick needles in me to open up the nerve endings, which promoted quicker healing.

I beat the rush hour traffic back across the Bay Bridge, made a brief stop at home to change my clothes, and headed for the Sports City Cafe in Cupertino, a restaurant I still share ownership in with Ronnie, Keena Turner, Eric Wright, and former defensive back Carlton Williamson. I wanted to look spiffy when I greeted my offensive line at the door and escorted them to the table for the meal I'd promised them.

I was really looking forward to this dinner. It seemed like ages since I had hosted the line. Frank Pollack and some of the other new guys had never had a teammate take them to dinner like this. I told them to order whatever they wanted, though I had second thoughts about Bubba's order. Bubba likes to eat, and when you say order anything, he takes that to mean one of every item on the menu.

The offensive linemen enjoyed the attention and recognition because about the only time they're singled out on the field is when they get called for a penalty. Other than that, they toil in relative anonymity. But they gave their all for Joe and us running backs, so taking them to dinner was like having a big family get-together.

They were as maligned as the running backs when our running game didn't work, but believe me, we had some talented linemen. Left guard Guy McIntyre, who made the Pro Bowl for the second straight year in 1990, used to block for Herschel Walker at Georgia. Right tackle Steve Wallace blocked for Bo Jackson at Auburn.

Harris Barton had moved from right tackle to right guard that year, and it took a while for him to get acclimated to his new position, which might have accounted for our running game's slow start. But Harris is a great technician and he has great position when he gets on top of a defensive player. I think if we had utilized Harris more on pulling plays he would have been one of the most devastating run blockers in the NFL.

Center Jesse Sapolu is steady, but I think he is more of a guard than a center. He's a great cut blocker, very quick, with great pulling ability. I don't think that he was real comfortable at center. He's not the prototype center that Randy Cross was, but Jesse was getting better every week. I don't know what his feelings were, but he didn't have much choice in the matter.

Bubba Paris, our left tackle, had teetered on the brink of Pro Bowl status every year. Bubba was a massive talent and he used his weight to his advantage when blocking people, and eventually wore them out. However, after a particularly brilliant game against a Pro Bowl defensive end like Reggie White, he would play mediocrely against a lesser opponent. Eventually he also wore out his welcome with the San Francisco coaches because he couldn't meet a 326-pound weight requirement at the start of that team's 1991 season. Bubba was picked by Indianapolis, but they released him with three weeks left in the season. He finished the 1991 season on the roster of the Detroit Lions. The irony here is that the Lions made the NFL playoffs and the 49ers didn't.

Critics used to point to the San Francisco offensive line as being the weak link, but if that was true why had we been first or second in total offense nearly every year? They must have been doing something right.

One of the criticisms against the 49er offensive linemen was that they cut blocked, which means that they'd roll up at an opposing player's legs. But contrary to popular belief, that is not illegal. The name of the game is to put people on their backs, and that's what our line tried to do. Many of their runs are designed around that type of block.

I tried to let the offensive line know that I cared about them. One year I bought them all Browning automatic shotguns for Christmas, a collector's limited edition with suitable inscriptions. The shotguns cost me $12,000, but that is really a small token of my appreciation when you realize how much easier they made my job.

I always try to build up a positive rapport with my linemen because I believe that it's necessary for our team's success. If they have confidence in my running ability and know that I care and appreciate them, then we're going to function better as a team.

It's like when you're kids and you form a club, and you and your little mates pierce your fingers and press them together. The intermingling of blood is supposed to bond you for life. That's the way I felt about my offensive line at San Francisco, and the way I still feel about them. I have a new line blocking for me now, and I feel the same way about my Raider linemates. There's a special bond between a running back and his offensive line.

So we had a nice dinner, swapped a few stories and had a few laughs, the way any brothers would do. The bill was a little more than $400, which was pretty reasonable considering how big our linemen were.

◆
16. The Pursuit of the Dream

Everyone would like to leave an imprint on history, whether it be with a work of art, a book, or a significant contribution to humanity. Something that people will remember you by.

Football players are no different than anyone else, only our vehicle for immortality is the playing field, that hundred-yard by fifty-yard patch of grass where we are judged by what we do and what we don't do—today. If we don't do well right now, we can be certain that our jury will issue forth a chorus of boos.

Football players are always in a hurry-up mode because we have so precious little time to make our mark on history. Our athletic prowess is with us for only a brief, fleeting moment and then it's gone, like a soft summer breeze. I think the average career expectancy for a pro football player is just a shade more than 3.3 years.

The San Francisco 49ers were poised on the brink of making professional sports history. They had won back-to-back Super Bowls, and it appeared that they might have a chance to make a third straight world championship. No team had ever won three Super Bowls in a row—not the Green Bay Packers, not the Cleveland Browns, not the Miami Dolphins, not the Pittsburgh Steelers. No one.

If we could become the team to represent the National Football Conference in Tampa in January, and emerge victorious, it would be the closest we players would ever come to immortality. Time would have stood still for us and it would have given future generations of champions a benchmark to strive for.

The team that came the closest to accomplishing that feat is the Packers under Vince Lombardi; only bad timing prevented them. The

179

1965 Green Bay team defeated the Cleveland Browns 28–12 for the NFL championship, but unfortunately for the Packers, former NFL commissioner Pete Rozelle didn't think up the Super Bowl until the following year. The 1966 Packers beat the Kansas City Chiefs 35–10 in Super Bowl I and then repeated the following season in Super Bowl II with a 33–14 thrashing of the Oakland Raiders.

Miami won the Super Bowl in 1972 and 1973, and Pittsburgh won back-to-back Super Bowls twice, in 1974 and 1975 and in 1978 and 1979. The 49ers joined that elite group on January 28, 1990, with our 55–10 win over Denver in Super Bowl XXIV.

The Dolphins' bid in 1974 to win their third straight world championship was short-circuited in the first round of the playoffs by my new team, the Raiders. Clarence Davis's last-second catch of a desperation throw by Kenny Stabler gave the host Raiders a 28–26 victory. The Raiders also spoiled the Steelers' plans for a Three-peat in the 1976 AFC Championship Game with a 24–7 win over Pittsburgh. The Steelers' second try for three straight Super Bowl victories never got off the ground, as they finished the 1980 season with a 9–7 record and failed to reach the playoffs.

As we approached the 1990 playoffs, I looked back on our season, and all I saw was a momentous struggle. It was like we were a marked team, and I'm not just talking about my injury or our opponents. There were opposing owners who construed Eddie DeBartolo's generosity toward his players as arrogance. They were upset because he flew the team to Kauai in June of 1990 for our Super Bowl ring ceremony. No other team had ever had a free five-day Hawaiian vacation accompany its Super Bowl ring ceremony. So the other owners were motivated to do something to keep Eddie in line, and the best way to do that was to keep us from going to the Super Bowl again.

Then there was our team itself. Sometimes success breeds contempt among players, and we become our own worst enemy. Different people handle success in different ways. We had to guard against becoming complacent and to keep reminding ourselves how much dedication and hard work it had taken to get where we were.

Those were the factors we were up against as we looked forward to the playoffs. The guys we lined up against also didn't like the idea of us having a monopoly on the Vince Lombardi Trophy. Hell, they were getting tired of watching Pete Rozelle hand it to us. The opposing players also were aware of all of the perks we got from management, and I'm sure that it rankled many of them.

So the 49ers knew going into the season that nobody was going to step aside for us just because we were the two-time defending Super Bowl champions. For some of the lesser teams in the throes of rebuilding programs, a victory over the San Francisco 49ers would make their season and possibly even save some coach's job. And if some team should knock us out of the running for a third straight title, and then go on to win the Super Bowl, I'm sure that that coach could write his own ticket. Why, he could even become a television analyst for some seven-figure salary.

But until they blew the whistle for the opening kickoff in Super Bowl XXV, we were the defending champions, and we would remain the defending champions until the final whistle of that silver anniversary game.

We closed out our season with a 13–10 loss to New Orleans at Candlestick and a 20–17 victory over Minnesota in the Metrodome on December 30. How cold was it in Minnesota on December 29? It was so cold that I didn't leave my room after we came back from practice. I thought my lungs would freeze up if I did. I didn't play in either of those games, as I had injured my knee in the first half of our 26–10 victory over the Rams in Los Angeles in our second meeting on December 11. Actually, I hurt it the previous week against Cincinnati, but I didn't say anything because I wanted to play against the Rams. The night before the Rams game, the knee was really throbbing.

In that game, I became the 49ers all-time leading receiver with 508 catches, eclipsing former leader Dwight Clark's mark of 506 catches. Jerry Rice entered the 1991 season as the team's third all-time receiver with 446 catches. So it was only a matter of time before he replaced me in the team record book. His first catch in San Francisco's 24–22 win over Seattle on December 8, 1991 gave him 509 catches, and counting. If someone has to beat me, I'm glad it's J.R.

Fourth on the all-time list is Billy Wilson, who currently is a scout for San Francisco. Wilson, who played for the 49ers from 1951 through 1960, had 407 catches for 5,902 yards and 49 touchdowns. I think his is a very significant record because he set it in the days of the 49ers' fabled "million-dollar backfield"—Hugh McElhenny, Joe Perry, and John Henry Johnson—when the team was predominantly a running team. Also, he did it when there were only twelve and fourteen league games. Billy is an extremely popular member of the 49er family, and one of its most loyal. He recently waged what looks like a successful battle against cancer, which curtailed his scouting activities for a while. But he's back on the road, thrashing the bushes for future Jerry Rices and Roger Craigs.

Because we defeated the Vikings again, and with relative ease, we were rewarded with a bye in the first round of the playoffs. We had a league-best regular-season mark of 14–2, which meant that everyone had to come to us. Football on the road would be but a memory this time around.

We knew we would be facing either the Philadelphia Eagles or the

Washington Redskins first. People think that ballplayers have a prefer-
ence when they reach this level, but most really don't. Whichever team
we faced would be tough, because every team that makes it to the
playoffs turns it up a notch. We had already beaten the Redskins 26–13
in the second game of the regular season, so I guess if we'd been able
to make a choice we would have chosen them.

But there was something about beating the Eagles and Buddy Ryan
that gave us a certain amount of satisfaction. I think that Joe enjoyed
showing up Eagle quarterback Randall Cunningham because the eastern press made such a big deal out of him. But other than that, we
were just happy to be in the playoffs again.

As it was, the Redskins defeated the Eagles, and headed out to Candlestick Park to play the two-time defending Super Bowl champions.
Right away, the oddsmakers made us the favorites by a solid touchdown. After all, it was Joe Montana versus Mark Rypien.

I didn't tell anyone, but the extra week off was a godsend to me. My
knee began to perk up, and after missing the last two games, I knew
that I would be able to make a contribution in this game.

Although I was still taking therapy for the injury, I was getting a little
rambunctious in practice. I could sense my knee getting stronger, and
the frustrations of a mediocre season were starting to surface. By the
Wednesday before the game, I was starting to stretch my practice runs
out to fifty yards. I would zip past the line of scrimmage and just keep
going. I also was getting my patented high-step back again.

If I run all of the plays out in practice I create a rhythm, and it is
something I can carry over into the game. Because I hadn't been playing, I felt sort of obligated to prove myself to my teammates. After all,
I was one of the team leaders, and I was supposed to lead by example.
That helps acclimate the younger players. But when you're sitting on
the bench, you can't help acclimate anyone.

So I ran out my plays. I could tell that it was irritating Coach Seifert,
because several times he hollered at me to take it easy. He wanted me
for the game, not back on the injured list. But I was confident that my
knee would hold up, so I kept running them out. I know my body, and
I knew that it was sufficiently healed and that I would be fresh going
into the playoffs.

During the week, Walter Payton called me up, and we discussed the
way he handled his body when he was on the injured list. He also
cautioned me against overdoing it, but I knew I was back. My body
told me so.

A Candlestick Park crowd of 65,292, the second-largest home crowd
in 49er history, was buzzing with excitement when they made the pregame introductions. In the first quarter, Rypien teamed up with veteran
Art Monk for a 31-yard touchdown, giving the Redskins a 7–0 lead and

an infusion of confidence. But we came right back with a 74-yard drive, with Rathman going over from the 1 yard line for the score.

The second quarter was vintage Joe Montana, as he took the team on scoring sorties of 80 and 89 yards, giving us a 21–10 advantage at the half. At halftime, our coaches told us that we had them on the run and to guard against the long pass. But we already knew that.

Our final score was perhaps our most entertaining touchdown of the season. With fifty-seven seconds left in the game, defensive end Charles Haley ripped the ball from Rypien's hands, and it popped into the outstretched, heavily bandaged paws of nose tackle Michael Carter. The 300-plus-pound Carter was a silver medalist in the 1984 summer Olympics—only his event was the shot put, not the hundred-yard dash.

Carter took off toward the goal line, his chunky legs churning and his eyes bulging out of their sockets and a posse of equally massive Redskin offensive linemen in hot pursuit. After what seemed to be an excruciating amount of time, he finally collapsed unscathed into the end zone, where he was mobbed by his defensive teammates. Seifert quipped that they timed his 61-yard touchdown fumble return with a calendar, not a watch.

The next morning we had a team meeting, and then watched the New York Giants systematically dismantle the Chicago Bears, 31–3. It was just as we figured, us against the Giants. Our December 3 regular-season game, which we won 7–3, was acknowledged as one of the hardest-fought games of the 1990 season.

The United States declared war on Iraq the Wednesday before our playoff game with the Giants, and the media immediately wanted to know our views about playing the game while our nation was at war. George assembled us before we went out on the field to meet the media on Thursday, and told us to keep our comments strictly to football.

Naturally, the first question tossed my way was whether the NFL should cancel the game. Inasmuch as I had been cautioned about commenting, and in view of the fact that my opinions would have absolutely no effect on what the NFL did or didn't do, I simply said, "I'm sure that everything will work out well for the U.S. But I can't get into that question because I'm not in a position to talk about it."

The war was on our minds, but we had to stay focused if we wanted to get to a third straight Super Bowl. The country had its war to fight and we had ours.

I had been besieged with questions about how many times I was going to carry the ball. I told the media that I would do whatever it took to win the game, and that I looked forward to doing things that I hadn't been able to do earlier in the year. But I knew that I couldn't worry about Roger Craig and whether or not he was going to find his rhythm or get to carry the ball twenty-five times. I had to keep focused on the team goal of getting back to the Super Bowl.

I knew the Giants weren't going to change. They lived and died by brute force, so we could expect an intense physical battle. They had stuffed Chicago's running game the week before, so we knew our running backs were going to have to fight and claw for every inch they got. We appeared pretty equal on paper, so it was just a matter of who wanted it the most. They were going to come in with a vendetta, and at the same time they were going to be determined and well coached.

We knew we had one advantage, and that was that we believed in ourselves like no other team. We worked on the two-minute offense every Thursday in practice, and I don't think there was another team in football that executed it as well as the 49ers.

We also had Joe Montana, and that's another big plus. He's the type of quarterback who is going to make big plays. He's going to rise to the occasion. I consider him the ultimate Green Beret. Joe's going to go in and get the job done, and he's not afraid of taking a hit.

When I went to bed that Saturday night at the team hotel in Burlingame, I had some butterflies. I thought about us being the only team ever to win three Super Bowls. What if . . . Then I caught myself looking too far ahead and brought my mind back to the Giants game. As long as our team didn't look beyond that game, we'd be all right.

As we lined up for the pregame introductions, I was focused. The game was just as I had figured it would be, a war in the pits. George and Mike Holmgren decided early on that our best chance was with the passing game, so we only called five running plays in the first fifty-four minutes of the game. I don't draw up the game plan, but if I had I would have had more running plays, even if it was only to keep the Giants defenders honest and keep them from their all-out rushes against Montana.

Still, we held a 13–9 going into the fourth quarter. New York place-kicker Matt Bahr missed a 37–yard field goal attempt, and it appeared as if our lead might hold up. Because Phil Simms had been injured, backup Jeff Hostetler started the game at quarterback. But on their second possession of the fourth quarter, former Giant Jim Burt ran into Hostetler's knee and put him out. Matt Cavanaugh, his backup, who had not taken a single snap in the regular season, trotted out on the field, and we all figured that we had them where we wanted them. They went three downs and out.

The Giants kicked, and we took over with a little less than ten minutes to go in the game. On a third-and-ten play from our own 23, Joe rolled right looking for a receiver downfield. Giants defensive end Leonard Marshall got loose and blindsided Joe just as he was ready to let go of the ball. Steve Wallace fell on the ball for us, but Joe was still on the ground. He finally was helped off the field, and Steve Young took over. Later it was learned that Joe suffered a bruised sternum and a fractured little finger on his throwing hand, so even if we went to the Super Bowl, Montana wouldn't have played.

Hostetler came back and led them on a drive which culminated with a 38-yard field goal with 5:47 left. Now we were ahead by only one, 13–12, and ball control was the priority. That meant we would be running the football.

Up until that final drive I had only fumbled twice that season. But on my first carry, I fumbled. Fortunately, Bubba Paris was right there and recovered. I glanced up at the clock, pleading with it to go faster.

We reminded ourselves in the huddle to protect the ball, because we knew that the Giants would be trying to rip it out of our hands on every play. I gained six yards on one run and four on the next for a very critical first down. The clock was approaching the three-minute mark and all we needed to do was make one more first down and hold on to the ball. A very simple formula.

On a first-down play from the New York 40, Steve called my number on a trap play, the first one of the afternoon. It called for center Jesse Sapolu to block nose tackle Erik Howard, for tight end Brent Jones to fire out on linebacker Lawrence Taylor and take him out of the play, and for me to run up the middle through the hole created by the guards.

I did everything by the book. I cradled the ball with both hands and searched for a crack of daylight. All of a sudden, the ball wasn't there. My hands were clasped against my jersey and players were pulling at me as I tried to turn around and retrieve it.

Howard had broken through and gotten a helmet on the ball, knocking it backward to where Taylor was. It appeared to jump right to his hands, and the Giants had the football at their own 40-yard line with 2:36 left. Think of the worst nightmare you've ever had and multiply it by ten. I had the worst sinking feeling I'd felt since my father had died. I had committed the most unpardonable of sins for a running back—to fumble away the ball to the opposition with the game and the season on the line.

I've fumbled the football before, and I'll fumble it again. But never with so much on the line, so much at stake. I fumbled away my team's opportunity for a spot in pro football history. In front of my own fans at Candlestick. If only I could have burrowed a hole in the turf and crawled into it. If the Giants scored, and we didn't get back to the Super Bowl after all of our hard work, how did I explain it to my teammates?

Taylor said later, "I crashed through, the ball came off the back of Craig's arm, and I was there." He happened to be in the right place at the right time.

There were a lot of things we didn't do right that day, but history will say that it was my fumble that prevented the 49ers from going to the Super Bowl for a third straight time.

I kept praying on the sidelines that our defense would come up with a big play and we could get the ball back. I needed one of those eleventh-hour reprieves that the governor gives a condemned man. But it never came.

Bahr kicked a 42-yard field goal with no time left on the clock to send the Giants into Super Bowl XXV against the Buffalo Bills and prevent the 49ers from keeping our appointment with history. There was this feeling of total helplessness as I watched the ball sail barely inside the upright.

In the locker room afterward, I knew that my cubicle was going to be a center of attention. Every media type with an NFC credential was going to want a piece of me. I could've begged off and issued a written statement for the public relations staff to hand out, but that's not my style. If I can stand up and accept the accolades after a productive game, then I can sure as hell accept the blame after something like that.

I couldn't imagine a feeling worse than the one I was experiencing, other than being given the knowledge that I was dying. There was this heavy, sickening ball rolling back and forth through the pit of my stomach.

As I came out of the shower, the media parted and let me return to my locker. I had taken a long shower, but the sweat was already beginning to break out again. I kept a towel around my waist as I stepped into my underwear. "Why is everybody here?" I asked, as if I didn't know. And then the inquisition began.

I told the assembled media how I perceived the fumble, and I accepted full blame for it. I told them that I couldn't make any excuses and that I would live with what I'd done for the rest of my career—for the rest of my life, for that matter. The epitaph on my gravestone would say HERE LIES ROGER CRAIG. HE FUMBLED IN THE NFC CHAMPIONSHIP GAME.

That fumble meant more than just a loss. It represented the loss of three years of games to me, and to all of my teammates and coaches. Immediately after the game, I thought about the rookies who had never been to a Super Bowl, people like Dexter Carter and Eric Davis. I felt I had especially let them down. It was probably the lowest point in my football career. To come that close to going to the Super Bowl for a third straight time and to be turned away.

I also knew that the off-season was going to be an extension of that devastating moment. I knew that wherever I went, people were going to bring up the fumble and that I was going to have to answer countless questions about it. It was going to follow me, and I was going to have to relive that nightmare over and over again.

Ronnie Lott came up to me and, in a touching moment, told me that he loved me. He said he cared more for me as a human being than he did about what went on on the football field. I'm just appreciative that my teammates respected me. They lent me moral support through the entire ordeal—which is more than I can say for management. So, with the help of my teammates, I knew that eventually I would climb out of that hole.

But I didn't realize as I made my way into the safety of darkness that evening to be alone with my thoughts that the fumble was going to change my life. I didn't know then that my career as a 49er—as one of the best backs in the team's history—would end with that fumble, my last carry for the only pro team I had ever known.

That night I didn't want to see or talk to anybody—hell, I didn't even feel like talking to myself. I just wanted to go home and be surrounded by my family. Tom Rathman called me later in the evening to tell me that everything was going to be all right.

"It's okay, buddy," he told me. "It could have happened to any one of us. It could very easily have been me that fumbled." He reminded me that we went into the game as a team and we came out of the game as a team.

But I knew that everything wasn't all right, and Tom knew it too. He was just trying to be nice and cheer me up, like friends will do. I'm a very positive person, and something like that, with all of the blame focused on me, is very difficult for me to handle emotionally.

I kept reminding myself that it happened, that it was over and now it was time to move on. I knew that sooner or later I could put it all behind me and start looking forward to the next season. Who knew? Maybe I could score the touchdown that put the 49ers in the 1992 Super Bowl, and everyone would forget about this game. I've always been a very upbeat person, and I knew that you can always turn a negative into a positive. I was just having a little trouble figuring out how to do it this time.

On Monday we had a very subdued team meeting, and Coach Seifert told us he was proud of us and that we really gave Three-peat a helluva run for its money. He said we had nothing to be ashamed of. He said there would be other seasons and other opportunities for us to bask in that warm glow of victory.

After the brief meeting, we cleared out our lockers and went home. Some guys, I knew, were clearing their lockers for the final time, like nose tackle Fred Smerlas. He was mainly signed as an insurance policy in case Michael Carter's injury didn't respond to therapy, and Fred spent the majority of the year on the injured reserve list or the inactive list.

But that's the way it is every year when the season is over. You look around the locker room and silently say your good-byes and thank everyone, because each new season begins with a lot of new faces. Losing a chance at a third straight Super Bowl would ensure that there would be even more new faces come summer camp. Heads were bound to roll, and I wouldn't have to wait too long to find out which ones.

17. Good-bye
Frisco, Hello L.A.

Heads would roll, and mine would be one of them.

Everything had been special between me and the 49ers up until the fumble, and then it was as if all of the championships and the camaraderie and the family feelings had never existed. I think I'm still the same Roger Craig. I haven't lost any teeth and my heart still beats on the left side of my chest. But our romance had grown cold, leaving ashes of doubt.

I was at a shopping mall in Northern California recently, when an attractive young lady in a 49er jacket approached me and asked in an incredulous tone, "How could you? How could you sign a contract with the Los Angeles Raiders, of all teams?"

There has always been a built-in animosity between 49er and Raider fans, ever since the Raider team was a member of the American Football League and played across the Bay in Oakland. The Raiders played their first-ever game on September 11, 1960, at the 14,000-seat Frank Yuell Field.

The AFL and the NFL merged on June 8, 1966, and when they did, the rivalry between the teams became even more heated. To make matters worse, the Raiders were an instant success in Oakland, while the 49ers continued to struggle through the sixties and seventies. San Francisco fans, supposedly the more sophisticated and worldly, became jealous of the Raiders' success, which only served to increase the bitterness of the rivalry.

Ironically, the year that San Francisco finally won its first Super Bowl, defeating the Cincinnati Bengals 26–20 in Pontiac, Michigan, in 1982, the Raiders packed up and moved to Los Angeles in a hostile parting with the city of Oakland. But even geographical distance couldn't cool the rivalry.

So of all of the teams for Ronnie Lott and me to pick, Los Angeles is the choice that most perplexes my Bay Area fans. I'm not even sure I understand all the reasons myself. I signed my Raider contract at nine o'clock on the evening of April 1, 1991, just three hours before the expiration of the Plan B deadline. Maybe it was my April Fool's joke on the 49ers, whom I felt held me up to ridicule by placing me on the list of unprotected, Plan B players. Maybe it was my way of striking back at them.

I think to fully understand my decision and the emotional trauma I went through prior to my signing with the Raiders, you have to go back to January 20, 1991, that fateful Sunday we played the Giants for the NFC championship at Candlestick Park.

That day was the most traumatic of my life. I wish they could bury the memories of that afternoon in one of those time capsules, so I'll be long gone by the time they dig it up.

I know the 49er coaches and management will vehemently deny that it had anything to do with my status on the team, but you will never convince me that the fumble is not the reason I'm not a 49er anymore.

The day after our final team meeting, a Tuesday, I got a call from George Seifert asking me to come down to Santa Clara for a visit. There is nothing unusual about that; Bill Walsh used to do it all the time. Usually he would ask you what your plans were for the off-season and remind you to stay in touch and keep working out. But no one ever had to tell me to keep working out. That's part of my life-style, and as I was driving down to the team's Santa Clara headquarters from my home in Portola Valley, I reflected back on my year and decided that I might actually have trained too much.

I had trained strenuously before the 1990 season, running hills, doing sprints, and lifting weights, and I wanted to weigh around 210, but I came in at 205, about fifteen pounds below my usual weight, because I felt it would give me added quickness. Looking back, I think I was really too light. I was lean, and I looked good as a model, but as far as being a football player I needed more size. My wife kept telling me that I was losing too much weight and that my clothes were falling off me.

And there were several other factors working against me in 1990. First, both guard Guy McIntyre and center Jesse Sapolu held out and missed most of training camp. Therefore it took the offensive line nearly half the season to begin to jell. I had trained to have an All-Pro season, but I took a lot of pounding early. I needed more size to compensate for our lack of overpowering run blocking.

And I never seemed to be able to get into sync, even before my injury. Mike Holmgren, the 49ers' offensive coordinator, comes from Brigham Young University, where they emphasize a pass-oriented offense. Consequently we didn't spend a lot of time with the running game. George is a defensive-minded coach, and he let Mike call all the shots on offense.

Then there was Al Lavan, the running backs coach. I could never figure out what he expected from the running backs. I never really felt comfortable when I was out on the field, and I never fully understood my role. It could be very frustrating at times. I would be running well in the first half, getting in a groove, and then suddenly he would pull me out and put someone else in. Now, what kind of shit is that?

Against Cincinnati, I was having a pretty good game when Lavan replaced me with Harry Sydney. I normally run the "tiger formation," which is our one-back offense. But Lavan, or Holmgren, put Harry in to run it, and when he sprained his ankle they sent him back out there. I was miffed because I ended up with 97 yards on 21 carries. It was my most productive afternoon of the season, and I would have loved to have gotten to the century mark in yardage as a matter of pride. My line was rooting for me too, because whenever I went over a hundred yards rushing I would take them all to dinner. Instead, I got the hook.

It went like that for the latter part of the season. I never knew when I was going to get pulled out of a game. I would just get warmed up, and then Dexter Carter or Harry would come in for me. They didn't do that with Joe Montana or Jerry Rice. Why me? I just feel that they didn't take full advantage of my talents.

To me, Dexter Carter is pretty one-dimensional. He has that shifty quickness, and the 49ers should utilize his talents by using him on screen plays and isolating him one-on-one with a linebacker. But I don't believe you should run him up the middle. The team lists his weight at 170, but I think it's closer to 150. If they run him up the middle play after play, they'll burn him out before he's eligible for his NFL pension.

I wanted to say, "Talk to me, but don't play mind games with me. Just talk to me straight." It was really frustrating at times, but I never complained. I worked hard and trained hard for my role, just as if I was going to carry the ball thirty times a game. I've always faced every obstacle that came my way. I've paid my dues, so at least extend me the courtesy of an explanation. You owe me that much. But I never got it from Lavan or Holmgren.

Finally there was that special feeling we'd had down through the years, where we all performed together, with one heartbeat. In past seasons, there were never any of the petty jealousies and backstabbing that can rip a team apart. We all played hard because we never wanted to let our teammates down. We were one for all and all for one, no matter how trite that sounds. We were a family.

But in 1990 it was different. Maybe it was the tension of trying to Three-peat. I don't know. But I do know that the special locker room camaraderie was missing during the 1990 season. Guys were more into "me" and "I." That's the kind of thing that can divide a team.

There were fights in the locker room, behind closed doors, and guys seemed more worried about how much other guys were making than about winning football games. I'm not going to get into who the combatants were, but suffice to say it was a disruptive force in our quest for a third straight Super Bowl title.

Everyone seemed tight, coaches included, and you could almost see the tension. The pressure to succeed was created by ourselves. To be honest with you, the tension in the locker room took a lot of the fun out of the game. It was like one of those internal squabbles that polarizes families, pitting brother against brother. Ronnie attempted to cool everyone out, but it just didn't seem to work this time. Sometimes I think that when Bill Walsh left following the 1988 season, he took some of our good chemistry with him.

By the time I had arrived at Seifert's office, I pretty much knew what I was going to tell him. I was going to explain to him what I believed were the reasons our team never got to the Super Bowl. I was going to tell him about the running game and the locker room tensions. It was going to be a real constructive, no-holds-barred meeting.

When I got to his office he greeted me at the door, and we went in and sat down. Before I could start talking, he hit me with the fumble, my future, and Plan B. I told him that I was really feeling bad, and he said that that was understandable. He told me that as of that moment I was his starter, but that there would be open competition for my job once training camp started. There was no need to tell me this because I never thought that a player was guaranteed a starting job. Hell, I thrived on open competition.

But I was still feeling bad about letting my teammates down, and I didn't need this. Not at this time. The body was still warm, and he was paving the way for my successor.

Then he hit me with the fastball right through the middle of my heart. He said that they were placing me on the Plan B list of unprotected players, which meant any NFL team could negotiate with me. I couldn't believe my ears. I thought that this must be some kind of nightmare, and that maybe the fumble was part of it too. Not in my wildest dreams did I imagine they would put me on Plan B. It was like they stuck a dagger in me and ripped my guts out. That's the feeling I had after I left his office and went back home. I must have staggered down the stairs; I was in a daze.

To me Plan B is where all the guys hanging on by their fingernails end up, the free agents who can't quite cut it and the draft picks who proved to be mistakes, the old player who has had the last down of football squeezed out of him. I certainly wasn't hanging by my fingernails, nor was I squeezed dry.

Seifert explained to me that they were putting the older, high-salaried veterans on Plan B and were trying to protect some of the younger, lower-salaried players, whom he considered the future of the franchise.

I took that to mean all older players. But when the list was released, Montana's name wasn't on it. Nor was veteran tackle Bubba Paris, who had constantly fought a losing battle with his weight and had been bouncing from starter to backup. Neither was LeRoy Etienne, a reserve linebacker whose role was restricted to that of a special-teams player. The names Roger Craig, Ronnie Lott, and Matt Millen stood out on the list, like we were members of some Bum of the Month club.

Now you tell me how I can respect someone who does that to me? They knew that I was still hurting because of the fumble. To drop this on me only two days after the game was really insensitive.

I kept thinking that they'd made a mistake and that I would get a phone call from team owner Eddie DeBartolo, Jr., telling me that everything was all right, that my name had been mixed up with someone else's. Eddie and I were like brothers. If we had a problem, we could talk about it and work it out.

I knew it was illegal for the 49ers to negotiate with me during the Plan B period, but I figured a personal phone call from the team owner would be in order. Only Eddie never called. The only person I was getting support from was Vernessia. That's what so nice about having a great supportive wife and a loving family. They were able to ease some of the hurt I was feeling.

Still, I knew I had to get away. The media would have the Plan B list by now, and they would be lining up at my door to ask my reaction. I'm really not the type of person to duck adversity, but I was totally confused, so I couldn't give them a worthwhile response, anyway. Plus, I was too angry to guard my comments.

I finally decided that I had to get to the bottom of this. When I got back home after a brief family vacation, I left a message for Eddie D. at his Youngstown offices, telling him that I wanted to fly back to Ohio and talk to him. I told him that I was tired of playing these mind games and there were some things I wanted to get off my chest.

But I never got a response. A lot of other people called me, but Eddie never did. So I asked my agent Jim Steiner to set up a meeting. He checked and said that Eddie and club president Carmen Policy would be at the San Jose Airport on the Saturday prior to the start of the NFL meetings in Hawaii. They gave Jim the message for me to meet them at the airport.

I needed to meet for peace of mind. If we did meet, and Eddie explained the financial picture, NFL Commissioner Paul Tagliabue could fine the team or dock them a draft choice, or even both. I can understand the reasoning behind the league's policing of the matter, because teams could make a farce out of the Plan B machinery by setting up a deal with a player before they left him unprotected. But I wanted to know what was going on.

By this time the 49ers knew I had flown to Green Bay for a tryout with the Packers, and that both the Rams and Raiders were interested in me.

When I got to the airport, Eddie and I went up to a private room, and Carmen, general manager John McVay, and Seifert stayed down stairs. It was all very hush-hush, and no one outside of the parties involved and my agent knew we were meeting.

We talked for a long time. We reminisced about all of the good times we'd had, and all of the adversity we had overcome as a team. Eddie and I laughed, and I was as honest with him as I could be. I told him I was deeply hurt that he never called me, and about how displeased I was being placed on Plan B, and that I thought it could have been handled better and that all I wanted was a reasonable explanation. We're gladiators out on the football field, and our loyalty is unconditional. He told me that he wished I would stay and play with the 49ers. But he would neither confirm nor deny that I would be offered a lesser contract. The subject of money was never broached.

We shook hands, and when we came downstairs we had our arms around each other and were laughing. Eddie looked over at Policy and McVay and winked, like it was all in the bag, I was going to accept their terms and spurn the other offers. That's when I knew that football wasn't a game anymore, it was strictly business.

They had misjudged me as an individual. It seemed to me that they were more worried about how they'd look if I left than about my welfare. It was like they could care less how Roger Craig felt, regardless that he played eight hard years with nary a whimper.

I think they had decided that I didn't have any more football left in me. But I'm a different breed of player. I'm a young thirty-one. When I'm half in shape, I'm in better shape than most of the players on the team. I'm not a lazy person.

I realized then and there I couldn't let the emotional issues cloud my decision. I knew there were a lot of negative forces around with the 49ers, and that loyalty and promises didn't mean shit. So I called Steiner and told him to do what was best for my family and myself. I told him to handle it strictly as a business deal.

When Eddie got to Hawaii he talked to the media, and he told one writer that all we talked about at our airport meeting was the fumble and how remorseful I felt. He said that I couldn't face my teammates. But that's simply not true—they were the first ones to forgive me. And as I said, I've never been one to walk away from adversity. I don't believe in crawling under a rock. I welcome the challenge. He might have been trying to cover up the fact that we met and talked during the Plan B period.

Still, I wanted to give the 49ers every opportunity to welcome me back. I honestly wanted to be a 49er and stay in the Bay Area; that is where I want to make my permanent home, regardless of the circumstances. So I kept in constant contact with Steiner, and I told him to see what he could work out with them.

My 1991 contract called for $1 million in salary and a reporting bonus of $250,000. But as the Plan B deadline grew closer, Jim called back and said that the 49ers refused to budge on their final salary offer of $500,000, plus the reporting bonus. Can you believe that? They wanted to cut my base salary in half. They just didn't show me any respect.

What really ticks me off was that in all those productive years I had, like 1988 when I rushed for 1,502 yards, I never once made noise about holding out or renegotiating my contract. I put loyalty and team unity before everything else.

Even though I was on a level with the Eric Dickersons and the Herschel Walkers, I never made the big bucks that they did. Dickerson was scheduled to make $1.45 million with the Colts in 1990, and when that wasn't enough he took a walk. Walker, who was rarely used by Minnesota, made $2.25 million. I made $750,000 in 1990, which was considerably less than Joe Montana's $4 million and Steve Young's $1.1 million.

But I never complained, even though deep inside I felt that I was underpaid. I felt 1991 would be the year I was finally going to make top dollar, commensurate with my talents. I was going to enjoy the security a high-paid back can attain. I always believed in being faithful. I never made it an issue by holding out because I felt that that would be letting my teammates down. I couldn't hold out anyway, because I'm too impatient and I love the game too much.

I figured that eventually I would reach the upper echelon and I would be able to make the big bucks for two or three years. Plus, there were a lot of other special perks that came with playing for the 49er organization: up until then, they had always taken care of the players and made everyone feel like we were one big happy family.

So what happened? Just when I'm about to make the big money, they offer me a pay cut. I just never figured that it would turn out that way. As I said, I've never been a problem player.

I gave my heart and soul to the 49ers, and they misjudged my pride and dedication. There were times when the coaches would ask me to talk to the younger players, to explain the dedication and hard work it takes to become successful.

They even sent me to the airport to pick up rookies, so they would get off on the right foot.

In practice, I ran out every play—not because I enjoyed doing it, but because I wanted to set an example, to show the younger players what it takes to become a champion. The club even showed rookies and free agents a film of my workouts as an example of the training required to make it in the NFL. I wanted to establish a work ethic for the young players to emulate. I wanted them to say, "So this is the way it's supposed to be done."

That's my nature. I want to involve my teammates; I want them to turn it up a notch when they hit the field. That's what separates the winners from the losers in this game.

But the bottom line, I found out, is that football is strictly business. When you're a nice guy and loyal, it doesn't get you any Brownie points. When you're nice, they run all over you. I guess I should have been a rebel without a cause, some sort of renegade. Then maybe I would have gotten some respect.

A couple of days before the April 1 Plan B deadline, the 49ers sent former running backs coach Sherm Lewis over to my house to talk to me. They had been hearing the rumors about me visiting different camps, and they were getting worried that I might defect.

He told me to call Seifert and tell him what my intentions were. I told Sherm that the team had two months to talk to me and resolve the issues separating us. They thought everything was fine and dandy, but they had misjudged me. I told him that I had placed the entire matter in the hands of my agent. I probably called Steiner three times a day—after every anxiety attack.

On Monday, April 1, I got up early as usual and went to run this hill near my house. Normally, I would run with Jerry Rice and some other guys, but this day I wanted to be alone with my thoughts.

I can't begin to tell you what went through my mind. My heart was heavy, for I knew from my conversations with my agent that there was a good chance this could be my last day as a 49er. I'm not ashamed to tell you that there were tears streaming down my cheeks as I ran the hill. I felt like I was about to be cast out by my family, the only family I had ever known in this crazy business.

After about an hour, I headed toward Menlo Park and the gym where I regularly lift weights. Usually I skip into the main lobby and flash my grin at everyone, but this day there was no skip and there was no grin. I slipped quietly through the front door, found a weight machine, and started doing my reps. All the while my mind was racing a thousand miles a second, as I tried to figure out the solution to my dilemma.

I took a quick shower, left the gym, and started driving aimlessly. If you asked me what roads I took, I couldn't tell you. I reran my career in my mind. I replayed the past season, with the knee injury, and tried to figure how they determined that I was just about through as a player. Sometimes I made a left turn and sometimes I made a right.

Every once in a while I would take a call from Steiner on my car phone, and he'd tell me that the negotiations with the Raiders were heating up, and that the 49ers still hadn't upped their final offer of $500,000 plus the reporting bonus.

I knew now that it was just between the 49ers and the Raiders. The Packers had made me a nice offer, but it was not enough money for me to leave the West Coast. Can you picture me in a Green Bay Packer uniform? I couldn't. Besides, I had already spent enough cold winters in Davenport, and in Lincoln at the University of Nebraska. In Los Angeles, I would only be an hour away from home by air.

Ronnie Lott called me and told me to make sure I was making the right decision. He cautioned me not to let his decision to sign with the Raiders influence me. He said I had to do what was right for myself and my family.

At six o'clock the phone rang. It was Jim, calling to tell me to get to the airport right away and catch the seven P.M. flight to L.A. I knew then and there that I had played my last down for the 49ers.

I hurried to the airport to catch the flight. As it was, we were cutting it pretty close to the midnight signing deadline. I didn't get to Los Angeles until eight o'clock, and then I had to go to the Raiders' headquarters in El Segundo.

Surprisingly, I wasn't too nostalgic on the flight down. I guess I had released all of my emotions earlier in the day. This would be the dawning of a new era, and I was excited.

When I arrived at the airport, a Raider aide was there to greet me and drive me to El Segundo. When we pulled up at the offices, it was shortly after nine o'clock. There was a TV crew stationed out front, but I just gave them a big grin and a wave and strode inside the building. By the time the eleven o'clock news aired that night, the entire Bay Area knew that I was a Los Angeles Raider. News travels fast in California.

Al Davis was there to greet me, and the formalities were relatively brief. We exchanged pleasantries and they put the contract on the table. Steiner and the Raider brass had already gone over the details, so all that was left for me to do was to check the dollar amounts and put my signature on it.

It was done before ten P.M., and I was now officially a Los Angeles Raider, one of those silver and black thugs that offend so many of my NFL brethren.

I picked the Raiders because they made me a better offer than the 49ers, they play on the West Coast, and they showed me the respect that I believe an NFL player of my stature deserves.

I really never thought I'd ever leave the 49ers, but I felt that they had betrayed the respect I had shown them throughout my eight hard years on the field. They forced me to make the decision to sign with the Raiders.

They forced me to see that football is a business and that I had to do what was best for me, business-wise. I signed with the Raiders because it was a better business deal, and because Al Davis respected me for what I had accomplished during my NFL career.

That's why I'm a Raider and not a 49er anymore.

There are no guarantees that I will have a lengthy career in Los Angeles, but there is no doubt in my mind that I will. Everyone thinks that I chose Los Angeles because I want to develop a movie career after my playing days are over, but that had absolutely nothing to do with it. All I had on my mind when I signed was to play football.

As for my relationship with the 49ers, I guess that I'm still a little bitter. The way they handled it was an affront to my integrity. They never took into account the value I place on being loyal and on my intense pride. I think that the 49ers, especially Eddie D., listened to the wrong people when it came to assessing my remaining talents.

I believe the sole reason I was placed on Plan B was because of that fumble. They tried to tell me it was my knee, but they knew my work ethic, and they knew I would be back again. Nothing will ever convince me otherwise. If Roger Craig hadn't fumbled against the Giants, he would still be a 49er.

And that part really pisses me off, because I wasn't the only one who had an off day that afternoon. I've never felt it was all my fault.

What about the play itself? If center Jesse Sapolu had blocked Howard, the nose tackle, I wouldn't have gotten hit. And if tight end Brent Jones had blocked Lawrence Taylor out of the play, as he was supposed to, then Taylor would never have been in a position to recover the fumble. But I'm not blaming Sapolu and Jones.

What about the fake punt by the Giants? The Giants had fourth and one on their own 47 yard line, and everyone in the house except special teams coach Lynn Stiles knew they were going to run a fake punt. When you're behind in the fourth quarter and you only need a yard, that doesn't seem like too much of a gamble. But we had a punt-return call on instead of a goal line defense. Center Steve DeOssie centered not to punter Sean Landetta but to up-back Gary Reasons, who strolled 30 yards to our 24 before he was stopped. Four plays later Matt Bahr kicked a 38-yard field goal to close the gap to 13–12 and set the stage for the dramatic finale.

Later we discovered that not only did we have the wrong call on, but linebacker Bill Romanowski had come out injured on the previous play. We only had ten men on the field when they ran the fake punt.

So if you're going to start passing the blame around, pass some that way. Don't throw it all in Roger's lap. Without that field goal, the Giants couldn't have won it on a field goal following my fumble.

But, hey, I'm not about to blame anybody. It was a helluva game and we played our hearts out. It's just that when the gun sounded, the other team had two more points than we did. I never like pointing the finger because it is a team sport. The 49ers won four Super Bowls as a team, and they lost the playoff game against the Giants as a team.

I also believe that the 49ers—specifically Eddie D.—got some bad advice, whether it was from George Seifert or John McVay or from the medical people. I think somebody fooled Eddie into believing that I was washed up as a football player. If nothing else, it taught me the valuable lesson that this game is strictly a business. All of that rhetoric about being a close-knit family is just so much bullshit.

What upsets me most is that now I'll have to be away from my family for long periods of time. The kids grow up so quickly, and I'm only going to be able to see them once a week during the season. I would love to come home every night and see my new baby son, Alexander Julian, who was born last June 4, at Stanford Hospital. My family is going to stay in Northern California because I don't want the children to start all over again at a new school.

I also think the fans are hurt by what happened. I know the ones whom I've come in contact with ask me why, and then they wish me luck.

My biggest mistake, and I take full responsibility for it, was getting too close to management. I thought that being a member of a football team was a family arrangement, that when times got rough the team closed ranks and rallied around you. I thought that my relationship with Eddie D. was like a brother thing. I was wrong. If I had it to do all over again, I would never have allowed myself to get that close to management.

When it comes down to it, the bottom line is that you have to take care of yourself and your family. Life always teaches you valuable lessons, and each lesson should make you a better person. I guess after this one, I should be pretty close to being perfect.

But while I'm still hurt by the way things happened, I harbor no hard feelings nor do I have any ill will toward the 49ers. Some of my best friends still work for them.

A couple of days after I signed with the Raiders, I wrote Eddie a nice long letter. I told him how much I appreciated playing for his team and how I enjoyed all the good times we'd had.

*   *   *

I started looking forward to the new challenge almost immediately following my first Raider minicamp in May. I got my weight back up to 220 pounds and felt much stronger and, surprisingly, not any slower. It appeared that my old quickness was still there. Raider head coach Art Shell told me to cut back on my training as far as running the hills. He told me to leave something for training camp and the long season. So I did a lot of running in water.

I honestly believe that I have another three years of football left in me. I'm already starting to have fun out on the football field again.

It's a new experience, different colors, but football is football. I need to adjust somewhat, and the most difficult task, and the one I think is most important, was being accepted by my new teammates. Raider players are naturally suspicious about former 49ers.

You already know how I feel about not being a 49er, but you don't know how I feel about being a Los Angeles Raider. When I think about it, change for the most part is for the better. You can get too complacent, stagnant, in the same role year after year. Now, I'm not saying that is what happened to me, but it is a possibility.

Heck, maybe the 49ers did me a big favor. I feel that this change has breathed new life into me. It has given me an entirely different set of challenges, and that is what I thrive on.

As for my own peace of mind, things couldn't have worked out better. When someone has a grudge, the best thing is to get away from it and get into new surroundings. I need lots of positive feelings around me.

Before I left for camp, I had a long talk with Riki Ellison. He preceded Ronnie and me to Los Angeles by a year and won a starting job as an inside linebacker. Riki basically was confronted with the same problem that Ronnie and I were: the 49ers offered him a contract, offering to prorate his salary depending on how many games he played. He said see you later and signed a handsome three-year deal with the Raiders with no strings attached.

Riki told me how loose and close-knit the Raider players are. He said the team was a lot like the 49ers were when Bill Walsh was there. I've talked to a lot of players, and they've all told me that they wouldn't mind finishing their careers with the Raiders.

I shared time this last season with Marcus and Nick Bell, a rookie out of Iowa University. Isn't that irony for you? At one point during the 1990 season, I figured I was going to have to beat out Marcus to get my job back when I returned after my injury. The 49ers never acquired him, but I'm still trying to beat out Marcus.

With Bo Jackson now officially retired from football, the Raiders experimented a little last season with Marcus and me in the same backfield. It met with mixed results.

The Raider coaches worked overtime with quarterback Jay Schroeder, trying to get him to throw the touch pass. They traded away Steve Beuerlein, whom I thought was more in the Joe Montana mold, to Dallas because he had pissed off Al Davis when he held out during the 1990 season. Personally, my receiving talents were better suited for Steve.

But Jay got us to the playoffs in 1991, and can throw the long pass as well as anybody in the game. The offensive line with the Raiders did a heckuva job last season, and I led the team in rushing. Even though I didn't break the century mark rushing, I'm looking forward to next season. I'll have a much better command of the Raider system by then. I know it's really going to cost me a lot of money when I do rush for more than 100 yards in a game, so I've been scouting out one of those all-you-can-eat-for-$8.95 places. I'm trying to keep the overhead down.

The only regret I have is that I didn't get to wear my number 33 jersey for the Raiders. That belongs to Eddie Anderson, one of the best safeties in the NFL. Even though I feel more at home in number 33, I didn't feel right asking him to give it up. So I wore number 22 last season.

I suppose I could have offered him a bribe to trade numbers, like my former teammate Jim Burt did when he came to the 49ers in 1989. Burt had worn number 64 throughout his career with the Giants, and when he got to San Francisco he discovered that number was being worn by Rollin Putzier, a reserve defensive lineman. The two huddled in a corner of the locker room for a little while, and when they parted Burt had his old number back and Putzier had a new number. All it reportedly cost Burt was five cases of beer. But to me a jersey number is extremely personal, and I couldn't ask Anderson to give it up.

Besides, I kind of enjoyed making a fresh start, and that included a new number to go along with my new silver and black uniform.

As I said, I think I made the right decision for my family and myself, but time will determine that. I respect Al Davis for believing in me and giving me an opportunity. That's really all you can ask for.

There was a lot of irony during the 1991 season, not the least of which was the Raiders making the playoffs and the 49ers missing them for the first time since 1982. We had a chance to help San Francisco in the next-to-last Monday Night Football game of the season, when we played the Saints in New Orleans. If we beat the Saints, we prevented them from capturing the last NFC playoff berth and kept the 49ers' dreams alive for another week. Unfortunately, our offense had an abysmal night and we lost 27–0. That was the final blow that knocked the 49ers out of the playoffs. The first blow was when they decided they didn't need Ronnie and me anymore.

I suppose that I will look back a few years after I get out of the game and try to make some sense out of what happened. Maybe I'll sit around with Joe Montana and Jerry Rice, have a few beers, and we'll all laugh about it.

But I know one thing. There was nothing funny about the 49ers' determination in 1990 to scale heights never attained before in pro football. We almost made it. We got nearly to the summit, one step away from it all, and we fell back. It was a long three-year odyssey, fraught with obstacles and adversity. But we also had a lot of fun, and we had a sincere, deep affection for one another.

Some of us were naive; I know I was, especially about loyalty and commitment. But maybe that's why it all worked, what made the chemistry so special. I know there will never be another experience like it. Not for me anyway, for as long as I live.

This game, this life, is so unpredictable. Take the dream I had the other night, for instance. I dreamed that the Raiders traded me back to San Francisco. It all seemed so vivid and real.

Who knows? Stranger things have happened.

◆

Index